THE GOOD,
THE BAD &
THE MORAL
DILEMMA

Being in part the result of conversations with a somnolent gentleman in a railway carriage

THE GOOD, THE BAD & THE MORAL DILEMMA

G. R. EVANS

LION

Copyright © 2007 G. R. Evans
This edition copyright © 2007 Lion Hudson

The author asserts the moral right
to be identified as the author of this work

A Lion Book
an imprint of
Lion Hudson plc
Wilkinson House, Jordan Hill Road,
Oxford OX2 8DR, England
www.lionhudson.com
ISBN 978 0 7459 5268 0 (UK)

ISBN 978 0 8254 6250 4 (USA)

First edition 2007
10 9 8 7 6 5 4 3 2 1 0

A catalogue record for this book is available
from the British Library

Every effort has been made to trace and contact copyright owners for
material used in this book. We apologize for any inadvertent omissions or
errors.

Distributed by:

UK: Marston Book Services Ltd, PO Box 269, Abingdon, Oxon OX14 4YN

USA: Trafalgar Square Publishing, 814 N Franklin Street, Chicago, IL
60610

USA Christian Market: Kregel Publications, PO Box 2607, Grand Rapids,
Michigan 49501

This book has been printed on paper and board independently certified as
having been produced from sustainable forests.

Typeset in 10.5/12 OriginalGaramond BT
Printed and bound in Wales by Creative Print and Design

Contents

Preface

He'd had enough of king-sized situations, he'd only to watch Jack and Mary in their small, overworked world to see that it took a remarkable amount of energy and intelligence to hold down a personal place in the scheme of things. Now, instead of trying to combat famine over hundreds of square miles, he was going to spend two weeks of his professional time giving an old friend the first holiday he had been able to have with his wife since they were married.[1]

Elizabeth Jane Howard (b. 1923)

Should I walk to work today, or drive? News headlines about global warming are turning this from a question of personal preference to a 'moral' one, with the result that this morning's small personal dilemma prompts me to think about it as though it were huge. But that leads to another question. Should I concentrate my efforts to do good on those closest to me (I could give my daughter a lift to school), or try to make a difference to the whole world? I could become so paralysed with indecision that I am late for work.

Here is a practical manual that tries to make all this more manageable. It is written to reassure. For the demands of the modern world are mostly not new, but perennial questions that have been wrestled with again and again for centuries, though they may present new faces today. This book is full of questions; they are intended to be a challenge. Many of them present genuine dilemmas, precisely because no one has ever succeeded in resolving them once and for all. Everyone has to work the answers out for himself or herself.

The living of the 'moral' life probably has to begin from inside you and me, with my reflection on my ways of understanding life and your reflection on yours. This is the theme of Part I, which explores learning to care about what needs caring about, without having one's balance upset, and within a process of growing understanding. The middle chapter of this experiment in laying the foundations takes a short excursion into the traditional virtues. Do they still have a place? Is being virtuous a matter of what I do or what I am? Should I take responsibility for what I do or just obey the rules?

Life seen as a process of growing, a progression, a gathering of experience and advancing skills and understanding, may involve doing one thing at one stage, another later. Life lived in readiness for something new will always be exciting but it need not be stressful. The individual can practise an inward alertness, which is also a way of being at ease even when things are not 'easy'. It may even be possible to get to work on time without a brow furrowed with moral anxiety.

But morality also has to look outwards. It involves engaging with the world. Part II of this book begins by considering the very idea that there are other people, and examining some of the modern assumptions behind the idea of 'human rights'. It moves on to explore the complex ways in which I may 'belong' to different human groups, and the nature of the ties and responsibilities involved. Do I have to cooperate or can I opt out?

Part III explores some longstanding questions that seem to have distinctive aspects in the modern world. What is fairness? Is it fair that some people – and some whole societies – are richer than others? What are my ecological responsibilities towards the planet? What are the moralities of war? Should I do something about it when I see wrongdoing? Can I (and should I) stand up for principles I believe in or tolerate the different beliefs of others? Is there a way to do both, and should I try? Should I always tell the truth, and what is 'honesty'? Should I try to be kind? Should I be forgiving?

This is a book that makes no assumption about religious belief, but thinking about morality inevitably involves ideas that are also central to the world faiths. Part IV addresses two great underlying questions that have traditionally been treated from a religious point of view. The first is 'What is "evil" and where does it come from?' (Is the 'good' bound to win in the end?) The second is 'How much freedom of choice do I really have?' (Am I in some way 'fated', a mere plaything of forces much greater than me? If so, why blame me for the consequences of my actions?)

One of the questions that runs through the whole book is 'Can I make a difference?' I suspect that I – and you – can. Part of this process is the transformation of the inward self in the way it engages with life, other people and the wider world. Only I know what it is like 'in here', but while I continue to try to hide the things I am rather ashamed of from myself as well as others, I shall go on being in an interior muddle. So, trying to think clearly and understand what I have to balance in making moral choices, and being flexible in responding to the situations in which I find myself will probably make a difference to me too.

PART I

AN INNER LIFE

[Why do] I still seem to myself a subject of inexhaustible and fascinating anxiety? — a volcano in perpetual eruption? Am I alone in my egotism when I say that never does the pale light of dawn filter through the blinds of 52 Tavistock Square but I open my eyes and exclaim, 'Good God! Here I am again!' — not always with pleasure, often with pain; sometimes with a spasm of acute disgust — but always, always with interest?

Virginia Woolf (1882-1941), Am I a Snob?

Chapter 1

Ways of Living

To care and not to care

> Teach us to care and not to care
> Teach us to sit still.[1]
> **T.S. Eliot (1880—1965)**

Human beings do not stay where you put them. When T.S. Eliot wrote these lines in his poem 'Ash Wednesday', he threw out a challenge. It is not easy to achieve a balance once and for all between active engagement with the world and its needs, and the sort of detachment that makes it possible for doctors and nurses to work without getting too upset by the sight of pain and suffering to be useful to their patients. And even if I could learn to be 'still' in that way, remaining inwardly at peace might not turn out to be a way of 'arriving' at a place to stop. What if my 'steady state' should turn out to be more dynamic than static, full of change and onward movement?

Not minding about things so much that it gets in the way

In the late eleventh century Anselm of Canterbury (1033–1109) tried to work out how God himself dealt with this problem. A God who could get upset was inconceivable to him, for reasons we shall come to in a moment, yet we speak of God's 'mercy'. How can God be moved to be merciful if he feels no pangs of compassion? Anselm's solution was to suggest that although we feel the 'effect' of this mercy (*effectus*), God himself does not share the feelings of anguish of those to whom he shows mercy. He makes them feel better without any sensation (*affectus*) of his own.[2]

Why did Anselm see it as non-negotiable that God must remain tranquil? This was largely due to the influence of a system of classical philosophy which had been taken up by early Christianity and incorporated into the foundations of its account of the world.

Life seems to be a matter of opinion, mused Marcus Aurelius, the stoically inclined Emperor of Rome (r. AD 161–80). He made a practice of noting his private reflections, with a view to making them public, or, more particularly, making them available to his student son to guide him in life. Marcus Aurelius meant that it is up to the individual to interpret events and to decide how to respond to them. Getting upset about unwelcome happenings is a matter of choice. Unless you think of something in a particular way it will not trouble you, he insists.[3] Be like a rocky headland on which the waves continually break but which stands firm, the foam of each wave dying away, leaving it unmoved. When something distressing happens think how fortunate you are that your inner self is unhurt and that you are neither damaged by the present nor frightened of the future. It is all a question of the way you look at events. As Seneca (c. 4 BC–AD 65) writes in his *Moral Letters* (*Epistulae Morales*), you should make life agreeable to yourself by banishing all worry about it.[4]

Being 'stoical'

Marcus Aurelius' ideas were not his own original invention. About 300 BC Zeno (333–264 BC), a Phoenician Greek who came from Cyprus, taught a philosophical system that became known as 'Stoicism', because he taught in the *stoa*, or colonnade, in Athens.[5] This has provided a useful label ever since for an approach to exactly this way of living in a vigilant stillness. Cicero (c. 106-43 BC), once he had retired from being a public figure in ancient Rome to spend his time talking philosophy with his friends, set out – rather as Marcus Aurelius was to do – to write his own book of advice for his son, *On Duty* (*De officiis*). Stoic ideas seemed the best advice he could give him.

Stoic teaching offered a unified theory of everything. This was not as difficult to do as it would have been if Stoicism had confined its teaching to any particular set of beliefs. Stoics thought moral principles must be universal, by which they meant that there was not one morality for one race, nation or portion of humanity and another for a different one.

That seemed to be an accurate perception, in view of the frequency with which the basic ideas of Stoicism, such as freedom from attachments and an essential simplicity of life, appear in other systems, some of them remote in their origins from the philosophical debates of ancient Greece and Rome. So the Stoic way is not the only way of learning how 'to care and not to care'. In Hinduism, for example, with its comparatively free-form character, each person tries to live according to an ideal of personal duty to self and society; each person tries to purify what he or she is, not giving way to resentments or jealousies, not being cruel. The ideal for the Buddhist, too, is to live a life of simplicity, respecting the small and particular, and striving for freedom from entanglements, needs and dependencies.

Stoicism so thoroughly penetrated the heritage of the thought of Plato (428/427–348/347 BC) as well as Aristotle (384–322 BC) that, by the early Christian period, philosophical systems had largely become a compound of all three. This 'merger' has had an enormous influence on Western thought, largely because of the way Christianity took in some of its core principles. They became embedded in Christian theology and ethics without encountering the objection that they had not come from the Bible, for they often chimed very well with what was to be read there, especially in the New Testament, which was itself influenced in places by these ideas.

Stoics took moral principles to be an *applied* way of living a good life, in which what a person was like inwardly would be reflected in the way he or she behaved. By contrast, Aristotle tended to see reactions to unwelcome events as objectively real and not a matter of subjective choice. In *Problemata*, Aristotle considers a series of physical problems such as why do the frightened tremble? Why do the angry grow hot and the frightened cold?[6] Such involuntary physical reactions, according to Aristotle, are not determined by what one thinks or how one behaves.

The Stoic way of seeing this accords with Jesus' teaching that it is what emerges from a person, what he or she does, that defines the person and reveals his or her nature: 'Wherefore by their fruits ye shall know them' (Matthew 7:20).

No one else's actions can debase you, suggests Marcus Aurelius, but your own response may. Much the same principle is to be found in the New Testament. It is what comes out of his mouth that defiles a person, not what he puts into it (Matthew 15:18).

It is not so easy to sit still

Its widespread attractiveness over so many centuries does not mean that maintaining a tranquil mind is an easy skill to master, especially when something bad happens. Early in the sixth century AD, as the

Roman empire was in its chaotic dying days, the scholar and politician Boethius (480–524/25) found himself, in the turmoil of the times, under house arrest and facing a death sentence. He was understandably upset, but he saw that as a personal failure, for his training appeared to have deserted him when he needed it most. He felt that his Stoic philosophy ought to be more helpful than it was turning out to be. He wrote the *Consolation of Philosophy* to try to work out how to respond. He describes his 'vision' of a personified Philosophy, who appears to him in the form of a goddess. She reproaches him. He had once been her student, but seems to have forgotten all he had learned.[7] This is not the first time she has had to come to the rescue, she complains. Society has regularly persecuted philosophers, and Boethius is no exception.

Boethius tries to put into words the reason why he is unable to help himself by applying his philosophical skills. He and Philosophy used to sit in his library, discussing the natural world and the best systems of public administration, and now bad fortune has stripped him of the rewards he had earned by living a good, socially responsible life.[8] Philosophy's expression remains calm. She expresses her respect for Boethius' activities as a 'whistleblower', for he has been raising concerns about the improper behaviour of the Senate and that is in the public interest.[9]

She then leads him into a discussion of the way the world is ultimately governed and its purpose, and helps him to set within that fuller picture a better understanding of what makes a human being.[10] For, now that he is being tested by adversity, it has become apparent that there is a crack in the 'wall' of his understanding; he is finding that he is not properly fortified for life or against the blows it can bring. She gets Boethius to realize that he has forgotten the trick of positioning himself in the world so as to be no more lifted up by good fortune than cast down by bad. When he had good luck in life, he was bold and confident and used all sorts of teasing philosophical arguments, but now that he is suffering bad luck, he is not joking about it. He is imputing his distress to this change of fortune, but the change of fortune ought not to affect him at all.

Generation by generation, ideas like these were tried out in real life in the West, and some of the ways in which they might be problematic began to appear. There was a good side and a bad side to this way of living. The Stoic encouragement of the cultivation of the independence of the inner self, keeping a certain distance from what is enjoyed or experienced, has been approved again and again. When George Chapman (c. 1559–1634) wrote his dedicatory lines to King James I to accompany his new translation of Homer, he emphasized the significance – even for a king – of living within himself and not depending on outward things for his sense of identity and importance:

> Since perfect happiness, by Princes sought,
> Is not with birth borne, nor Exchequers bought,
> Nor followes in great Traines, nor is possest
> With any outward State, but makes him blest
> That governes inward, and beholdeth theare
> All his affections stand about him bare[11]

Yet commentators were often sensitive to the question whether the ability to ride out storms – and the general skill of remaining tranquil in more normal circumstances – was a real, robust way of engaging with the world, or a trick. This is still an important question, as Alain de Botton recognizes in his 2006 book, *The Consolations of Philosophy*, in which he deals with ways of coping with unpopularity, not having enough money, frustration, inadequacy, a broken heart, difficulties.[12]

Do I just want to avoid feeling uncomfortable?

Stoicism could and did appear hard and unfeeling. The modern Oxford English Dictionary (OED) defines 'stoical' in terms of 'austerity, indifference to pleasure and pain, repression of all feeling, and the like'. In the eighteenth century Alexander Pope (1688–1744) already found Stoicism lacking in human warmth, and wrote scathingly of the coldness of the control it seemed to require:

> In lazy apathy let Stoics boast,
> Their virtue fix'd; 'tis fix'd as in a frost;
> Contracted all, retiring to the breast;
> But strength of mind is Exercise, not Rest[13]

Shouldn't I be 'engaged' even if that is uncomfortable? There is obviously a good deal to be said for being able to stand away and think clearly, but is it selfish to keep calm in the face of disasters by detaching myself?

Put like this, Stoicism and similar systems can certainly seem like adjusting my perception of reality to protect my personal comfort. The eighteenth-century James Boswell (1740–95), biographer of Dr Johnson (compiler of the famous dictionary), wrote about one of his friends:

> Last night Demster came to me between ten and eleven and sat till one… He said he intended to write a treatise on the causes of happiness and misery. He considered the mind of man like a room, which is either made agreeable or the reverse by the pictures with which it is adorned. External circumstances are nothing to the purpose. Our great point is to have pleasing pictures on the inside… The great art is to have an agreeable collection and to preserve them well.[14]

To let my imagination conjure with other people's motives and paint them in strong colours and allow feelings of resentment to develop is to arrive at a point where it is not what people do that upsets me but my perception of what they have done. See the action in question in the right way, and anger vanishes. Where is reality if everything is relative and I am free to see it as I choose? So, if I find myself asking, rather irritably, whether this is anything more than a great game of self-deception, in which I keep reinterpreting reality so as to feel good about it, I am fooling myself; I have to be able to provide an answer.

There was a built-in protection in classical Stoicism against such self-referential, self-indulgent building of a comfortable zone in which to live. Although the Stoics believed that peace of mind was a fundamental requirement for happiness, they held that only those who lived virtuously could enjoy it. So, the balancing act of 'caring and not caring' was conducted according to moral principles and was not supposed to be a selfish exercise in avoiding unpleasantness for oneself. Deliberately distorting perceptions of reality so as to furnish one's mind with an 'agreeable collection' of pictures would not do. Nor would allowing oneself simply to stop bothering in the way John Ruskin (1819–1900) deplored when he found himself doing it: 'I have taken a fit of caring for nothing, and what is worse of lazy bed-keeping half awake.'[15]

Surely I should care about some things enough to do something active to protect or defend them?

Clinical detachment

It is fairly obvious that sometimes maintaining detachment may be better for the other person or for other people in general. A fireman, policeman or ambulanceman (or woman) has to be able to act with such professional detachment. It is no use trying to extricate an injured person from rubble after an earthquake if I have tears running down my face so that I cannot see what I am doing. If I am a nurse in an accident and emergency department of a hospital I have to be able to prioritize the treatment of the injuries that arrive without getting angry or allowing judgements about fault to get in the way. The novelist Sally Vickers gives one of her characters a moment of insight in her novel, *The Other Side of You*: 'Beware, beware of those who care! I, who cared so little for myself, had by way of compensation cared too much for others and they were the losers thereby.'[16] Caring can be intrusive, she is suggesting. Commitment and believing in people, things, ideas can, on the other hand, be positive.

There are difficult questions here, though.

If a drunk-driver causes an accident but he needs
more urgent treatment than his victims is it for
me to make a moral, instead of a medical,
judgement about who 'deserves' to be attended
to first?

Orderliness and moderation

The most important 'governing' principle involved in the balancing act in the classical world had to do with respect for orderliness and moderation. Restlessness is the sign of a 'disordered' spirit, says Seneca in his *Moral Letters*. In a late nineteenth-century lecture, Thomas Strong still responded vividly to this in his own more modern times:

There is to the Greek mind an element in [life] which is productive of surprise and painful disaster. This element is passion. Without being wholly and irretrievably evil, passion is still a dangerous and subversive force. It throws off rational control and hurries the man into action which he deplores in cooler moments.[17]

Feeling strongly

Should I try to cultivate the habit of not wanting anything very much, or should I feel free to be passionate in my interests and activities? A strong commitment or a strong attachment needs to be managed inwardly or it can become obsessive. It is a matter of getting the balance right.

Is 'passion' (feeling strongly about something) a bad thing, then? The ancient Greeks did not mean quite the same range of things by 'passion' as the modern English word connotes. They meant caring so much about something that it upset the balance of tranquillity, in rather the way Thomas Traherne (1636–74) uses it: 'I am not so Stoical, as to make all felicity consist in meer Apathy, or freedom from Passion, nor yet so Dissolute, as to give the passions all their liberty.'[18]

When Traherne wrote this, he was expressing his reservations about Stoicism, because it seemed to require people to avoid passionate commitment or extreme feeling. On the other hand, he could see the dangers of living entirely at the far edge of one's feelings. Enjoyment of pleasures without dependency on them seems to have been roughly what he had in mind.

> *Is this way of thinking helpful today in a modern world full of encouragements (and incentives) to take things too far? Is there still 'virtue in moderation'?*

Balancing

The work–life balance

When Jesus was the guest of the sisters Mary and Martha, Martha, over-busy with the practical preparations, complained that Mary was just sitting and listening to Jesus and not doing her share of the work. Jesus approved of Mary's choice: 'Mary has chosen the better part, which will not be taken away from her,' he said (Luke 10:42).

This is one aspect of balancing that most of us have to do at some time: out-of-work, idle and bored on a sofa watching daytime television; or tense with frustration on a commuter train twelve hours into the working day, waiting to get home to a brief evening before getting up early to start another day much the same.

In Carol Shields' 2002 novel, *Unless*,[19] a nineteen-year-old girl drops out of her university course to sit all day, every day, on a street corner with a bowed head, a begging bowl and a placard in front of her on which is written the single word of 'Goodness'. Her mother tries to make sense of this in a confusion of worry and regret, reviewing her own life and the lives of her family, her thoughts circling uneasily around the question of what, exactly, is 'good' about what her daughter is doing. She begins to think that Nora has withdrawn from normal life and disengaged from the world as a protest against her own powerlessness to do much about what she perceives to be wrong with the world.

Is it 'good' merely to turn one's back on 'wrong' so as to do no harm? But Nora *is* doing harm. She is distressing her parents and her younger sisters. It is also apparent to her mother that Nora has made a moral choice that depends on the rest of society continuing much as usual. Nora is actually sleeping in a hostel for the homeless where there is food and a clean bed each night. If everyone did what she is doing there would be no one to run the hostels.

Her placarded 'statement' and the self-abnegation of sitting behind it reflect something that many societies have considered to be valuable. Sitting behind the placard could be seen as a modern version of the centuries-old tradition of 'bearing witness'. It will 'make people think' as they walk past. In medieval Christian Europe, society was thought of as made up of specialist sections with distinct roles essential to the whole social process: some who ruled; some who defended the state by fighting in the armed forces; some who did the ordinary work that produced food and clothes and built houses; and some who withdrew from all these activities and prayed for everyone else, because everyone else was too busy to concentrate on having an inner life.

In the Christian West, pious people who could afford it endowed monasteries with lands to support monks and nuns in this activity. A similar value is still placed in Buddhist societies on such people who, not unlike Nora, live a life of contemplation and quietly hold out a begging bowl. In Buddhism, those who give by putting something into the bowl see themselves as benefiting not only from the 'work' of prayer done on behalf of the rest of the world by specialists who command a certain expertise. They also gain a 'borrowed virtue' of making it possible for them to be free to do so.

> *Cultivating detachment from my wants might*
> *prevent them from turning into spurious needs.*
> *But would self-denial make me a saint or a moral*
> *hero?*

Would material prosperity make people happy?

In the modern West, the general level of material prosperity has been rising for more than a generation, but the level of perceived contentment has not risen with it. Newspapers are not full of smiling, contented people who are happy that they have all they need. This would have come as no surprise to observers of earlier ages.

The ancient world would have disapproved of 'couch potatoes' on the principle that human beings were expected to be actively human and not to behave like vegetables. Many were particularly keen on achieving a mastery over urges more appropriate to animals than humans. Living virtuously was conceived in terms of learning how to live in a manner appropriate to human beings at their best, and thinkers of the ancient world had definite ideas about that.

The 'dynamic stasis'

This 'dynamic stasis' held the virtuous in the middle, between the gods, who were (even if some of them were thought to live in statues) thought of as essentially intellectual and rational beings, and animals, which were considered to lack powers of reasoning. Human beings maintained a precarious balance between those higher aspirations to which their rational selves were drawn and the low tastes towards which their bodies tugged them, and which they found hard to resist. Aristotle, for one, looked for satisfactions of a fairly elevated kind. He thought that happiness comes from the right exercise of the moral and intellectual functions of human nature, geared to the way of life one chooses. The philosopher's good life lies in thought; the statesman's good life involves action; the sensualist's good life is found in his pleasures. Epicurus urges the individual to 'live as a god among men' and 'in no way like a mortal animal'.[20]

At the bottom of the ancient hierarchy of living things were 'merely' bodily creatures – animals and plants without rational souls, which were seen as being incapable of anything but a lowly bodily life. The key idea here is that 'lower' desires, the likes of the

body and the senses, have a dangerous pull. Seneca remarks that a
sensible person lives in his mind and soul, and thinks as little about
the body as possible. It is a deprivation to do without bodily
pleasures at first, but such wants die away if not fulfilled and one is
the freer for it in due course.[21]

The tug of war

The ancient and medieval description of the natural hierarchy
became inseparable from the idea that matter was somehow 'bad'
and spirit 'good', that sexual urges in particular were liable to lead
people astray because of their inherently bodily character, their
strength and the difficulty of controlling them by reason. This view
of the world made its way into early Christianity. Paul says he
intends to 'punish [his] body and enslave it' (1 Corinthians 9:27).
The war between the 'beastly' body and the upwardly aspiring soul
was discussed a good deal in the most influential of the writings of
the major early Christian authors, who later came to be known as
the 'Fathers', particularly by Augustine.

It was common to see bodily things as 'dirty' and to cite the Bible
in support. Speaking of sinners, 1 Maccabees 2:62 calls their 'glory'
mere dung and worms. Philippians 3:8 claims that a Christian may
happily lose everything and regard it as so much 'filth', so as to 'gain
Christ'. Such ideas are often used by Augustine (AD 354–430) in his
sermons and letters. It remained familiar ground during the Middle
Ages, when there was much talk of the dunghill of the body. This did
not end with the Middle Ages, both because the imagery was
powerful and, perhaps, because it calls to deep and complex feelings
in human beings involving both desire for and rejection of the body
and the pleasures of the senses.

One of the areas in which modern life gives most scope to over-
strong desires involving the very old and familiar temptations
exercised by material things – and encourages them through
advertising – is in the endless temptation to acquire goods, especially
the latest and most fashionable goods. As a secular Roman planning
for the good life, Marcus Aurelius recommends that you avoid
keeping quails or getting excited about things of that sort.[22] He
would presumably have discouraged the active desire to acquire the
latest fashionable consumer goods in much the same way. Marcus
Aurelius also discourages his readers from showing off and being
fashionable.[23] Today he would be pointing reprovingly at the

'shopaholic' who spends much of his or her spare time shopping for new clothes.

Why? What is wrong with these ways of spending time and money? Is it because they draw me into inappropriate passions and enthusiasms for objects that are really not worth my time? Is this still an appropriate way to understand the desirability of the latest car or mobile phone? Is it because they unbalance me by encouraging me to see such acquisitions as more important than they are, as worth sacrifice? Is it because they distract me from applying my mind to higher things, and if so, what would be more worthy and higher objectives?

The reader who nods approvingly in agreement at this point will also have to ask whether enjoying a hobby such as making model aeroplanes, keeping racing pigeons or going to football matches is an unnecessary distraction from higher things. Is the acquisition of material possessions always a gratification of the senses, or can it involve a higher satisfaction, aesthetic, for example, or spiritual? And what is the difference?

Is it all right to enjoy the pleasures of the senses and material things as long as I do not become dependent on them?

Compromise

Are there basic principles, a moral 'guide' that will fit in a pocket and provide a solution when I want to behave well but am not sure how to do it? Is it possible to frame a calculus for deciding how to behave in a given situation? The Victorian theologian Henry Sidgwick (1838–1900) tried that, and very complicated he found it to be.

He suggested that 'Each is morally bound to regard the good of any individual as much as his own' unless it is a lesser good, in which case the balance would shift.[24] This derives from Jesus' second commandment, to love your neighbour as yourself, as does a development of it, the requirement to treat others as you would wish to be treated yourself. Let us say I have a mild wish to go to a football match and you are a lifetime supporter and very badly want to go. There is only one ticket. I give it to you. A second example of an attempt to identify a basic rule is his 'Principle of Deferred Gratification', which states that one should prefer a greater to a lesser good even if it means waiting for the greater one.[25] All this conjures up a picture of anxious people consulting a list of rules, ticking off points on their fingers and doing moral sums when faced with the urgencies of small daily decisions. That is obviously not realistic.

Very simple rules of thumb would be more practical for daily use. But the fact that clear rules would be useful does not in itself show that there are any such rules, absolutes, anything as strong as Kant's 'categorical imperative' – the idea that a certain sort of action may be morally 'necessary' or absolutely forbidden and not dependent on circumstances. Sidgwick's approach recognized something important – that moral decisions frequently involve 'balancing' considerations against one another, and that each person as a 'moral agent' has a responsibility to do that for himself or herself, looking for the best thing to do in the circumstances.

Does this mean compromising? Should I compromise if that means, according to the OED, 'a coming to terms, or arrangement of a dispute, by concessions on both sides'? That must depend on the nature of the concession, whether it would endanger truth or honesty, or as the OED puts it, 'a putting in peril or hazard, endangering, exposure to risk or suspicion'. The 'good' is the morally right and it cannot properly give way to the expedient, Cicero insists.[26] But there may be concessions to be made that do not compromise my integrity or imperil the truth.

Is it possible for my enjoyment to be innocent when I am spending money on my own pleasure that I could be giving to charity?

The humming-bird approach

Is there value in sheer enjoyment even if it is not productive of profounder thoughts or deeper insights? I go for a swim and enjoy the sensations. Is that all right or should I be concentrating on the benefit to my health, and not enjoy myself too much?

An ideal that has been persistent in the history of Western civilizations has been that the good man or woman should live a medium, middling or moderate life at the proper point of balance between being an animal and being a rational, intellectual being, cultivating the mind and spirit, satisfying the body's needs and enjoying the pleasures of the senses in a reasonable manner. Some things that seem innocent enjoyments in moderation become harmful in excess.

The maintaining of an inward equilibrium has its counterpart in the need to 'balance' the external events and factors that seem to threaten it. Contentment can be seen as an 'equals sign' between the things that would otherwise be tugging me one way or the other. I face a disappointment. I could 'even it up' by thinking of compensations. I cannot afford to go on holiday this year. When did I last have time to spend at home? Is such a balancing exercise just a way of limiting my disappointment or is it a moral activity?

A humming-bird flies hard in order to hover at the mouth of a flower. Its 'dynamic stasis' is a living 'equals sign'.

Perfecting
Life as a journey to a better future

> Once you've discovered the trick of what you are, you just have to live up to it. That's it, isn't it... I'm just talking about how one is from day to day. All life must be some kind of movement or other, only we're meant to see why we're going, it doesn't just happen to us – we – move – isn't that the point?[27]
> **Elizabeth Jane Howard (b. 1923)**

It is not surprising that so many explanations of the right way to live see life as a journey. We live along a line of time and cannot go backwards. Is it possible to progress towards a state of perfection while on this journey? Richard Hooker (1554–1600) used that kind of language in the sixteenth century: 'There is in all things an appetite or desire, whereby they incline to something which they may be: and when they are it they shall be perfecter than now they are.'[28]

What he meant by 'perfect' was probably closer to 'complete' than to its usual modern English sense. Because of the way he was educated he would also have been influenced by Aristotle's thinking on this point. Aristotle was especially interested in the idea that every living thing has a built-in tendency to unfold in a particular way until it becomes what it ought to be. An acorn will grow into an oak and not a chestnut tree because that is its potential.

Parents can see their individual children unfold in something of this way as they grow up, not just into adult humans but into the particular adult humans they have it in them to be. Some patterns of conduct seem to conduce to that process of 'perfecting'; others hinder it. An adolescent who becomes addicted to drugs could drop out of university and die an early death. The musically talented will not simply unfold into concert pianists. They have to do a lot of piano practice.

What is fulfilment?

Another early modern author describes the whole scheme of progression like this:

> We know that every Creature has a private Good and Interest of his own; which Nature has compel'd him to seek by all the Advantages afforded him, within the compass of his Make... Now, if by the natural Constitution of any rational Creature, the same Irregularitys of Appetite which make him ill to Others, make him ill also to Himself; and if the same Regularity of Affections, which causes him to be good in one sense, causes him to be good also in the other; then is that Goodness by which he is thus useful to others, a real Good and Advantage to himself.[29]

Here is a 'world of thought' in which loving myself and loving my neighbour are kept in balance within a dynamic progression of growth and perfecting.

Does being good to others make me 'better'?
How?

The contrast with modern ideas of self-improvement

To turn from this approach to the approach of modern self-improvement or to business management models of 'staff development' is to enter quite another realm of expectations – harder, competitive – in which striving for self-improvement involves the businesslike setting of goals, and in which other people feature chiefly as part of a personal plan to get on in life.

The Olympic rower Steve Redgrave moved into consultancy in this area when he gave up competitive sport and wrote *You Can Win at Life*:

> This book was inspired by the reactions I get when I talk to sportsmen and women and to business audiences. One question

that often gets thrown at me is: 'Now you are going into business yourself, are you structuring things the same way as you did in sport?'... This book is about how you, too, can get where you want to go.[30]

In this business version of life too there are steps and stages designed to assist 'progression':

visualizing and defining your dreams and desires;
recognizing your potential;
setting your goals;
training your body and mind;
staying ahead;
leading or being a member of a team.[31]

When this is set alongside the gentler, more reflective, urgings of the examples taken from earlier writers, the contrast of outcomes is striking. The objective here is to 'win at life' within the framework of the world of business. The framework of 'personal development' is narrowed, to become a poorer thing than growing or progressing to become fully what I am capable of being or designed to be. Having an eye for the good of others, keeping in balance their good and my own, has a different air and a different purpose, too. And the ambitious 'winner at life' is not very easily going to be able to 'care and not care', since if he stops caring urgently about it he will not win.

The modern reader in the West is likely to be challenged by this sort of offer of help with the process of 'growth'. This, not the earlier literature, is likely to be on a station bookstall or in a glossy paperback at the airport.

What is wrong with 'staying ahead' at all costs?

Does 'perfecting' have to involve effort, struggle and the overcoming of hardship?

As a schoolboy at Rugby, Matthew Arnold (1822–88) had problems with some of his schoolwork. His father wrote to urge him on: 'Nothing is to be done without Trouble, – but that I would have you... set your neck to the collar, and pull very hard, and then the Coach will at last get up the Hill.'[32]

Should behaving well really be like pulling a horse up a steep hill?

Is there a place for the idle moment?

A series of approved 'Homilies' was published in the Church of England in the course of the sixteenth century (1547 and then 1562–63). The idea was to make sure that, even if the parish priest was incapable of preaching adequate sermons, there would be something worthwhile for the congregation to listen to. He could just read them a homily.

One of these officially approved ready-made sermons is on the subject of 'Idleness'. It insists that human beings are not 'born to ease and rest, but to labour and travail'. This way of thinking came from the Old Testament. The story in Genesis describes how, after Adam and Eve had disobeyed him, God sent them out of the Garden of Eden to work hard for their livings (Genesis 3:19). Since then, people are 'born' to a life of hard labour and should expect nothing else, though the sinfulness of human beings distorts their expectations and makes them only too happy to be lazy, warns the Elizabethan homilist. This is especially a danger for those who are well off and consider it a perk of their social position that they should not have to labour away at living. According to James Mackintosh (1765–1832), society is easily led to consider 'idleness to be no evil at all, but rather a commendable thing, seemly for those that be wealthy':

> Desirous that my own leisure should not be consumed in sloth, I anxiously looked about for some way of filling it up, which might enable me, according to the measure of my humble abilities, to contribute somewhat to the stock of general usefulness.[33]

Does 'trying hard' need to be seen as an earnest worried endeavour in this way? Buddhists call a consciously maintained state of mind – observant, aware, self-critical, considerate of others – 'mindfulness'. This is defined in the OED as 'the meditative state of being both fully aware of the moment and of being self-conscious of and attentive to this awareness'. The classical world glimpsed something like it in the notion of what the Romans called *otium*, 'leisure', a quiet, reflective way of living in which a person may conduct himself purposefully and virtuously.

'That we may feel the importance of every day, and every hour as it passes, and earnestly strive to make a better use of what thy goodness may yet bestow on us, than we have done of the time past', is Jane Austen's way of putting something like this in her 'prayers'. Both the worried and the not-worried approaches are visible in what she says. There are glimpses of the quiet awareness 'mindfulness' involves. She speaks of 'that temper of forbearance and patience... which... will secure to us the best enjoyment of what this world can give'. Nevertheless, she is worried about the need to examine one's faults and failings at the end of every day. 'Another day is now gone, and added to those, for which we were before accountable,' she frets.[34]

> *Should I watch the clock? Should I make good use of*
> *my time? Can biding my time be a good way to use*
> *it?*

With a similar note of anxiety, Jeremy Taylor (1613–67) recommends his readers to be careful in the use of their time:

> He that is choice of his time will also be choice of his company, and choice of his actions, lest he first ingage him in vanity and losse, and the latter by being criminal be a throwing his time and himself away and a going back in the accounts of eternity...[35]

> Avoid the company of Drunkards and busie-bodies, and all such as are apt to talk much to little purpose: for no man can be provident of his time, that is not prudent in the choice of his company.[36]

Jeremy Taylor liked to see people get up early:

> Let your sleep be necessary and healthful, not idle and expensive of time, beyond the needs and conveniences of nature; and sometimes be curious to see the preparation which the sun makes, when he is coming forth from his chambers of the East.[37]

I may warm to these exhortations or laugh, but I can see that they need not be burdensome requirements if viewed in the context of a gentler and more relaxed, but still alert, 'mindfulness'.

Should I seek to be perfect (no half measures),
making sacrifices if necessary, or could perfection
turn out not to be something so extreme?

What if painful struggle is not my choice but is thrust upon me?
This is all very well as long as life goes steadily on without upheavals
and disasters such as serious illness. What if life is hard? What if I
am made redundant with no prospect of another job, or the local
factory is closed down, or I or a member of my family falls ill? It is
the response I make, not the things that happen, that seems to affect
me most.

For example, how should I respond if I am told I have a mortal
illness? Do I try to see this as helping me to grow towards that full
humanity which is a person's end?[38] John Betjeman (1906–84)
describes a reaction to this kind of bad news in which there is an
apparent 'denial', a pretence that nothing has changed (which is
itself a way of coping), a promise that through the change will run a
comforting normality. The patient and his wife leave the
consultant's offices:

> The heavy mahogany door with its wrought-iron screen
> Shuts. And the sound is rich, sympathetic, discreet.
> The sun still shines on this eighteenth-century scene
> With Edwardian faience adornment – Devonshire Street.
>
> No hope. And the X-ray photographs under his arm
> Confirm the message. His wife stands timidly by.
> The opposite brick-built house looks lofty and calm
> Its chimneys steady against the mackerel sky.
>
> No hope. And the iron knob of this palisade
> So cold to the touch, is luckier now than he
> 'Oh merciless, hurrying Londoners! Why was I made
> For the long and painful deathbed coming to me?'
>
> She puts her fingers in his, as, loving and silly
> At long-past Kensington dances she used to do
> 'It's cheaper to take the tube to Piccadilly
> And then we can catch a nineteen or twenty-two.'[39]

Both in the Middle Ages and at the end of the eighteenth century among Evangelical Christians, 'death-bed scenes' were a popular literary device for encouraging readers to turn bad times to good. In earlier centuries the usual thing was to practise seeing life as a mere preparation for an eternity whose arrival would be welcomed, not feared.

Are there other ways of being positive about such bad news?

The stages of life

Are older people under higher moral constraints because they ought to have learned from experience? They have also lost some of the inhibitions of shyness and timidity and may feel free to take challenging conversational and social risks, like the old woman in Jenny Joseph's poem 'Warning',[40] who wears purple with a red hat and behaves outrageously with complete insouciance.

How old I am obviously affects what I may 'rightly' do. When I was a child I was not allowed to drive a car. A small boy who sneaked out of the house with the car keys and drove the family car down the road would be doing something 'wrong' in the eyes of the law. Now I am grown up and have passed my driving test, I have a driving licence and I am free to drive down the road whenever I like. But, if I live to be ninety and my eyesight fails, it will stop being all right to drive a car down the road.

In some religions, life is divided into more or less formal stages, with a particular purpose identified at each stage as the right thing to concentrate on with a view to making the right kind of inward progress. In Hinduism, for example, life is seen as having well-marked periods of this sort, with different duties appropriate to each. In the first stage a person's task is to learn. Ideally, for the Hindu, this would mean actually spending time as an apprentice to the 'good' life, living a life of simplicity and self-denial with a teacher; keeping oneself from evil thoughts, words and deeds; and studying the culture of one's society. The aim is to learn, in the profoundest sense, to 'speak the truth', in other words, to see the world clearly and be honest about it. This sort of apprenticeship to the good life is recommended in other religions, too. There is something of the guru in the Jewish rabbi, and Jesus seems to have stood in a similar relationship to his disciples.

In Hinduism, the second stage of life for most people involves marrying and founding a family, in which there are plenty of opportunities to practise unselfishness, and husband and wife are, ideally, partners assisting one another's progress. The third stage of life begins when grandchildren are born and the pious Hindu may retreat to a life of contemplation and study. This prepares a person for the fourth and final stage of life, a withdrawal from the world into a monastic life in which he or she cultivates the presence of the divine. This is a period of final preparation, taking forward the learning of youth in the light of mature experience.

As I grow older should I 'feel the benefits' of a lifetime of virtue (supposing I have lived one)? Should I have become something better than I was when I was young? Should those good habits have become what I am? Or am I still going to be struggling with the same bad habits I had when I was young, still subject to unaccountable fits of anxiety and harmful temptations?

Should I look forward to a 'retirement' that will be a letting-go of responsibilities and all these worried endeavours? A high-pressure life, in which time has to be found for both work and family as well as for reflection, is nothing new. In the world of antiquity (from the first century BC to the sixth century AD), busy civil servants and politicians were often quite frank that they longed to retire from public life so as to have time for serious thought about the purpose of life and the way the universe works.

To seek *tranquillitas* in freedom from business may not be an unequivocal moral good, in Cicero's view.[41] He knows many who have retired because they can no longer endure the dubious goings-on of public life, and think they can best find that quiet life on their private estates. He has longed for this himself. These escapees want no one giving them orders, and they long for their freedom.

Cicero discusses the citizen's duty to remain in the fray, though he himself had been glad enough to get out of it on his retirement.[42] The modern worker who chooses early retirement is faced with a similar dilemma. What will be best not only for me but for my workmates or colleagues and the rest of the world?

Cassiodorus (c. 490–580) had been a senior civil servant in the days of the end of the Roman empire. He retired to spend his time thinking about God, and he published a commentary on the Psalms:

> Once I had put from me at Ravenna the responsibilities of office
> and those secular cares which leave a nasty taste, and could
> savour the honey for the soul which is to be found in the
> heavenly Psalms... I plunged myself avidly into reading them so
> that I could sweetly drink in those sayings after the most bitter
> activities.[43]

Pope Gregory the Great (c. 540–604) wrote a set of rules for those who held pastoral office (*Regula Pastoralis*) in which he set out a method of 'considering' things, which would enable those with practical responsibilities to strike a balance between their duties and the need to maintain an active inner life – an essential for spiritual leaders such as bishops (and himself as Pope). They were battling with much the same problem in the Middle Ages. The theme was taken up again by Bernard of Clairvaux (1090–1153), in his 'On Consideration', in which he points out to a later Pope, Eugenius III (1145–53), the importance of not allowing all his time to be taken up with trivial business, to the neglect of time for reflection, contemplation and 'consideration'.[44]

So there is another option, less extreme than withdrawing from the world to do nothing but think and pray, and that is a quiet, untroubled vigilance.

> And here, resolving to harass my self no more, I am preparing for
> a longer journey than all these, having liv'd 72 years, a Life of
> infinite Variety, and learn'd sufficiently to know the Value of
> Retirement, and the blessing of ending our days in Peace.[45]
> **Daniel Defoe (c. 1659—1731)**

Have I made a difference?

> I went to London to be private. My birthday being the next day, I
> now arrived at the sixtieth year of my age. Upon this, I began a
> more solemn survey of my whole life, in order to make and
> confirm my peace with God by an accurate scrutiny of all my
> actions past as far as I was able to call them to mind.[46]
> **John Evelyn (1620—1706)**

Evelyn was not facing the sudden news that he had a terminal disease, or the fairly exact prognosis of a modern medical diagnosis. He was just thinking about growing old. The practicalities of putting the past behind and getting on with your life with repeated fresh starts and an optimism that this time you will be able to make a difference, change with age. Eventually, there are more years behind than there are likely to be in front. John Evelyn seems to have felt that this required some anxious surveying, that the task he now had to tackle was a review of past actions so as to make sure nothing could still be held against him by a God with an account book.

This totting up of the negatives was the obverse side of a positive, sometimes risk-taking, practice of using opportunities to be active in the world, to 'do some good'.

> A life of action and danger moderates the dread of death. It not only gives us the fortitude to bear pain, but teaches us at every step the precarious tenure on which we hold our present being.[47]
> **William Hazlitt (1778—1830)**

When William Hazlitt wrote an essay on the fear of death he called for something rather different from Evelyn's detailed reckoning. He encouraged his readers to think more radically about the value to be placed on life:

> The most rational cure after all for the inordinate fear of death is to set a just value on life. If we merely wish to continue on the scene to indulge our headstrong humours and tormenting passions, we had better begone at once: and if we only cherish a fondness for existence according to the benefits we reap from it, the pangs we feel at parting with it will not be very severe.[48]

Am I afraid of death or of the process of dying?

Chapter 2

Ways of Behaving

Good, bad or indifferent?

> On the one hand there is the seething mass of desire. On the
> other, above it and separate, there are the lordly principles of
> ethics, which exist to control it. I believe nothing but confusion
> comes from this picture… I substitute for this a model in which
> there is just a plurality of concerns.[1]
> **Simon Blackburn (b. 1944)**

This comment about the goodness or badness of what I do is not as
alarmingly neutral as it sounds. It is not really being suggested that
it does not matter:

> Among these concerns are ones that have the kind of status that
> leads us to talk of virtue and vice, duty and obligation. These are
> the concerns we expect of each other, so that if we do not share
> them, or weight them properly, we are regarded as having fallen
> short.[2]

A battle of opposites?

The traditional vices and virtues usually appear in pairs. This has
encouraged generations of the would-be-good to think that most
behaviours have 'good' and 'bad' versions. Prudentius (348–c. 410)
in his *Psychomachia* or 'psychological conflict', describes a great
'battle of the virtues and vices', in which virtues and vices fight
'dressed up' as soldiers with names like Faith and Worship-of-the-
Old-Gods; Chastity and Lust; Patience and Anger; Humility and
Pride.[3] Others join in the fight, not always neatly paired, but
definitely on one side or the other, representing Honesty, Sobriety,
Fasting, Modesty, Hope, Reasonableness; these confront Deceit,
Self-indulgence, Greed. Greed comes with quite a gang of

personified unpleasantries, such as Worry, Hunger, Fear, Anxiety, Lying, Pallor, Corruption, Sorrow, Sleeplessness, Filth.

Alan of Lille's late twelfth-century epic poem *Anticlaudianus* sets up a battle of vices and virtues in imitation of Prudentius. Children's computer games, and films, plays and television dramas in which the 'Goodies' fight the 'Baddies' contain modern versions of this battle.

So this has remained a favourite way of conveying in a dramatic narrative the endless warfare in the human psyche that everyone seems to experience to a greater or lesser degree – to judge from its popularity as a picture of things century after century. All these descriptions of adversarial confrontations between virtues and vices assume that good and bad are polarized and opposed – and that it is the job of each of us to take sides and join the fight. If this has seemed an accurate picture over so many centuries, it would mean that growing more perfect is going to be quite a struggle and even when the battlefield is strewn with the corpses of these aggressively bad behaviours, they are not finally and decisively flattened.

When is good and bad behaviour 'relative'?

Yet good and bad behaviours seem, in some ways, to be relative. Observing the same behaviour on your part, I might call you extravagant or I might praise you for your generosity. I might accuse you of meanness or I might praise you for being thrifty. It seems to depend on my point of view. Even John the Baptist and Jesus experienced this kind of ambivalence in the way people talked about them:

> For John came, neither eating nor drinking, and they say, 'He has a demon'; the Son of Man came eating and drinking, and they say, 'Behold, a glutton and a drunkard, a friend of tax collectors and sinners!' Yet wisdom is justified by her deeds.
> **Matthew 11:18—19**

And perhaps the same adaptation of behaviour to the circumstances is to be seen in Jesus' own conduct. Jesus taught his disciples to be patient with one another, forgiving quickly and turning the other cheek (Matthew 5:39). But when he saw the Temple full of traders who were turning a place of worship into the equivalent of a modern commercial shopping mall, he threw them out, with a fierceness that seems to have been marked by anger (John 2:15). There is an important practical question here.

If I cultivate a 'virtue' or a good 'habit' am I safe in assuming that it will always lead me to do the right thing?

Some basic virtues

Islam has its own set of virtues which are particularly respected, partly based on the pre-Islamic Arab approval of generosity, courage, loyalty, veracity and patience.[4] Within the Christian tradition, two sets of prescribed virtues have been particularly important.

The list of Roman 'civic' virtues Cicero drew up was taken as one of the main starting-points for Christian good behaviour. These were prudence, justice, temperance and fortitude. Macrobius (395–423), in the fifth century, enlarged on each of the principal virtues in Cicero's list. Inside prudence he discovers reason, understanding, circumspection, foresight, docility and caution. Fortitude (or courage) evinces for him magnanimity, faithfulness, security, magnificence, constancy, tolerance and firmness. In temperance are to be found modesty and sobriety. From justice come innocence, friendship, harmony, respectfulness, religion, proper feeling and humanity.[5] This breakdown of aspects of the core virtues – themselves aspects of a single citizenly virtue which we might now describe as 'propriety' rather than 'honour' – suggests that a unitary virtue, embodying all the others, is likely to have a particular shading or colouration in a given time and culture.

This underlines the essential capaciousness or stretchiness of patterns of good behaviour, and the way they begin to overlap and to merge, on the way to becoming a single, unitary 'integrity'.

Basing itself on the New Testament, early Christian theology added three more core virtues: faith, hope and charity. Paul mentions these in several of his letters to young churches (1 Corinthians 13:13; 1 Thessalonians 1:3; Galatians 5:5–6; Colossians 1:4–5). Thomas Aquinas (c. 1225–74) suggested they have a natural sequence. Once you have faith, you begin to have hope and that leads on to love.[6]

But identifying the virtues and vices was not cut and dried, even in the New Testament period. Paul lists 'every kind of wickedness' (Romans 1:29), including evil, covetousness, malice, envy, murder, strife, deceit, craftiness, gossip, slander, God-hating, insolence, haughtiness, boastfulness, inventing of evil, rebelliousness towards parents, foolishness, faithlessness, heartlessness, a general lack of rightness in conduct.

Cicero's list, with its Christian additions, was borrowed and much used in succeeding centuries in the West, and as societies and their expectations changed people began to ask whether the vices and virtues should be modified too.

'Think not that morality is ambulatory; that vices in one age are not vices in another; or that virtues, which are under the everlasting seal of right reason, may be stamped by opinion', said Thomas Browne.[7]

Changing expectations about the virtues

Changing cultural expectations and social norms are bound to throw up new activities. William Fulbecke (1560–1603?), in *A Booke of Christian Ethicks* describes 'the true difference between Vertue and Voluptuousness', with a list of vices including dissembling, blaspheming, deceiving, flattery and dicing.[8] These match quite well with the vices we have just been considering, but among them are emphases that seemed particularly important in late sixteenth-century England, such as trying to curry favour with important people and gambling. Robert Boyle (1627–91), a century later, lists the qualities of 'the Christian Virtuoso' as they appeared to his generation, as greatness of mind; noble aims; courage or valour; constancy and patience in afflictions; bounty or liberality; forwardness to oblige; readiness to forgive; a just and impartial estimate of riches; humility; and contempt of all that is base.[9] By the nineteenth century, a robust confidence that times change made it possible to say:

New occasions teach new duties:
Time makes ancient good uncouth;
They must keep upward still, and onward,
Who would keep abreast of Truth.[10]
James Russell Lowell (1819—91)

So 'Shock! Horror!' headlines would not have fixed on the same alarms in every age or culture, if there had been newspapers to carry them. What, then, is the test to apply if I want to adjust the rules of good and bad behaviour? Can I argue that some at least of the virtues and vices of Cicero and the New Testament have become less absolute with the passage of time and change of cultural expectation?

And if things can change over time, are the same ways of behaving right for everybody now? How can I tell whether there are things that would be good if someone else did them but which are not appropriate for someone like me? Am I free to set my own standards and see moral questions from a personal standpoint?

Are there things it is 'good' to do now but which might not be 'good' in future generations, or which were once 'bad' but are so no longer?

Is a virtue what I do or what I am?

The virtues are values we embody, live and enact.[11]
Andr Comte-Sponville

Does the goodness or badness of a person's actions affect his or her value as a person and consequently someone's 'entitlements' in life? Small children are told that Father Christmas will not bring them presents unless they have been good. Could a virtuous person be more 'deserving' than someone who does not behave well?

The question whether virtuous people deserve more favourable treatment has been raised in the modern world in connection with the allocation of scarce medical resources in the National Health Service. Does a choice have to be made between providing care for someone whose illness is not his or her 'fault', and someone whose lifetime smoking is a probable cause of the lung-cancer which needs treatment; or whose bad eating habits have led to obesity and thence to diabetes; or who has cirrhosis of the liver as a result of hard drinking or alcoholism? It has even been suggested that an obese patient should be told treatment will be available only after weight-loss when there is no medical reason not to provide it straight away.

Do I become what I do?

The philosopher Immanuel Kant (1724–1804) thought the practice
of good manners would improve people's morality. We all have
habits, customary patterns of behaviour, which our friends may or
may not tell us frankly are 'good habits' or 'bad habits'. The hard
question is whether – as many popular tales have suggested over the
centuries – we are inwardly and outwardly marked by the way we
live, until we almost become what we have done. Habits reflect or
express what we are, so they could provide a useful clue to
'progression' towards perfection. When I look in the mirror do I see
lines of bad temper, arrogance or hardness, or gentleness and
benevolence, as my character 'shows' in my face?

Aristotle's theory was that a virtue is a characteristic, a regular
way of going on which becomes 'second nature' to an individual,
and indeed helps to mature the individual towards that full
humanity which is a person's 'end' or purpose.[12] Built into this
theory is the idea that the habitual activities of a living thing not
only express what it is, but progressively help to *make it what it is*.
A horse is doing what it ought when it eats grass and gallops about
until it dies at last in a perfection of horsiness. The most important
meaning of the word 'perfect' here is 'complete'. (The English word
comes from the Latin verb *perficere*, to complete.) Behind these
activities seem to lie the tendencies or characteristics which give rise
to habits. For a habit is something I *often* do, or it would not be
a habit.

Could the way I behave go further, and somehow enter into what
I am and alter the 'real me'? The idea that a virtue is not so much a
mode of behaviour (what I do) as what I 'am' was already well
developed in the classical world. Aristotle made a distinction
between 'virtue' as the innate potential (*dunamis*, Latin *potentia*);
and actual virtuous behaviour (*energeia*, Latin *actus*).[13] Cicero
defined virtue as a 'habit of mind' which accords with reason and
nature.[14] The Latin word *habitus* gave rise to the modern English
word but it means much more than 'habit'.

The question whether my habits change me or become 'what I
am' was discussed a good deal in the Middle Ages. In the twelfth-
century book by Peter Abelard, *Know Thyself*, the key idea is that
'sin' or wrongdoing consists not in having the will to do evil but in
consenting to it.[15] In the thirteenth century, Thomas Aquinas
insisted that virtue cannot be something which is in people by nature

because it is capable of being removed or eradicated by sin.[16] In his view, vice and virtue are 'caused' in us by the way we behave, rather than being innate.[17,18]

> 'The actual possession of one virtue is preferable to the bare
> speculative knowledge of them all',

asserted Robert Boyle in the seventeenth century.[19] What would such 'actual possession' involve? The English word 'virtue' comes from the Latin 'virtus', a power or 'force', but it has something of both the tendency to behave well, and the actuality of doing it:

> What is a virtue? It is a force that has or can have an effect.
> Hence the virtue of a plant or a medication, which is to cure, of a
> knife, which is to cut, or of a human being, which is to will and
> to act in a human way. These examples, which come from the
> Greeks, say more or less what is essential: virtue is a capacity or
> power, and always a specific one. The virtue of hellebore is not
> that of hemlock; a knife's virtue is not that of the hoe.[20]
> **Andr Comte-Sponville**

Mixed motives and diminished virtues

There are complications to be thought of before I go much further down this road. Perhaps I think with satisfaction that I am doing the right thing, but it is also advantageous to me so I score no points for disinterestedness (assuming that disinterestedness is itself a virtue). Perhaps I do what in some circumstances would be the right thing, knowing that this time it is likely to cause harm to others, so my motive for doing it is compromised. Perhaps I fail to do the right thing, because I guess (rightly as it turns out), that the result will be better for everyone that way. Should we do evil so that good may follow, asked Paul? (Romans 3:7–8). Perhaps I postpone doing the right thing in the confident expectation that events will move on and I shall not need to do it in the end. How does this fit with the idea that what I do becomes what I am?

Virtues can be greater or lesser, suggests Thomas Aquinas,[21] though he also thinks that it would not necessarily be more virtuous to do something to an extreme; virtue for him, and many classical authors, is essentially 'measured', something moderate.[22] Medieval writers warmed much more enthusiastically to extremes, describing with relish how people roll in the 'mud' of bad behaviour with the enthusiasm of pigs in a wallow.

We also have to ask whether virtue is a unitary thing or whether there are separate particular virtues, allowing someone to have 'good habits' in one way but not in another.[23] Is virtue a single thing or is it like a bouquet of flowers which you can make up at a florist containing any flowers you think will make a harmonious bunch? Are the virtues a 'set' or can I 'specialize' in just one or two if I want to be good? How would that affect my growing into the kind of person I shall become?

'He who has one virtue has them all and he who lacks any virtue has none', says Augustine.[24] Aquinas thinks virtues are linked (*connexae*), at least in the case of faith, hope and charity, which means you cannot have one without the others.[25] This is a way of saying that integrity may involve a sort of wholeness and completeness and internal consistency of such virtuous habits.

Everyone has seen how modern politicians lose sight of the way this cluster hangs together, one high expectation of good conduct reinforcing another. Then 'sleaze' begins to creep in, contaminating the propriety or honour of public life with cronyism and the buying of privileges, leading eventually to the dismantling of the protections that make a community a 'humane' place to live.

There is also the phenomenon of the personal downslide. It is easy to get into debt in the modern West by spending too much on credit cards and taking out loans you cannot really afford, encouraged to see a certain level of consumption as an entitlement, and the possession of fashionable cars and mobile phones as a mark of social standing. It can be tempting to try an easy fix. Loan sharks are only too willing to help. At the extreme end of this downward spiral, in the streets of a modern city, individuals with drug habits, desperate for easy money, mug people and steal mobile phones. The pattern was obvious even in the sixteenth century as this Homily describes:

> We see how easily such a man is induced, for his gain, to lie, to practise how he may deceive his neighbour, to forswear himself, to bear false witness, and oftentimes to steal and murder, or to use some other ungodly mean to live withal.[26]

Can manners be 'good'?

The good Hindu is courteous, hospitable and treats his or her family well. Is this good manners or virtue? 'Courtesy' in modern English usage can seem like a mere veneer on the surface of life. The OED defines it as 'graceful politeness or considerateness in intercourse with others', 'courtly elegance and politeness of manners'. Good manners seem at first sight a small-scale way of behaving well, something I can definitely do to make a difference, if only a modest difference. 'Silly cow!' shouts a youth in a hood as a woman with a child in a push-chair gets in his way in a shopping centre. Is he bad-mannered or 'bad'?

> Politeness doesn't care about morality, and vice versa. If a Nazi is polite, does that change anything about Nazism or the horrors of Nazism?[27]

Are good manners a virtue, or a range of virtues? Or are they something less, a matter of tone of voice and minor pleasantness of manner, the opening of life's doors and the giving up of life's seats for others to sit on, rather than the grand passions of fortitude, justice and their like?

'There is a theory of manners that uses the fiscal image of balancing the books', remarks Lynne Truss in *Talk to the Hand*.[28] This approach sees good manners as transactional, designed to ensure that society runs smoothly and without episodes of fisticuffs when tempers fray. The recent introduction of ASBOs (Anti-Social Behaviour Orders) in Britain has been designed to impose sanctions on (mainly) young people who behave in ways that prevent this protection of good order from working as it is designed to do.

Does being good make you happy?

> What a necessary Means Vertue is, how sweet, how full of Reason, how desirable in it selfe, how just and amiable, how delightful.[29]
> **Thomas Traherne (1636—74)**

Francis Hutcheson (1694–1746) outlined a theory of 'Moral Goodness' in his *An Inquiry into the Original of Our Ideas of Beauty and Virtue in Two Treatises* (1725). For him, one important test was how beautiful actions are, and another, how disinterested. Self-interest may make us behave badly, he suggests, but it cannot fool our sense of the beauty of goodness.[30] Beauty, goodness, truth, justice and mercy all come together in setting the standards of a satisfactory life as vividly for him as they did for Plato. The same complex of associations is found in other early modern writers, such as Daniel Defoe:

If a perfect Calm possesses the soul; if Peace and Temper prevail, and the Mind feels no Tempests rising; if the Affections are regular and exalted to virtuous and sublime Objects, the Spirits cool, and the Mind sedate, the Man is in a general rectitude of Mind; he may be truly said to be his own Man...

For the divine Spirit is an Influence of peace, all calm and bright, happy and sweet like it self, and tending to every Thing that is good both present and future...

But... if at any time the Mind is ruffled, if Vapours rise, Clouds gather, if Passions swell the Breast, if Anger, Envy, Revenge, Hatred, Wrath, Strife... the Man is possess'd, the Devil is in him.[31]

Am I happy when I am good?

Chapter 3

Personal Responsibility

Some complex moral decisions have to be taken very quickly. I see someone being attacked in the street. Do I challenge the muggers? Do I ring the police on my mobile phone and risk being mugged myself and having it stolen? Do I walk away very quickly so as not to get involved because my family would want me to come home safely? How long do I have to think all this through before the muggers have knocked their victim to the ground, kicked him and run off with their spoils?

Some moral decisions are made after months of agonizing. Should I find a care home for our mother? Will that mean I cannot help with the cost when my teenage children go to university so that they will graduate with big debts?

Other people may be free with their advice. 'I wouldn't do that if I were you.' They may put pressure on me. 'If you do that I'll never forgive you.' But all that really means is that we take what they say into account in doing our own sums and balancing the factors before we decide and act. Other people can help or advise or try to influence us, but in the end my decision-making is the expression of a lifetime of being who I am and yours expresses who you are. You and I are on our own when it comes to deciding what to do.

It may not feel like that. 'Carers', who never get a break from looking after a handicapped child or an elderly parent who is developing senile dementia, can feel as though they have no choice. But they may, even if the room to manoeuvre seems to be only in the wrong direction. For sometimes a person burdened with too much responsibility for too long simply walks away. That is a decision, and it proceeds not only from a balancing of factors but also from the innate characteristics and developed personality of the individual. A different sort of person, finding the situation intolerable, might react by neglecting or even injuring the child or adult cared for, when the caring has become too heavy a responsibility; or even 'ending it all' for everyone concerned. One mother in 2006 committed suicide by jumping off a bridge with her twelve-year-old autistic son. A different sort of person again might not let things reach that stage but make active efforts to get help; another might take those efforts beyond the individual case and start a pressure group, a support group or a hostel offering respite care.

How can I possibly keep my balance between caring and not caring and make progress towards perfection when it seems there are no obvious right answers? Personal responsibility may involve doing one's best in the circumstances and not wasting energy on self-reproach, but surely there are some guidelines I can rely on?

Innate directives

> Let any plain, honest man, before he engages in any course of
> action, ask himself, Is this I am going about right, or is it wrong?
> Is it good, or is it evil? I do not in the least doubt but that this
> question would be answered agreeably to truth and virtue, by
> almost any fair man in almost any circumstance.[1]
> **Joseph Butler (1692—1752)**

In the book of Genesis, which forms part of both the Jewish and the Christian scriptures, is a description of the process by which human beings came to know right from wrong. In the story, God tells them not to eat of the fruit of a certain tree, which is the tree of the knowledge of good and evil (Genesis 2:17). Persuaded by a serpent, first Eve then Adam eats the fruit. God drives the first humans out of the Garden of Eden immediately, for now they are like God himself in their knowledge of good and evil (Genesis 3:22).

In some systems an understanding of right and wrong is believed to be innate. Islam sees human beings as the creations of a God who gave them a built-in awareness of the difference between right and wrong. The idea that certain key principles of right conduct are built in means that on the Day of Judgement no one will be able to argue that he did not know what he was supposed to do. So there is no excuse even for those who may try to claim they did not have the appropriate teaching.

Within Christianity, Jesus' description of the surprise of the 'sheep' and 'goats' as they are identified at the Last Judgement and sent off to their reward or punishment (Matthew 25:32–46) can also be read as a hint that the knowledge of the rights and wrongs of the way to behave is inborn:

It is irrational and impious to suppose that Almighty God... would give to his Creatures Instructions, Commands, and Advices, which were puzzling, obscure or uncertain, when their Eternal Salvation was depending upon their conceiving and applying them aright.[2]
Jean Barbeyrac (1674—1744)

Augustine of Hippo noticed signs of greed and jealousy in tiny babies and (without the benefit of modern scientific thinking about the instinct for survival) came to the conclusion that selfish behaviour was not only innate but sinful. In city streets and supermarkets and at home mothers chide and try to reason with toddlers who are having difficulty in reconciling 'I want' with 'You mustn't'.

'You know you should!' How do I know?

Thinking for myself

He gives away all he has to the poor.
You do some voluntary work.
I am too busy to think about this at present. Remind me next week.

It throws an enormous responsibility on me if I have to work out my position on every front, and answer every moral question from first principles. It is going to test to the limit my capacity for knowing when to care and when not to care, how to balance things and what direction to head in, so as to grow more perfect.

Knowing myself and being myself

How well do I know myself? Low self-esteem can be as much a form of unhealthy self-regard as conceit.

'Knowing yourself' was a fashionable activity in classical antiquity. It was linked with the search for balance and tranquillity, but, especially in the Roman world, it was also a call for realism. 'Describe yourself to yourself as you are' is the way the Roman poet Juvenal puts it in his *Satires*. He has in mind the 'Know Thyself' recommended by the Greek philosophers, but his formulation has a robust Roman air.

The internalization of moral judgements by making honest reference to one's own self-knowledge appealed to later generations too, but with a slant appropriate to the changing times.

The practical problem is that what I see when I try to 'know myself' is bound to be influenced by the expectations of the time I live in. William Kidd's little pamphlet on individuality reached its twenty-sixth thousand in the printing of 1863, so it was evidently striking a chord in the hearts of Victorians who wanted to break out from the comparative strait-jacket of contemporary social expectations. 'How refreshing it is to meet with a person of integrity who is purely natural and who is sufficiently honest of heart to be independent of the World's opinion as to his sayings and doings!' he said.[3] Kidd continued enthusiastically:

> Nature makes us vagabond: the World makes us respectable.
> Commend me to Shakespeare's vagabonds... His sweet-blooded
> and liberal nature blossomed into all fine generosities as naturally
> as an apple-bough into pink blossoms and odours. Surely it would
> be better if we could have, along with our modern enlightenment,
> our higher tastes and purer habits, a greater individuality of
> thought and manner?[4]

But even the charming 'vagabondishness' of the sort that blossoms into 'fine generosities' involves striking a balance between the claims of 'me' and those of the rest of the world.

Fashionable expectations in the West have travelled a long way since then in the direction of positive encouragement of individuals to 'be themselves' and form their own moral codes. Everyone can now feel free to be 'vagabond' in the sense that society's expectations no longer maintain a general framework of respectability; many of the old marks of respectability now look absurd or unnecessarily repressive in their expectations. It is as though the moral corsets had been removed and, after the sigh of relief, everyone realized that now each person had to rely on his or her own 'moral muscles'.

> *Should I feel free to 'be' whatever I like? (Is being a*
> *nurse 'better' than earning a huge bonus in a job in*
> *the city and giving some of it to charity?)*

Indulging myself or controlling myself

In the modern West there is a good deal of commercial persuasion to put myself first. '*Because you're worth it!*' coos a model in advertisements for expensive cosmetics, encouraging consumers to feel justified in spending a lot of money on their appearance. '*Be good to yourself*' says another advertisement. But if I am a member of the Buddhist or Sikh community living in the West I may see this as a dangerous encouragement to be self-indulgent. One Buddhist 'rule' is to avoid using mind-changing drugs, including alcohol, to the point where their use may cause one of the other rules to be broken. Sikhs, too, embrace an ideal of self-discipline, as a means of teaching themselves to be contented, humble and forgiving, and of purging themselves of anger, greed and pride.

A life spent considering nothing but my own advantage would probably include days of gloom like the one on which John Ruskin wrote in his diary in 1877: 'Wednesday Dark, with small rain I rheumatic – disconsolate, scornful of myself – more uncomfortable than ever yet – in fading interest in all things'.[5]

He did not always feel like that. He left his mark on Victorian society with an energetic programme of public service work, including fostering the provision of teaching for ordinary working men; and he was a prolific painter and writer. But it seems that he might have answered the question 'What should I do?' in different ways on different days, depending on his mood. I, too, am sometimes not really 'myself'. I have 'off days', behave out of character, do things that make me ashamed of myself.

The small boys cast away on an island in William Golding's novel *Lord of the Flies* confront this problem early in the story as they realize they are on their own and all the familiar controls of their lives have vanished. They have to work out a form of organization from first principles:

> 'We'll have to look after ourselves.'
> Secure on the other side of Ralph, Piggy spoke timidly.
> 'That's why Ralph made a meeting. So as we can decide what to do...'
> Jack spoke.
> 'We've got to decide about being rescued.'
> There was a buzz. One of the small boys, Henry, said that he wanted to go home.

'Shut up,' said Ralph absently. He lifted the conch.
'Seems to me we ought to have a chief to decide things.'
'A chief! A chief!'
'I ought to be chief,' said Jack with simple arrogance, 'because
I'm chapter chorister and head boy. I can sing C sharp…'
'Let's have a vote…'
This toy of voting was almost as pleasing as the conch. Jack
started to protest but the clamour changed from the general wish
for a chief to election by acclaim of Ralph himself. None of the
boys could have found good reason for this; what intelligence had
been shown was traceable to Piggy while the most obvious leader
was Jack. But… there was the conch. The being that had blown
that, had sat waiting for them on the platform with the delicate
thing balanced on his knees, was set apart.[6]

*How am I going to make moral decisions if there are
no external rules to consider and my inner landscape
is so changeable?*

Conscience

Is my conscience an inner 'judge', which is simply part of me, a
learnt part of my inner checks and balances, or a divine monitor,
God giving me a direct nudge? 'What is conscience?' has never been
an easy question to answer. Robert Boyle, who had a lifelong interest
in the question of conscience, provided a pension for Robert
Sanderson (1587–1663), Bishop of Lincoln, so that he could prepare
for the press a series of lectures he was giving on the subject. No
consensus has emerged.

In *Paradise Lost*, John Milton (1608–74) has God explaining that
conscience is his own voice acting as an 'umpire':

I will place within them as a guide
My umpire conscience[7]

Jeremy Taylor agrees that conscience is the voice of God:

God is especially present in the consciences of all persons good
and bad, by way of testimony and judgement: that is, he is there a
remembrancer to call our actions to minde, a witnesse to bring
them to judgement, and a Judge to acquit or to condemne.[8]

The problem with this explanation is that conscience may apparently prompt different people in different ways.[9] I may be as firmly convinced that I know what God wants as someone who completely disagrees with me is that God is telling him or her the opposite. That seems to suggest that I am my own judge and you are your own judge, and divine prompting has nothing to do with it.

Another way of looking at the operation of 'conscience' is to see it in its relation to maintaining peace of mind. C.S. Lewis (1898–1963), exploring the way the Roman poet Horace used the Latin root of the English word, suggested that having a clear conscience means knowing nothing against oneself, *nil conscire sibi*.[10]

Yet another approach is to ask what it would mean to have a 'clear' conscience. If I am living an open life and have nothing to hide can I say I have a clear conscience? This is another way of understanding conscience which has its origins in the classical world. Seneca says that everyone who has been up to no good wishes to hide the fact, but a good conscience loves the light. Thomas de Quincey (1785–1859), who had plenty on his conscience, says much the same:

> Guilt and misery shrink, by a natural instinct, from public notice: they court privacy and solitude; and, even in the choice of a grave, will sometimes voluntarily sequester themselves from the general population of the churchyard, as if declining to claim fellowship with the great family of man.[11]

> *Am I hearing my voice or God's when my conscience bothers me?*

Integrity

Do I have personal integrity? Someone with integrity has been seen as possessing a consistent inner self. The root meaning of integrity is 'wholeness', from the Latin *integritas*. This wholeness has several aspects. A person who has integrity is 'complete', or at least on the way to becoming so.

An important idea here is that the wholeness may be full of detail and variety as long as all the complications are in balance and in harmony. One of the dictionary definitions of 'integrity' is 'having all parts in due connexion', being 'in an unbroken or undivided state' or 'constituting a complex unity' (OED). Integrity seen in this way has something of the quality of a work of art, which forms a whole even though it is made up of hundreds of brushstrokes or sounds, and the composition is satisfying though it may be far from symmetrical.

The biblical idea of personal wholeness includes the notion of being healed, made healthy. To the woman who was healed of a longstanding haemorrhage when she touched his garment, Jesus said that her faith had made her 'whole' (Luke 8:48), as the Authorized Version translates it. To the cured leper who came back to say thank you he said, 'Your faith has made you well' (Luke 17:19). This idea of healthiness is associated with soundness, being unmarred and undamaged, unimpaired, unviolated, innocent.

And what, in a practical sense, will be the result if I attain such personal integrity? How will it make me behave? The dictionaries have descriptions. I will show soundness of moral principle, be upright, honest, sincere, truthful. I will be known for my fair dealing. I will be careful not to fall into thinking that my perspective gives me an adequate vantage point. Integrity has to be balanced, unselfish and generous in the views it takes of things.

Should I be glad when I have an uncomfortable conscience?

Should I always do what I am told?

Are moral rules something I should look for as 'given' in existing moral codes, or can I make them up? What happens if each individual sets his own standards and rules and sees moral questions from a personal standpoint?

What are the rules?

The first problem is finding out what the rules are. Various sets of detailed instructions have been laid down within the religions of the world. To be an adherent of a particular religion usually means accepting a code of conduct. These rules of right and wrong are seen as divinely or supernaturally 'given'. That does not necessarily mean that believers in any of the world religions know what is expected of them in every situation.

The original codes can grow dated in various ways. For example, the ten commandments of Judaism (Exodus 20:2–17; Deuteronomy 5:6–21) say that God has expectations about the way his people will behave towards him, and about the way they will treat one another.

They are not to worship other gods or make idols to worship or use God's name to swear with; they are to respect their elders and not steal from one another, or commit adultery or covet one another's possessions. But the details given are not necessarily applicable today. The ten commandments presume a particular sort of household in which there are servants and even slaves, and the 'head' of the household owns everyone in it including his wife and children, just as he owns the farm animals. Modern households in the West are very different in structure. Coveting other people's 'oxen' (specified in Exodus) is not a frequent temptation in the modern West, though wishing to 'keep up with the Joneses' and imitate my neighbours by buying whatever they have just bought – a new car, a new television – may be.

An alternative way of responding to the imperatives of one of the great 'codes' is to seek for the essentials, the simplicities, the basics. Jesus made a summary of the ten commandments (Matthew 19:19). They mean, he said, that I should love God wholeheartedly and love my neighbour as myself. The philosopher Spinoza (1632–77) applied that to his own time. 'The only knowledge commended in Scripture is that which everybody needs in order to be able to obey God in the way required by that precept [love of one's neighbour]',[12] and 'It is evident, then, that so far as Scripture is concerned, we are under obligation to believe only what is indispensable for carrying out that command [to love one's neighbour].'[13]

When Jesus gave his summary, someone immediately asked Jesus who his neighbour was. It seems that the questioner hoped that there might be people he need not 'love'. The habit of looking beneath the details for the essentials makes it harder to fool ourselves. Jesus made that obvious when he told the questioner the story of the Good Samaritan, which we shall meet in later chapters.

Could running up debts on a credit card to buy things
you cannot afford but which are currently in vogue,
be a breach of the commandment which forbids you
to covet what your 'neighbour' has?

The pattern of influence of each set of moral principles embodied in a holy book, or a religious tradition, has not only been affected by cultural change and technological development over time; it has also been affected by decisions taken in other religions. The Jewish laws set out in the Old Testament were reviewed in early Christianity and a decision was taken not to require Christians to follow all the requirements of the law of the Old Testament. Islam adopted elements of the Old Testament and the New. The Koran describes the episode of the giving of the commandments to Moses without giving the full list:

> God said to Moses:
> 'I have chosen you of all mankind to make known My messages and My commandments. Take therefore what I have given you and be thankful.'
>   We inscribed for him upon the Tablets all manner of precepts and instructions concerning all things, and said to him:
> 'Observe these steadfastly, and enjoin your people to observe that is best in them.'
> **Koran 7.143—146**

In any case, the codes set out in the holy books – the Old Testament, the Koran, the Christian Bible (whose contents were more or less agreed only about the fourth century) – were not always unambiguous in the first place. Over many centuries of interpretation they have tended to develop a range of emphases. For example, Orthodox Jews and certain Christian sects have been extremely strict about Sabbath Observance. Some Jews, for example, 'observe the Sabbath' to the point of not even switching on a light (though they may pay someone else to do so on the family's behalf). Those in the Christian tradition who have taken Sabbath Observance particularly seriously have not maintained the specific observances enjoined in the Old Testament but 'kept the Sabbath' (in their case Sunday, the day of Jesus' resurrection) by avoiding all amusements and concentrating on worship.

'Sunday Observance' for Christians at one time meant going to church three times on Sunday, with Sunday school and no games for children. 'What is to become of the Sabbath-day school?' asks Mrs Proudie, as she manouevres in Trollope's *Barchester Towers* to get an ecclesiastical preferment for her own protégé, in a cathedral close where the canons are more interested in the beauty of the music in the cathedral than in what she regards as the plain duty of Sunday Observance for the congregation.[14] These attitudes linger. From this mindset has come the continuing British restriction on opening shops for normal shopping hours on Sundays.

On the face of it, these variations would be puzzling features of the traditional moral codes of the world religions, if the right way to approach moral decision-making is by simply following rules.

Why is it not always obvious what is the right thing to do?

What is the ultimate authority of 'rules'?

Then there is the question of the authority of rules or laws. 'Who's going to make me?' asks the defiant adolescent boy, towering over his father. For much of history and in many contemporary societies there would be a general expectation that ultimately God, or some supernatural authority, could very well do that, that behind moral codes lay the sanctions of a divine lawgiver. Why should anyone take any notice of moral rules that curbed selfish conduct, unless such sanctions existed and were feared?

The classical philosophies of Greece and Rome left wide open the question what supernatural power or powers might exist, and even envisaged the existence of naughty and unedifying gods. They were concerned with the origin and structure and nature and purpose of things. But they went beyond the scope of modern science to the purpose of life, and whether there is a supernatural power in charge of the universe. They were also concerned with practical living, moral as well as metaphysical systems. Were these moral systems religious too?

How far can religion and morality be separated? The laws of a society normally have force because they are created by visible authority which polices their enforcement and has courts in which to try offenders and prisons in which they can be punished. Can moral rules have force unless there is a God behind them offering the same assurance of authority, and a structure for requiring enforcement? To think like that is to make a comparison that is not necessarily appropriate.

The force of moral laws that claim to have divine approval is clearly not the same in every religion, or in every era, or from all points of view. In the Old Testament, the ten commandments of Exodus 20 forbid things. There is a running theme of 'Thou shalt not...', as well as some positive precepts. The sanctions imposed on those who broke the commandments were expected to be severe. In some countries, fundamentalist Islam still takes it to be God's law that a woman 'taken in adultery' should be stoned. By contrast the

New Testament records Jesus speaking of a 'light yoke' and a 'burden' of requirements about good behaviour which could easily be carried and was scarcely a burden at all (Matthew 11:29–30). He summarized the ten Jewish commandments in a positive way, in the form of the requirements to love God wholeheartedly and to love one's neighbour as much as oneself (Matthew 22:36–39).

There is a considerable range of possible attitudes to the role of religion in the design of a moral system. At one extreme lies a fundamentalist certainty that all commandments in sacred writings (for example, the Bible or the Koran) are to be taken at face value as absolute imperatives of personal behaviour. Groups within a given religious community may claim to know with especial clarity what God expects. In the modern developed West are still to be found communities of Christian believers who take a very hard line on certain moral rules cited from biblical texts, treating them without an understanding of the way a text came into being or the changing meaning of terms. Sometimes they are reading the text only in translation, with all the loss of nuance that makes inevitable. For example, Conservative Evangelical Christians may insist that God's laws in the Bible are absolute, arguing that countenancing homosexual practices is of such importance that it is appropriate for a government's chance of election to depend upon its position on such matters. The Anglican Communion was threatened with schism in 2007 over the ordination of practising homosexuals to the priesthood or episcopate. Rowan Williams comments on the extreme passions aroused:

> I mention the gay-baiting Archbishop of Central Africa, who recently absolved, without trial, Bishop Nolbert Kunonga of Harare – a crony of Robert Mugabe accused of incitement to murder, intimidation and mishandling funds. Malango has also been accused of persecuting and smearing the Rev. Nicholas Henderson, a London vicar who was chosen last summer as Bishop of Lake Malawi.[15]

Peter Tatchell, gay human rights campaigner, writes eloquently of the homophobia he has encountered among Christians:

> Leviticus 20:13 says that queers are an abomination and should be put to death. Christian churches followed this murderous

incitement for 1,800 years. We sodomites were stoned to death in
antiquity, burned alive during the medieval inquisition and, in
Britain, hung from gallows until the mid-nineteenth century.

One of his main concerns is that homosexuals are 'rejected and
reviled by their families, driven to depression and suicide'.[16]

Tatchell's experience is a warning that an absolutist approach to
the condemnation of particular patterns of behaviour is likely to
generate fresh moral questions by thrusting all sorts of other moral
norms out of sight. One moral question, like a young cuckoo in a
nest, has thrown all the others over the edge. Here the duty of
parents to nurture their children, recognized as a 'natural law', is
engaged, only to be denied by parents who have 'rejected' children
with homosexual tendencies because of the way they read the Old
Testament book of Leviticus in an English translation.

At the other extreme of this spectrum lies a perhaps wholly
personalized choice of self-imposed rules with no underlying
religious assumptions at all. The question is whether a wholly
'rules-based' approach is the most helpful, with its inevitable over-
simplification of complex context and circumstances and its
tendency to encourage me to look anxiously over my shoulder to see
if punishment is bearing down on me for some infringement.

Is 'Am I keeping the rules?' the right question?

'Selective obedience' – and making the selection
How can I cope with conflicting requirements? Can I pick and
choose? To the conscientious and thoughtful, human life can come
to seem an endless process of moral decision-making, as dilemma
after dilemma presents itself. This great complexity of the human
response to a set of rules and a requirement of obedience has led to
debate about the desirability of a more selective obedience, in which
the individual takes a decision for himself or herself based on a
reasonable appraisal of the contents of moral codes.

It was asked from New Testament times whether all the Bible's
'laws' have to be obeyed by Christians, including those of the Old
Testament – even the law that one must tithe (give a tenth) of the
herbs in the garden.

Spinoza even thought the rules could safely be interpreted by
individuals according to their private opinion of what was required:

> I would not charge the sectaries with impiety for adapting the
> sayings of Scripture to their own opinions, for as they were originally
> adapted to the understanding of ordinary people, so it is permissible
> now for each individual to adapt them to his own opinions, if he
> finds by so doing that, in matters requiring justice and charity, he
> can obey God with a greater unity of mind and heart.[17]

This approach had, as Spinoza knew, many dangers, for it left wide
open the possibility that individuals might convince themselves that
all sorts of interpretations were 'right'.

> *What will happen if I decide not to do what I am*
> *told but what I think is best?*

Obedience

Restful though it might be just to 'do what I am told', I have to take
responsibility for deciding what to do for myself or I am a mere slave.
When I cry 'Good dog!' I am approving of the animal for doing what
it was told to do. A 'bad dog' is a disobedient dog. And on the whole
a 'good dog' appears to be a happy dog, basking in the approval of
the great authority in its life, its master or mistress, cheerfully
occupying its place in its pack.

A common factor in the approach to being good which takes
morality to be inseparable from religion has been the idea that the
first requirement is obedience to divinely appointed instructions.
Spinoza went as far as to claim 'that men are saved only by
obedience' is 'the basic doctrine of theology'.[18] That seems to make
human good behaviour hard to distinguish from canine good
behaviour. A dog's 'morality' is not usually defined by thinking for
its canine self and deciding what it is 'right' to do, personally
speaking. Does this approach make sense for human beings? Is
unthinking obedience a good idea for people as well as dogs?

To a degree that appears not to be fully matched in canine nature,
as far as we can observe, the human self rides on a sea of changing
personal response to circumstance, some of it conscious, some
unconscious. People have a capacity for thinking about
consequences, an ability to weigh pros and cons, a self-image that
can be damaged for much longer than the moment when a dog
wearing a 'hang-dog' expression looks 'apologetic' in an apparently
almost human way, by 'feeling bad about themselves'.

Human beings may have wants and expectations that can become obsessive and damaging, but which can also disappoint if they are fulfilled. Human beings can become vain if given too much approval for doing what they are told. They may despair if these bolsters of reinforcement are removed.

Obedience became a keynote of Benedictine monasticism in the West, under the Rule provided for his monks by Benedict of Nursia in the sixth century. The monk gave up self-will. He did what the abbot told him, praying, reading, working as instructed, and in this, it was promised he would find freedom for his soul.[19]

The modern English word 'duty' has been defined in terms of obedience, with something of this flavour, as 'the action and conduct due to a superior; homage, submission; due respect, reverence; an expression of submission, deference, or respect' (OED).

To enter a monastic order is to take a vow of obedience. A monk or nun under a vow of obedience gives up self-will and simply obeys the abbot or abbess, following the Rule of the Order. The sixth-century Rule of St Benedict puts it like this:

> Hear, my son, the precepts of the master... Receive this instruction of your father who loves you and obey it... In this way you will return through the effort of obedience to him from whom you have slipped away through disobedience... You who renounce your own wishes in order to fight for the true King, the Lord Christ, take up the powerful and glorious arms of obedience.[20]

The immediate obedience is to be to the abbot, and specifically to his instructions, which he is supposed to offer with gentleness.

By the twelfth century Bernard of Clairvaux was writing about problems that had arisen in knowing how exactly to take this. Obedience no longer seemed so straightforward. Monks asked whether all precepts of the Rule are to be followed equally strictly, or whether some could be dispensed of; whether the abbot himself had to obey the Rule, since he was first and foremost a monk himself; whether he could have authority either to compel his monks to an obedience going beyond the Rule, or to let them off parts of it.

The reason why all these questions were being asked was that most people who enter religious life find obedience hard. Perfect obedience, suggests Bernard, knows no bounds. It does not seek to stop at the boundaries of the law. It is much too wholehearted for that. And he points out an important difference between being obedient for fear of punishment and being obedient for positive reasons, out of love.[21]

The problem is that self-will is not so easily abandoned, even by those who freely choose to try:

> Almost the first thing that the Mistress of Novices explained to me was the importance of being exact about even the smallest details of the Rule. She said, 'You must give up your own tastes and habits and allow the Rule to mould you according to the pattern of the Order to which you belong.' As I was extremely lively and much attached to my own way of looking at things, I found this difficult.[22]
> **Monica Baldwin (1896—1975)**

It has long been recognized that obedience can be experienced as a kind of freedom. It takes from me the exhausting task of repeatedly having to make moral decisions. Sometimes, whatever I decide, I am going to be left with painful regrets, unless I believe I really had no choice but to obey. How easy and restful just to do as I am told.

Can I be forced to do wrong?

Sometimes an order from an employer, superior or manager is in conflict with other rules I feel bound by, as when a doctor is told to withhold a treatment because the hospital management has overspent its budget. In the modern West such dilemmas can be acute enough, with dismissal of an employee who refuses to obey orders out of conscience, or a trial in a military court for a soldier who refuses to fight in a war he believes to be illegal, as some have done in the case of the Iraq war.

More terrible examples have been faced in the modern world:

> In July 2002, 'Michael' was abducted by the rebel Lords Resistance Army (LRA) in Northern Uganda. Two years later he escaped. In this ongoing chapter of recent history, the LRA, led by the fanatical Joseph Kony, has abducted 25,000 children. In his army, boys are given a choice: kill or be killed, while girls are used as sex slaves. Few survive. Those who don't die from malnutrition or dysentery are murdered by rebels or hacked to death by other child soldiers.

The rebels came in the night to the village where I lived with my grandmother. They took me from my bed, just as they had done with so many other children. For the first two days I had my hands tightly bound, but as we approached the Sudanese border they loosened my hands and gave me bags to carry. All the time I kept my eyes down – I was terrified. I knew that I would soon be given my first 'assignment'.

I didn't have to wait long. When the LRA see someone riding a bicycle, they have a policy of killing them. People on bicycles pose a threat, as they can ride to the next village and raise the alarm. We came across a man on a bike and I was told to beat him to death with a piece of wood. I didn't hesitate, because to do so would have meant sacrificing my own life. Boys who are unable to kill (and there are many) are subsequently killed themselves.

After several months I was given a gun. They told me to smear shea butter over my hands, feet and forehead. This, the rebels said, would give me the courage to kill, but it would also make me fall to the ground should I try to escape. I believed them.

I don't know how many people I killed while I was in the bush. I would use my gun and fire indiscriminately into the crowds as we raided villages for food and children. Many people died because of my actions.

Finally, after two years, I began to doubt the rebels. Myself and another boy decided to escape. During the next attack on a village we took our chance; we ran and ran until after two days we found ourselves at the government barracks. They interrogated us and sent us to a returnees' rehabilitation project supported by Oxfam.

My conscience is not clear, and will never be. Inside I feel terrified of what I have done and regret it deeply. The nightmares haven't started yet, but I can't stop thinking about what happened in the bush. I've written to my grandmother to ask her to take me back, but have not yet heard from her. Perhaps she doesn't want to see me because of what I've done.

I know that because I've committed atrocities people may see me as a perpetrator, but I'm also a victim because I did not choose to kill.[23]

Would it really be my fault if I was 'forced' to do what I believed to be wrong?

Gurus, counsellors and life-coaches

> Dr Rowan Williams was talking eloquently about society's
> expectations of the Church of England and said words to the
> effect that society was missing the point in expecting the Church
> to be in the business of moral leadership. At this the man from the
> Daily Mail practically fell off his chair. Surely moral leadership
> was the whole point of the church?[24]
> **The Guardian**

Where is the boundary between the internal moral guidance of conscience and the external rule of the law? Who is allowed to tell me what to do? The State? Religious leaders (but what if one is telling me to become a suicide bomber)? Only God speaking inside me? The Roman Republic eventually became an empire in the late first century bc, and citizens were expected to show respect for the emperor as though he were a god. This was the ancient world's equivalent of the modern Western 'cult of celebrity', but it also assumed that authority should be treated with deference. People were expected to set aside personal and religious scruples and conform if someone authoritative in a significant and important 'office' told them what was right. This was a problem for the Jews and Christians of the day, who could not in conscience treat the Emperor as a god.

Rowan Williams was sceptical about the effect his opinions as Archbishop of Canterbury were likely to have on most people in the UK. 'I wonder whether when an archbishop condemns something, in the bedsits of north London somebody says, "Oh I shouldn't be having premarital sex." I'm not sure that's how it is.'[25]

But in the same period life-coaches and counsellors of various sorts, modern counterparts of the rabbi/guru, were thriving because it was possible to build an industry on people's need for someone to turn to for guidance. In a way, adherence to a code, with its simplification of complex moral issues, and a dog-like attempt to hand over responsibility for all these choices and just do what one is told, has its modern equivalent in the search for a guru, a counsellor, a life-coach. For the modern Western expectation is often that if I find myself in difficulties I shall seek 'counselling'.

*What balance should I aim for between listening to
advice and guidance and deciding for myself?*

'Oughts' and stewardship

'Ought I to make good use of my time?' 'Ought I to give more of my
income to charity?' are questions a worried and well-meaning
person has probably asked himself or herself a good many times. But
the fact that they all begin with 'ought' does not mean they are
asking the same kind of thing, or that they 'ought' to be a source of
anxiety. Some 'oughts' seem to involve a notion of stewardship.
'Ought I to make good use of my time?' is a question that presumes
that I should live so as to fill every hour with purposeful activity, as
though life had been entrusted with a certain amount of time and I
'ought' not to waste it. But experience shows that shapeless time,
time to reflect and even do nothing at all, time to lie fallow, can turn
out to have been important 'unconscious thinking' time. 'Ought I to
give more of my income to charity?' is another kind of 'ought'
question with a dimension of stewardship. For who am I to hold on
to so much property when others are poor and needy?

Ought I to keep my promises?

Whether I 'ought' to keep my promises depends on an
understanding of the word 'obligation', in which the obligation
arises from a covenant or contract. A contract is a mutual agreement,
though if it is thought of as being made between me and God I can
see that the parties are not going to be equal. God is portrayed in the
Jewish, Christian and Islamic scriptures as giving his
commandments unilaterally, not negotiating them with human
beings in search of a mutual agreement. And when they are
disobeyed, he is angry not at breach of an agreement but at plain
disobedience to his orders. The Koran speaks of disobedience at the
end of the passage in which Moses is given the Tablets containing
the commandments:

> I shall show you the home of the wicked... if they see the right
> path, they shall not walk upon it: but if they see the path of error,
> they shall choose it for their path; because they disbelieved Our
> signs and paid no heed to them.
> **Koran 7.146**

According to Genesis, God first made a covenant with Noah. The world was in a crisis of misbehaviour and so it was to be flooded and a fresh start made, but Noah was a righteous man, so he and his family, and two of each creature, were to be saved. Noah's part of the bargain was to trust God and build the Ark (Genesis 6:18). When the waters subsided, God sent the creatures in the Ark out to 'multiply', and he made a fresh covenant with Noah and all the creatures that he would never flood the earth again. The sign, which was to remind God and reassure his creatures that there was not going to be another flood, was to be the appearance of a rainbow when the weather looked stormy (Genesis 9:12–17).

With Abraham, Genesis says, God made another covenant, whose sign was to be his change of name, for formerly he had been called Abram. Abraham, his male kin and servants and slaves, for their part, would be circumcised, and that would be a mark that they were God's 'people'; in return God would give them the land of Canaan to be their land for ever (Genesis 17:1–27).

These early contracts were superseded in a way reflected in the kind of language found in Jeremiah. The new agreement was to involve an obedience that was not mere outward signs and observances, but an inward stance:

> I will put my law within them, and I will write it on their hearts; and I will be their God, and they shall be my people. No longer shall they teach one another, or say to each other, 'Know the Lord', for they shall all know me, from the least of them to the greatest, says the Lord; for I will forgive their iniquity and remember their sin no more.
> **Jeremiah 31:33—34**

There is a third understanding of this contract in the Bible, in the New Testament. Mark 14:24 describes Jesus at the Last Supper he shared with his disciples, taking a cup, giving thanks and giving it to his disciples to drink from. 'He said to them, "This is my blood of the covenant, which is poured out for many."' It was agreed by the early Christians that 'in speaking of "a new covenant", he has made the first one obsolete' (Hebrews 8:13). People began to ask whether that meant that obedience to the ten commandments was no longer required. What is the position now, they wanted to know? The early Christians took a decision recorded in Acts 15 that some of the old observances, such as circumcision, would not be required for their members. Baptism would replace it.

In modern life this contractual way of thinking has to be adjusted to fit a different society. First it has to be modified in recognition of the fact that contracts between people are meant to be between equals, and the law will try to ensure that where there is an imbalance of power between the parties the weaker one is not put at a disadvantage, for example by being forced to accept unfair terms. Broken promises within this contractual framework may be taken to wipe out the duty of the other party to fulfil the promises on his or her side.

A reciprocal promise most people make at least once during their lives is the one that creates a marriage. There are many promises that are not reciprocal, where I promise to do something for you or you promise to do something for me with no expectation of return. What is the basis of this kind of commitment?

In what way am I 'bound' when I have given my word?

The inner life, the central themes

Teach us to care and not to care
Teach us to sit still
Even among these rocks
Our peace in his will[26]
T.S. Eliot (1880—1965)

This is the second time in his poem 'Ash Wednesday' that T.S. Eliot presents his paradoxical challenge, this time with another idea looming behind it, that inward peace is not necessarily dependent on outward circumstances. He seems to be suggesting that even when times are hard, acceptance can bring peace. He describes this acceptance in terms of giving up personal wishes to the will of God. For those without religious faith, such acceptance is a more demanding discipline.

Grant me the serenity to accept the things I cannot change;
courage to change the things I can;
and the wisdom to know the difference.[27]
Reinhold Niebuhr (1892—1971)

A calm weighing of matters that can cause a great deal of worry and distress can take the anxiety away. This sort of 'mindfulness' can make me feel better and perhaps also be better in ways that are not only good for me but also beneficial to the people whose lives I touch and affect.

The New Testament contains passages of great beauty and power to comfort:

> Peace I leave with you, my peace I give to you. I do not give to you as the world gives. Do not let your hearts be troubled, and do not let them be afraid.
> **John 14:27**

> Do not worry about anything, but in everything by prayer and supplication with thanksgiving let your requests be made known to God. And the peace of God, which surpasses all understanding, will guard your hearts and your minds in Christ Jesus.
> **Philippians 4:6—7**

What you can take from this is for you to determine, for it is private and personal. Life seen as a process of growing, a progression, a gathering of experience and advancing skills and understanding, may involve doing one thing at one stage, another later. Life lived in readiness for something new will always be exciting. And as we shall see in what follows, it leads to ways of living that are public and visible and affect other people and the world at large.

In the New Testament, Jesus is recorded as saying that someone who entertains a wrong action in his heart is as guilty as he would be if he had done it. To lust after a woman is already to have had sex with her in the mind (Matthew 5:28). On this view, moral rightness has as much to do with the attitude, the inwardness of the doer, as with the action itself.

Is it enough for me to mean well and do my best?

PART II

SELF AND SOCIETY

... the effect of her being on those around her was incalculably diffusive: for the growing good of the world is partly dependent on unhistoric acts; and that things are not so ill with you or me as they might have been, is half owing to the number who lived faithfully a hidden life, and rest in unvisited tombs.

George Eliot (1819—80), *Middlemarch*

Chapter 4

Other People

Apartheid in South Africa kept the ethnic groups separate to the disadvantage of the 'blacks', as did local laws in the southern states of the USA for several generations after the American War of Independence (1775–83). This meant regarding some people as not fully human beings and denying them civil rights other people can take for granted. It is as easy for me and you to slip into thinking in such ways as for governments to do it, and it may be even more painful to an individual to be treated as not quite human when it seems to reflect a personal prejudice.

What makes us human?

From at least the sixteenth century there was a fashion for reading travel books. Some described real voyages, some imaginary, and some were an early form of science fiction. This kind of writing seems to have been made more popular by the opening up of the New World to the West in the sixteenth century. There was more trade and travel in the East, too, and Western travellers in the seventeenth and eighteenth centuries began to speak of it as somewhere culturally 'different'.

In such books the opportunity is taken to meet people – or science-fiction creatures – from other cultures and sometimes from other planets. By their oddities of appearance or action, or their surprise at the behaviour of their human visitors, they make the reader think hard about what it is to be human. For instance, the *Micromegas* of the French satirist Voltaire (1694–1778) has two travellers from Sirius and Saturn meeting members of the human race for the first time. One of them, Micromegas, is very, very big – 120,000 'French feet' high – compared with the five feet or so of the average human. He exclaims at the realization that God 'has given intelligence to forms of matter which seem so negligible'.[1]

Voltaire wanted to give his readers a jolt. For we, too, know that a conversation is more likely to feel as though it is 'between equals' when we can look the person we are talking to in the eye. If I ask 'Does he take sugar in his tea?' over the head of the wheelchair user to the person who is pushing him I am treating the man in the wheelchair as though he was not fully 'one of us'.

Something like this happens in *Gulliver's Travels*. Jonathan Swift (1667–1745) completed this satirical novel in 1725. In the course of his journeyings Gulliver arrives in a land of giants. They have never seen anything so small, but otherwise looking just like themselves. They are 'surprised at so much wit and good sense in so diminutive an Animal'. They think he must be a toy. Their king, 'when he observed my Shape exactly, and saw me walk erect, before I began to speak, conceived I might be a piece of Clock-work… contrived by some ingenious Artist'.

Gulliver has some difficulty in getting the inhabitants to take him seriously as a rational creature like themselves. But, he says, when the king 'heard my Voice, and found what I delivered to be regular and rational, he could not conceal his Astonishment'.[2]

Swift thus presents a challenge to the giants' frame of reference for determining who is to be dealt with as an equal. Puzzled about Gulliver, the giants ask for help from their scientists. The scientists apply scientific principles as the science of their day and culture understands them. Among these is the strikingly modern notion that a test of the place something holds in the natural order is its fitness for its purpose:

> His Majesty sent for three great Scholars… These Gentlemen, after they had a while examined my Shape with much Nicety… all agreed that I could not be produced according to the regular Laws of Nature; because I was not framed with a capacity for preserving my Life, either by Swiftness, or climbing of Trees, or digging Holes in the Earth.

They inspected his teeth and saw that he was carnivorous:

> … yet most Quadrupeds being an Overmatch for me; and Field-Mice, with some others, too nimble, they could not imagine how I should be able to support myself, unless I fed upon Snails and other Insects; which they offered by many learned Arguments to evince that I could not possibly do.

The scholars were contemptuous of Gulliver's attempts to explain that where he came from everyone was his size and the plants and animals were in proportion.[3] Their norms remained fixed within their own familiar frame of reference. Since he did not seem to fit into the expected categories, they invented a special category for him as a sport of nature, which they claimed was a 'wonderful Solution of all Difficulties, to the unspeakable Advancement of human Knowledge'.[4]

Not one of us?

It is obvious that there are physical differences – of skin and eye-colour, size, build – characteristics which may cluster in distinctive ways among genetically related sub-groups of human beings. It is much more contentious to suggest that there are innate differences of intelligence or ability associated with race because that way lies the temptation to try 'eugenic' selection.

A special value has sometimes been put on characteristics alleged to be more predominant in one race than another, and those not possessed of the characteristics in question have been treated as sub-human. In Nazi Germany fair hair and blue eyes were taken to indicate Aryan ancestry and membership of what came to be conceived as a Master Race, and it was a short step to justifying the attempted extermination of the Jewish population in Germany in the period of World War II (1939–45).

There is a disturbing history of that kind of assumption being used as a justification for treating one group (or race or tribe) as inferior to another, and therefore of less value to the world. It is only one step further to what is now called 'ethnic cleansing'. Ethnic cleansing was not new even at the time of the Holocaust of World War II. Alexis de Tocqueville (1805–59) pointed out that the white settlers in America were able to 'exterminate the [North American] Indian race... without violating a single great principle of morality in the eyes of the world'.[5] Nor was horror at the revelation of the reality of the Nazi Holocaust sufficient to stop it happening again. Ethnic cleansing has reappeared since in the Balkans in the nineteenth and twentieth centuries, and in parts of Africa, often driven by the boiling up of fierce longstanding hatreds between races sharing lands, sometimes sharpened by religious differences. There were both Roman Catholic and Orthodox Christians and followers of Islam in Yugoslavia, and a great deal of long-established unresolved conflict surfaced, as it did between the Sunni and Shia Muslims in Iraq after the Western invasion of 2003.

Sub-human?

We may feel all the repugnance of a person in the 'enlightened' modern West at state-approved discrimination, but still be capable of slipping into an assumption that the 'other person' is not really human because he or she does not fulfil certain current social expectations of full 'normal' functioning. To speak in a patronizing way to the person in a wheelchair, the person with a different accent, or less education, or less money, the person with the 'wrong address' or in the 'wrong clothes', may be to dehumanize that person by implication, even if I have no thoughts of 'cleansing' society of such 'misfits'.

To suggest that there is a degree of severe handicap beyond which a person is not really 'human' would be to start down a road at the end of which the value of the human person could no longer be regarded as non-negotiable. Nor have civilized societies been willing to say that there is a point at which the loss of the personality and competence that can come with dementia, or other incurable or terminal illnesses, takes away some ordinary human rights. A person who can no longer make rational choices may keep 'choosing' to wander away across a busy road. Freedom of movement and a degree of self-determination may have to be restricted for someone's protection if a person can no longer conduct the ordinary affairs of life. But that loss of autonomy should be kept to a minimum. I may be glad to live in a society that lives by such principles if I have to take to a wheelchair myself, or become homeless, or develop Alzheimer's disease. Then my full 'humanity' now can decide what should happen to my future possible diminished self.

But the ethical dilemmas that arise in the modern world are not all so easily resolved. IVF (in-vitro fertilization) allows for the possibility of selecting an embryo genetically compatible with a sibling who needs, for example, a bone-marrow transplant, so that a child is born to save a brother's life. The question is whether it is ethical to make one person an instrument of another's benefit and what the balance of benefits to the two will be, since the parents, not the children, are going to make the choice.

Outsiders and outcasts

In the city where I live, there are many homeless people. I often see one of them sitting on the pavement, back to a wall, with a dog crouching beside him on a lead made of a piece of string. A dog is useful for keeping warm when you have to sleep in a doorway on a winter night. I hear 'Spare some money for a cup of tea?' as I walk past. If I think about it consciously at all, I tell myself that the money will be spent not on tea but on alcohol or heroin, and that quite a lot of the street people are known to 'work' the city by pretending to be destitute, making quite a good living. At one time in East Anglian towns on different days of the week, numerous young mothers could be seen begging, each with a baby. A priest I know says he no longer wears a 'dog collar' and a nun I know has given up wearing a habit in the street, because to do so is to invite aggressive and intimidatory begging.

Occasionally, though, I notice someone crouching down to talk to one of the homeless, and apparently having a real conversation with him or her, a helpful conversation. I have an uncomfortable feeling I should do that.

In a café I look up from the book I am reading as the smell of someone who has not washed for a very long time wafts in. The odour is coming from what looks like a tramp. On the other hand he has a very clean suitcase, which he carefully positions by a chair at the next table before going off to buy his own coffee. He takes out of the suitcase and places on the table a pristine book on philosophy. I revise my opinion. He is not a tramp but an elderly academic. I give him a cautious smile of recognition as a 'colleague' as he returns with his drink. He is 'one of us' after all. Unlike the homeless man sitting under the bank cash machine with a large dog wearing an old scarf rakishly as a collar, he does not frighten me.

An immensely influential tradition of expectation that stretches from the civilization of ancient Greece to the modern world was that human beings are essentially 'reasonable people' – rational animals capable of rational analysis, of weighing up their options against canons of rational behaviour when they decide what to do.[6] There was optimism that to exercise one's powers of reasoning was a safe way of identifying this best and most reasonable course of action.

Reason can be misapplied, rejoined the Christian tradition, in a fundamental challenge to the optimism of many classical philosophers who believed that reasonable people would run things well and for the general good, for anything else would be unreasonable. Satan was very clever, pointed out Christian theologians. He knew how to use reasoning for nefarious ends. 'The serpent was more crafty than any other wild animal that the Lord God had made' (Genesis 3:1). He suggested to Eve, playing on her vanity and aspirations, that God had forbidden the eating of the fruit of one particular tree because he did not want human beings to become his equals: 'God knows that when you eat of it, your eyes will be opened, and you will be like God, knowing good and evil' (Genesis 3:5).

Satan and malevolent human beings are quite capable of using their intelligence in ways that subvert good order in society and work against human welfare, said Christian theologians. 'I think he will be remembered... as a clever man whose undoubted intelligence was put to malevolent effect,' commented Paddy Ashdown on Slobodan Milosevic's death in his prison cell on 11 March 2006, during his trial at the Hague on war crimes charges.[7] Milosevic was instrumental in prompting the events that broke up the former Yugoslavia in the 1990s. He used his powers of thought to nationalist ends, which he himself argued were good ends, but which resulted in thousands of deaths.

Putting reasonableness at the heart of things, as moralists have done for many centuries, creates a good few problems. The people begging on the streets who are not really destitute could be said to be using their wits to earn their livings in a perfectly rational, if deceitful, way. The smelly old don is arguably rational in his view that philosophy is a more important use of his time than washing his vest.

And not all human beings are mentally competent throughout their lives. In the modern world we have become aware of a danger that that may lead to discrimination. A baby cannot be reasoned with until it can understand what you say to it, but eventually it will grow up and join the rest of the human race as a more or less rational animal. Not all human beings become, or remain, able to do that. An autistic child finds it difficult to enter sympathetically into the thoughts of others. A mentally handicapped adult may not be able to 'reason' in a way that involves abstract thought. An elderly person with dementia may behave 'unreasonably'. Are these not 'real people'?

Does a frozen embryo, which has not yet developed
to the point where it can think, have human rights?

Feral children and innate innocence

Should someone who 'cannot help' being unreasonable or behaving badly be punished for his or her actions? In the past it was suggested some were born bad, had 'bad blood', had even 'inherited' criminal tendencies. The modern West blames the parents and tends to see problem behaviour in terms of nurture, to the point where politicians have even suggested identifying babies born into certain families as potential criminals and treating them accordingly.

By contrast, the idea was put forward in the early modern period that there was something 'noble' about the simplicity of the 'noble savage', a human being who did not have a trained mind, but whose innate fundamental rationality would nevertheless emerge, and prompt him to live with dignity and virtue. Jean-Jacques Rousseau's *Émile (On Education)*, published in 1762, begins with the idea that everything God makes is good as it leaves his hands but degenerates as human beings get to work upon it. He proposed an experimental education for the little orphan Émile designed to spare him this fate. The fictional version of this is Voltaire's 'Ingenu', about a character who has miraculously grown to adulthood without being thus damaged:

> Having learnt nothing at all in his childhood, he had not acquired any prejudices… He saw things as they are, whereas the ideas with which we are imbued during childhood make us see things our whole lives through as they are not.[8]

The ancient world mistrusted extreme feelings and generally approved of keeping emotions under rational control. Modern attitudes in the West may see the place of emotion differently. Children are taught at school to make a personal response to a passage of writing or a painting or a piece of music in which their feelings about it are taken to be as important as cool critical analysis. We understand better and are more sympathetic to the way conduct can be influenced by stress, exhaustion, problems in coming to terms with a traumatic event and painful associations, all of which interfere with calm reasonableness – and sometimes the more so in people who are not well equipped for reasoning, or trained to do it.

A child who is diagnosed with attention deficit disorder may be given drugs to calm him down. Is this right? His friend who has not been diagnosed as suffering from a 'disorder' but behaves in the same way is given an ASBO. Is this right? A small child whose elder brother has been given an ASBO is put under the supervision of Social Services because he is thought 'likely' to behave anti-socially as he grows older. Is this right?

The present-day balance

All this leaves us at the uncomfortable heart of the question what it means to be human. Is there a point when the loss of the personality and competence that can come with dementia or other incurable or terminal illnesses takes away some ordinary human rights?

The British Rabbi Julia Neuberger discusses the elderly, the mentally ill, the young and vulnerable, the prison system, the 'outsiders' (immigrants). She is critical of the tendency for governments to react to popular anxieties without thinking through the principles on which they are acting, or their implications. 'We are putting more and more people into prison, but we have less and less idea about whether we are trying to punish, rehabilitate, contain, or simply forget about them,' she comments.[9] Yet there have been numerous discussions of the purpose of imprisonment. It is not as though no one had ever thought about them; rather that society, she implies, has lost sight of the importance of knowing about all that groundwork already done.

Modern developed societies go to some trouble to protect the interests of people who cannot 'think for themselves', robustly defending their claim to be fully human and to have all the rights of the cleverest and most well-adjusted. But the moral responsibility of such individuals can be difficult to determine and to legislate for fairly precisely because they are not, in the ordinary sense, reasonable. And against that protective tendency run the headlines in tabloid newspapers, the panics and formation of lynch-mobs over society's 'misfits', the mentally ill being 'cared for in the community' when it is feared that they may be a danger, the calls for pre-emptive restrictions upon people who have not yet done anything wrong, in case they might.

Is it only if it is possible to agree who is really human, fully human, 'one of us', that it is possible to talk of 'human rights', and assert that everyone is entitled to have those human rights respected equally?

Human Rights

'Rights' is not simply the plural of 'right'. Having 'rights' is different from 'doing right'. This book is about how to do right, but doing right in the modern world takes into account respecting other people's 'rights'.

There is sometimes an outcry in the tabloid newspapers when someone who, it is said, does not 'deserve' it, has his or her human rights protected. For example, someone who would otherwise be deported cannot be sent back to his country of origin if it is known that he is likely to be tortured there.

> Of liberty, reform, and rights I sing –
> Freedom I mean, without or church or king;
> Freedom to seize and keep whate'er I can,
> And boldly claim my right – The Rights of Man!

At the time of the French Revolution, Mary Alcock (c. 1743–98), penned these 'Instructions, supposed to be written in Paris, for the mob in England':

> Such is the blessed liberty in vogue,
> The envied liberty to be a rogue,
> The right to pay no taxes, tithes or dues,
> The liberty to do whate'er I choose;
> The right to take by violence and strife
> My neighbour's goods, and (if I please) his life;
> The liberty to raise a mob or riot
> (For spoil and plunder ne'er were got by quiet);

She adds the further worried warning that these undesirables would not be content with living off a society which was soft on them and taking advantage of its benevolence, but would become politically active and attack the society which had treated them so well:

> The right to level and reform the great;
> The liberty to overturn the state;
> The right to break through all the nation's laws
> And boldly dare to take rebellion's cause.[10]

A similar popular indignation can be heard today, at the idea that people who 'do not deserve it', who 'exploit the system', should be able to rely on having their human rights protected.

> *Should criminals and suspected 'terrorists' have their*
> *human rights protected?*

Only 'targeted' rights?

Should people enjoy the same rights whether they have 'earned' them or not? In Jesus' parable of the labourers in the vineyard, a number of hired labourers contract to do a day's work for an agreed day's pay. At the very end of the working day the owner of the vineyard takes on more workers. When everyone goes to collect his wages, these get the same as the ones who have worked all day. They complain, 'These last worked only one hour, and you have made them equal to us who have borne the burden of the day and the scorching heat' (Matthew 20:12). That was the deal, says the owner of the vineyard. If I want to be generous to these others, what is that to you?

There is a pragmatic as well as a moral argument for even-handed generosity and treating everyone the same: 'Disregard and contempt for human rights have resulted in barbarous acts which have outraged the conscience of mankind', states the Preamble of the Universal Declaration of Human Rights.[11]

The Universal Declaration of Human Rights dates from discussions of 1948 about the need for protections of human rights, in the light of experiences of World War II. The central thrust was the notion that 'Recognition of the inherent dignity and of the equal and inalienable rights of all members of the human family is the foundation of freedom, justice and peace in the world'.[12] Unless this fundamental is protected by law, people may feel 'compelled to have recourse, as a last resort, to rebellion against tyranny and oppression'.[13]

The ease with which hard-won protections can be eroded has become clear in the early twenty-first century 'war on terror'. One of the problems with overriding the human rights of other people in an emergency is that it may be your turn next. The incarceration of terrorist suspects at Guantánamo Bay after the attack on the twin towers in New York seems to have involved clear breaches of the fundamental rights laid down in international law decades earlier. If they can be arrested without being told what for and kept in prison indefinitely with no chance to defend themselves, so can you.

Despite the complete outlawing of torture by the Universal Declaration of Human Rights of 1948, and under the same pressures as led to the breach of human rights at Guantánamo Bay, torture began to be used in the first years of the twenty-first century to get 'terrorist suspects' to confess. Some were flown ('rendition' was the term used) to countries known to be less fastidious about using torture, so that they could not be said to have been tortured on USA territory. Military doctors, setting aside their agreed professional duty as doctors to seek to do no harm, and to try to heal the bodies and minds of human beings without questioning their merits, assisted in 'coercive interrogations of detainees, including providing advice on how to increase stress levels and exploit fears'.[14]

Embedded in these practices was a presupposition that suspects were already known to be guilty. 'We know they're guilty so it's fine to torture them.'[15] Political leaders spoke without qualification of 'bad people'. One consequence has been exactly the escalation of resentment and terrorist activity in the communities most under 'suspicion' that the Universal Declaration of Human Rights was concerned about.

> *Are there circumstances in which the right to fair and*
> *humane treatment for 'suspects' should be set aside?*
> *Should people with alleged 'personality disorders'*
> *which might prompt disruptive behaviour or*
> *suspected links to criminal gangs or 'terrorist' groups*
> *be detained to protect 'society' even though they have*
> *committed no offence?*

The Universal Declaration of Human Rights takes the principles it articulates to be of universal validity, and for all time.[16] Those who framed the text appealed to a general sense of their self-evident correctness and 'rightness' – though their ideas about that probably owe a good deal to principles that were forming two centuries earlier in the Enlightenment in the West and were shaped in their turn partly by the ideals of the classical world. They are certainly not 'for all time' when compared with some of the assumptions of former centuries.

> *Are there basic and inalienable human rights?*

Equality

All human beings are born free and equal in dignity and rights.
They are endowed with reason and conscience and should act
towards one another in a spirit of brotherhood.
Article 1, Universal Declaration of Human Rights, 1948

Equal is not the same as identical. Cicero says that in a just society
each should be treated appropriately. The most pressing question
when it comes to deciding what is just and fair is likely to be whether
everyone is to be treated on a basis which gives them equivalency,
rather than crudely as equal-sized bricks in the 'wall' of society. A
perception that there are differences between me and you is not
necessarily unfair. It is the starting-point of an effort to 'even things
up'. For instance, if you walk with a limp, I might match my pace to
yours so that I do not get ahead. But I had better do it tactfully or you
might be insulted. A marathon runner and a person in a wheelchair
could not compete in a race that gave them both a chance to win,
without some 'handicap' for the marathon runner. But it is
important to go no further than removing the inherent inequalities
as far as possible.

Privilege and discriminating in favour
In George Orwell's novel *Animal Farm*, the animals, who represent
the 'working classes', overthrow the farmer who rules their lives.
They plan to run the farm themselves in a new, enlightened way, for
their common benefit. 'All animals are equal' is their motto. The
pigs become the leaders. But quite quickly the pigs begin to claim
that their onerous responsibilities as leaders entitle them to special
treatment and various advantages, and the cry speedily mutates into
'All animals are equal but some animals are more equal than others.'
As Orwell wryly recognizes, even in communist societies (those he
had in mind in this story), which attempted to outlaw class
distinctions and the resulting inequalities, it became commonplace
for those who attained positions of power to be accorded privileges.

Some people may be given special treatment, as though they are
superior and that gives them rights and entitlements others do not
have. This is a pattern common in societies with 'aristocracies' of
various sorts, and few societies fail to create or allow such special

categories, even informally. In the modern West the cult of 'celebrity' is an example. A 'celebrity' who travels with an entourage of personal trainers, stylists and life-coaches expects first class treatment.

Does special talent or ability make someone more valuable and therefore entitled to special treatment? In *Gulliver's Travels*, the Luggnuggians are a people of the East. Among them there are Immortals, individuals born at random among the population and identifiable by a spot on their foreheads, who will never die. In the story, Gulliver is extremely excited when he is told about them and 'cryed out as in a Rapture; Happy Nation, where every Child hath at least a Chance for being immortal! Happy People who enjoy so many living examples of antient Virtue, and have Masters ready to instruct them in the Wisdom of all former Ages!'

He envisages these fortunate individuals as having 'their Minds free and disengaged, without the Weight and Depression of Spirits caused by the continual Apprehension of Death'. He is surprised not to have seen any of them at Court, for surely a sensible ruler would 'prove himself with a good Number of such wise and able Counsellors'. Yet, he reflects, perhaps the 'Virtue of those Reverence Sages was too strict for the corrupt and libertine Manners of a Court'.

His hosts ask him how he would himself have spent his life if he had been one of these Immortals. He is optimistic that he would have used such special privilege for the highest ends. 'I would first resolve by all Arts and Methods whatsoever to procure myself Riches.' Then 'I would from my earliest Youth apply myself to the Study of Arts and Sciences, by which I should arrive in time to excel all others in Learning.' Lastly, he would set himself up as a historian, keep a careful 'record' of 'every Action and Event of Consequence that happened in the Publick, impartially draw the Characters of the several Successions of Princes, and great Ministers of State; with my own observations on every Point'. After the age of seventy, he would not marry, 'but live in a hospitable manner' and 'entertain myself in forming and directing the Minds of hopeful young Men, by convincing them from my own Remembrance, Experience and Observation, fortified by numerous Examples, of the Usefulness of Virtue in publick and private life'. He would form a close brotherhood from among his fellow Immortals, and they would discuss together what they had learned in the course of their

long lifetimes' observations.[17] Swift the satirist saw as clearly as
George Orwell how unlikely it was that such high-mindedness
would last.

*Should the Directors of a company travel First Class
on expenses while I, as an employee, have to pay my
own fares as a commuter?*

Some politicians say that a child who has been to a state school
should be given a university place in preference to her friend who
got the same examination results but went to a fee-paying school.
The friend may not be so sure that that is fair. 'Positive
discrimination' (which deliberately favours those who are classified
as disadvantaged in some way) tends to diminish the achievement of
those who are perceived to have succeeded only because special
allowances were made for them. It can seem unjust to those who did
not benefit from such allowances.

*Are there circumstances in which some should be
more equal than others?*

Respect and human dignity

If I am going to try to treat other people in a way that respects their
own dignity I probably ought not to stand on my own dignity too
much. Showing respect may be more than protecting reputation (my
own or anyone else's); it may mean having regard to the way another
person sees his or her situation. I realize you are blind and need to
cross the road, or see that you are in a wheelchair and need to get
into a building with a revolving door. Should I just seize your arm
or the handle of the chair, or ask first what you want me to do?

It is important to be open to a diversity of cultural expectations
too. There are well-established but different expectations in various
world religions about treating other people with respect. The
Buddhist rules of life expect a good Buddhist to consider before he
speaks whether his proposed remark may do harm by damaging
someone's reputation. Judaism also recognizes a duty not to shame
someone else publicly. Exodus 23:1 emphasizes the importance of
protecting a person's reputation. Leviticus 19:17 forbids tale-bearing
and the making of unkind insinuations.

Is it all right to enjoy a good gossip?

Setting a good example

Modern celebrities sometimes seem to set a bad example, for example, by boorish behaviour or being known drug-addicts or heavy drinkers. The television programme *Celebrity Big Brother* became a prime exemplification of this in early 2007 when the crude, apparently racist remarks of one of the contestants caused public indignation and some of these minor celebrities were recognized to be far from worthy of adulation, even if they were famous.

In many societies there is at least one class of whom more is expected by way of *good* behaviour and setting an example than of the 'ordinary run' of people. Some publicly choose to make an especially profound commitment and to live accordingly. This may mean trying to live a life more demanding in various ways, in terms of the behaviour expected. For example, in Buddhism, it may involve fasting, being celibate, avoiding the enjoyment of music, dancing, perfume, elaborate or fashionable dress, comfortable domestic furnishings. In Christianity a monk or nun takes vows of poverty, chastity and obedience.

What would happen if everyone tried to set an example by behaving better than other people?

Avoiding discrimination

In the modern West from the last decades of the twentieth century legislation was enacted to protect 'minorities'. These are not necessarily literally minorities, merely groups that had previously been somewhat socially disadvantaged, such as women, those of different ethnic origin from the indigenous population and the disabled. The range of such groups or categories has been widened in the European Community to include, for example, outlawing discrimination by age.[18] The underlying ideal is that all categories of people are to be treated equally and no one is to be discriminated against and treated as less human than others, *because of something over which he or she has no control*.

Two areas where this moral duty has developed furthest as a social expectation are the attempt to outlaw sexual and racial discrimination.

'Roles' of the sexes in society

'What is generally accepted as a virtue in women, is very different from what is thought so in men: A very good woman would make

but a paltry man', wrote Alexander Pope.[19] For most centuries it had
been taken for granted that men and women had differences which
went beyond sexual differentiation into the intellectual and social.
Alexander Pope suggests here that this means that a man and a
woman may be admired or respected for different things. A similar
set of differentiated expectations is obvious in John Evelyn's loving
portrait of his daughter Susanna on her marriage, in his
seventeenth-century *Diary*:

> She is a good child, religious, discreet, ingenious, and qualified
> with all the ornaments of her sex. And she especially has a
> peculiar talent in design and painting both in oil and miniature,
> and a genius extraordinary for whatever hands can pretend to do
> with the needle. She has the French tongue, has read most of the
> Greek and Roman authors and poets, and uses her talents with
> great modesty. She is exquisitely shaped and of an agreeable
> countenance.[20]

Even George Eliot (1819–80), herself a woman novelist writing
under a man's name, wondered aloud whether some women really
had the necessary mental stamina for serious thought. She wrote of
'The small brain and vivacious temperament [of women of "the
Gallic race"] which permit the fragile system of woman to sustain
the superlative activity requisite for intellectual creativeness'.[21]

Daniel Defoe included in *An Essay upon Projects*, a project to set
up 'an academy for women':

> I have often thought of it as one of the most barbarous Customs in
> the world... that we deny the advantages of Learning to Women.
> We reproach the sex every day with Folly and Impertinence,
> while I am confident, had they the advantages of Education equal
> to us, they would be guilty of less than ourselves... The Soul is
> placed in the Body like a rough Diamond, and must be polish'd,
> or the Lustre of it will never appear.

He is, however, aware of the danger that this plan might prove a
engine of social change. He is anxious to run this academy in such
a way as to 'protect the Reputation of the House, that persons of
Quality and Fortune might not be afraid to send their Children
thither'.[22]

The depth and persistence of the social assumptions about differentiation of roles is pointed up sharply by the Norwegian playwright Henrik Ibsen too:

> HELMER. It's outrageous. That you can betray your most sacred duties in this way.
> NORA. What do you count as my most sacred duties?
> HELMER. And I have to tell you! Are they not your duties to your husband and your children?
> NORA. I have other equally sacred duties.
> HELMER. No, you don't. What 'duties' might you have in mind?
> NORA. My duties to myself.
> HEMER. You are first and foremost a wife and a mother.
> NORA. I no longer believe that. I am first and foremost a human being just as much as you, – or, at least, that I'll try to become one.[23]

In the modern world a variety of different assumptions persist in different cultures. In some Islamic societies there remains a degree of rigidity in educating the sexes separately, and placing women under the control of men both before and after they marry.[24] This goes with presumptions about what a 'good woman' should do with her life. In Sikhism differentiation of the roles of the sexes derives from social expectation rather than from religious requirement. At the same time, in society at large, men have begun to complain that it is they who are disadvantaged, and boys are said to be confused about how 'to be boys'.

> *Should I expect different things of men and women?*
> *Should I treat my sons and daughters differently and*
> *in what ways?*

Racism, immigration and multiculturalism

I remember feeling quite sad for a dejected racist whom I saw, some years ago, near the Aldwych station in London, viewing with disgust a thousand posters pasted everywhere carrying pictures of the obese – and holy – physique of Guru Maharajji (then a great rage in London). Our dedicated racist was busy writing 'fat wog' diligently under each of the pictures. In a short

while that particular wog would be gone, but I do not doubt that
'disgusted of Aldwych' would scribble 'lean wog' or 'medium-
sized wog' under other posters now.[25]
Amartya Sen (b. 1933), *The Argumentative Indian*

Jesus' story of the Good Samaritan (Luke 10:30–37) is set in a
multicultural society, in which the Samaritans were a despised and
oppressed ethnic minority. The priest and the Levite, by contrast,
held positions of authority and dignity in the society. They were the
ones who hurried past on the other side of the road to avoid getting
involved. Try substituting 'politician' and 'celebrity' for the priest
and the Levite and a member of an ethnic minority for the
Samaritan, and read the story again. The Good Samaritan, the least
well placed of the passers-by, showed practical kindness. He 'did
something'. And he did it without considering who the injured man
was.

Unconscious prejudice

Prejudices can be unconscious, or can catch me unawares. I get on a
bus and quickly choose a seat. I do not consciously ask myself who I
want to sit next to, but now I look round, who did I half-consciously
avoid? That noisy gang of teenagers? That old man who looks as
though he might smell? The faces that are a different colour from
mine?

Culture and race are not the same, yet a racial difference is easily
taken to imply a cultural difference and with it a degree of inferiority.
Black applicants for jobs have commented that if they have a British-
sounding name they may get short-listed, and if they have a non-
British-sounding name they get rejection letters.

Charles Lamb (1775–1834) shows how easy it is to misunderstand
one's own motives. Lamb's 'Imperfect sympathies' was first
published in the *London Magazine*, August 1821, and entitled 'Jews,
Quakers, Scotchmen, and other imperfect sympathies'. (Lamb
borrowed the penname of Elia from a fellow clerk of his at the South
Sea House.) He admits that he is not free from unreasoning
prejudices himself: 'Old prejudices cling about me.'

In the Negro countenance you will often meet with strong traits of
benignity. I have felt yearnings of tenderness towards some of
these faces, or rather masks, that have looked out kindly upon

one in casual encounters in the streets and highways... But I
should not like to associate with them, to share my meals and my
goodnights with them – because they are black.[26]

This does not seem to have been 'racism' as we would reckon it
today. It is not the 'blackness' but the 'otherness' he seems to dislike,
when it comes to doing more than exercising toleration at a safe
distance. He feels much the same about Quakers, who probably
tended to be of his own white race:

I love Quaker ways and Quaker worship. I venerate the Quaker
principles... When I am ruffled or disturbed by any occurrence,
the sight, or quiet voice of a Quaker, acts upon me as a ventilator,
lightening the air and taking off a load from the bosom... But I
cannot like the Quakers (as Desdemona would say), 'to live with
them' (*Othello*, I.iii.248). I am all over-sophisticated... I must have
books, pictures, theatres, chit-chat, scandal, jokes, ambiguities,
and a thousand whim-whams which their simpler taste can do
without. I should starve at their primitive banquet.[27]

Despite these frank admissions, Charles Lamb dismisses the idea
that he might be accused of being chauvinistic, a person convinced
that his own kind is 'best' and hostile to people of other races or
nationalities: 'Those national repugnancies do not touch me, nor do
I behold with prejudice the French, Italian, Spaniard, or Dutch.'[28]

In a comment with a very modern ring, one which goes to the
heart of the present debate about multiculturalism, he disapproves of
people wanting to retain their cultural distinctiveness. 'If *they* are
converted, why do they not come over to us altogether? Why keep
up a form of separation?' This is the line of argument used today to
suggest that immigrants should be required to take a citizenship test.
It also seems to assume that a culture can be regarded as a fixed
thing, with norms of acceptable behaviour that will always be
substantially the same.

Should culture-protection or culture-blindness be the aim?
Yet the fashion in the UK until recently was to seek to protect and
strengthen the 'cultural identity' of an adopted child by restricting
adoption to parents who would 'match' and could reinforce that
sense of identity in the growing child. The trend now seems to be

moving in a different direction, one which discourages the
protection of cultural differences in each immigrant 'community'
and tries to insist that immigrants learn English and accommodate
their habits to British norms. Which is right? Should politicians
leave these questions to personal choice or seek to impose norms? It
is not turning out to be easy to define 'Britishness'.

> *Should adoptions be restricted to adoptive*
> *parents of the same race and culture as*
> *the child?*

Amnesty International stresses the rights of indigenous peoples in
lands such as Australia and the United States – lands that have been
taken over by people from another race – not to be treated differently
and in a disadvantageous way. Here is yet another problem of
cultural identity. North American Indians have been allowed special
areas ('reservations') in which to behave according to their tribal
norms, but that automatically singles them out from other American
citizens when it comes to participation in national life. And it
becomes an attempt to 'freeze' those norms at a particular moment
in their development. It does not, for example, make allowance for
the history of migration of the native Indian peoples across the
American continents, by 'requiring' reservations to protect cultural
patterns of a particular earlier period.

Immigrants: a blessing or a curse?

Sometimes a flow of immigrants has been prompted by an
emergency situation somewhere in the world, and the immigrants
are really fleeing dangers at home. A series of group immigrations
from Commonwealth countries into the UK after World War II was
often associated with such disturbances: Caribbean, Pakistani,
Ugandan Asians, Cypriots. In some cases (the Ugandan Asians, for
example) the immigrants had formerly been immigrants to the
country from which they were now fleeing, and both choices of
refuge had been the result of the patterns of empire created by
Britain in its imperial and 'commonwealth' periods. What a nation
did generations earlier may affect its life for many years, even
centuries. Yet when there was trouble in response to the perception
that too many people were arriving (such as race riots) 'politicians
demanded greater controls on immigration, blaming the victims not
the aggressors'.[29]

Patterns of economic migration raise further questions. Economic migrants may be perceived as 'spongers', seeking to better their standard of living by moving to a richer country. Or they may be perceived as a valuable asset to the country they go to, as in the case of those who are qualified as doctors or nurses.

> There can hardly be an American born who cannot recite the five thundering lines inscribed on the Statue of Liberty: the hectoring command – 'Give me your tired, your poor,/Your huddled masses yearning to breathe free,? The wretched refuse of your teeming shore. –/ Send these, the homeless tempest-tossed to me:/I lift my lamp beside the golden door…'

In the USA, with its historic tradition of welcoming immigrants, the first generous throwing open of the door changed subtly but crucially so that the reality did not match the generous offer:

> They touched the hearts and minds of millions of Europeans – always the poor, often the persecuted, very often the fugitives from military service. They were spurred to pack a few belongings… to climb about box cars deep inside Russia or Hungary or Lithuania or Germany and be carried to the great ports: Constantinople, Piraeus, Antwerp, Bremen. This was at a height during the two decades at the beginning of the twentieth century. But they were vetted on arrival in the USA and those on whose backs was chalked an H for 'possible heart disease' or a T, 'the expulsion sign of tuberculosis' were sent back.[30]

Alistair Cook describes the repeating pattern of rejection of newcomers:

> … with every wave of new immigrants there was always a booming counterwave of protest… every breaking wave of new immigrants made a rude sound to the residents, and they protested, then they discriminated.[31]

Each country that finds itself the desired new home of would-be immigrants has to decide whether to adopt a policy of assimilation or a multiculturalism that respects cultural and other differences in its growing mixed population. Canada still attempts a bold inclusiveness, asserting a thoroughgoing multiculturalism in which a further factor has had to be accommodated; for the original American Indian population was overrun and overruled by the migrants, who came at first mainly from French and English speaking Europe and arrived on the east coast, but now increasingly arrive on the west coast, from the Far East.

> The 1971 Multiculturalism Policy of Canada confirmed the rights of Aboriginal peoples and the status of Canada's two official languages... Acceptance gives Canadians a feeling of security and self-confidence, making them more open to, and accepting of, diverse cultures... With no pressure to assimilate and give up their culture, immigrants freely choose their new citizenship because they want to be Canadians... Our diversity is a national asset.[32]

When people migrate, intending to live permanently in another society, their acceptance there will depend partly on the pervasiveness of prejudices that arise from ignorance or misunderstanding. Moral attitudes need to be clear and honest here, or people get hurt.

Should rich countries accept trained professionals, such as doctors and nurses, from countries which need them, in order to fill gaps in their own social need for these professionals?

Chapter 5

A Tangle of Ties

Multiple belongings

> Where there is hatred, let me sow love; where there is injury,
> pardon; where there is doubt, faith; where there is despair, hope;
> where there is darkness, light; where there is sadness, joy.
> **Francis of Assisi (1182—1226)**

The moment I look beyond my own inner life I have to begin to
think about the impact what I do will have on other people. I have
to ask whether the moral issues that arise in my inner life are the
same as the ones that present themselves in my relations with others.
Francis of Assisi's list of ways in which I could make a difference is
deceptively mild-looking and simple.

He suggests that I can behave in individual and group encounters
in ways that make the other person feel better. Can I, conversely,
make things worse like the eleven-year-old William Brown in the
book *More William*?

> At this point William's father received a note from a neighbour
> whose garden adjoined William's and whose life had been
> rendered intolerable by William's efforts on the bugle.
> The bugle was confiscated... Darkness descended upon
> William's soul... 'I'd like to do somethin',' he confided to a rose
> bush with a ferocious scowl. 'Somethin' jus' to show 'em.'[1]

Tug and counter-tug

*What affections, loyalties and responsibilities am I
balancing?*

I can maintain a balance of obligations at home to make sure that
the tasks of keeping the household running are fairly distributed.

But should the children get their pocket money if they do not help with the washing up? I might sow temporary 'hatred', not love, by withholding it.

I can do something about sharing out wealth in society through giving to charity. But how much of my disposable income should I give away, and how do I choose which charities to give to, and will my contribution really turn despair to hope for anyone thousands of miles away to whom the gift is completely impersonal?

It is one thing to do a small amount of good in these ways, however uncertainly; quite another thing to be able to change society or the world at large, on a grander scale. Can I do that?

*What if the 'call' to try to make a really big
difference is going to make me neglect
my family?*

'Though your little nephew hang on your neck... though your father fling himself upon the threshold, trample your father underfoot and go.' This dramatic challenge comes from a letter of Jerome (347–420), writing to Heliodorus in 374.[2] He was only saying – with his customary fierceness – what Jesus had said: that his followers should be ready to leave home and family for his sake. Jesus promised a compensating reward:

> There is no one who has left house or brothers or sisters or
> mother or father or children or fields, for my sake and for the sake
> of the good news, who will not receive a hundredfold now in this
> age – houses, brothers and sisters, mothers and children, and
> fields... and in the age to come eternal life.
> Mark 10:29—30

But the ten commandments of the (Jewish and Christian) Old Testament say we should honour our parents, and obedience to parental authority is also a keystone of Islam.

In every encounter there is a balance to be struck, and sometimes it is not a straightforward choice between putting the family first and answering a 'higher' call. It is a problem for everyone who has ever grown fed up with the monotony of a regular job and wondered whether to give it up in favour of an uncertain life doing something to 'benefit humanity'. Yet making a gesture, a sacrifice of personal comfort and career prospects for a 'higher good', may affect other people I am close to or responsible for. If I take the family to live a 'sustainable' and 'eco-friendly' life in the country my children may miss their friends and the stimulus of city life.

Working parents who can hope for promotion only if they put in long hours and hardly ever see their children will then earn more to pay for their children's needs. Many women have to decide whether to stay at home with their children full-time or go back to work. They have to balance extra earnings and career satisfaction involving tiredness and stress, against a life with plenty of time for the children, but with the prospect of boredom and a future when the children have grown up and life seems 'pointless'.

How am I to balance the tug of personal relationships against other obviously worthwhile claims on my time and energy? This is not just a question of finding the right 'work–life' balance, though that is part of it. The littleness and intensity of daily life is 'where I live'. I probably spend a lot more time making decisions about what to do in personal encounters in family life, with friends and colleagues at work, than in worrying about what I can change in society at large, or the state of the world. Yet there are even bigger frames of reference to be considered, and a system of ethics that cannot take them in cannot be adequate for conducting my whole life.

Margaret Thatcher was famous for maintaining that there was no such thing as society. She did not mean that there need be no arrangements or rules to enable people to live and work together to their mutual benefit. She was raising a much deeper and more subtle question. What she said – speaking from the point of view of a Conservative Prime Minister of Britain in the 1980s – was in fact a contribution to a long-running, old debate about whether 'society' is an entity in its own right to which individuals may have to sacrifice their personal wishes for the general good.

The only freedom which deserves the name is that of pursuing our own good in our own way, so long as we do not attempt to deprive others of theirs, or impede their efforts to obtain it. Each is the proper guardian of his own health, whether bodily, or mental or spiritual. Mankind are greater gainers by suffering each to live as seems good to themselves, than by compelling each to live as seems good to the rest.'[3]

John Stuart Mill (1806—73)

Does belonging to a society (or even to a group or community) make a difference to the decisions I make about what it is right or wrong to do? If it does, I need to be clear what claim the group has on me and why something I am free to do by myself might not be a good thing to do if I am acting as a member of a group.

A family is a group; so is a teenage gang, 'the people at work', a club, a church or mosque, a nation. I chose to join some of these groups. Others I did not choose to join, but I am still treated as a 'member'. In some cases I was able to agree the terms. In others I was not. Some of these groups I can leave; some I cannot. How do I reconcile all the different obligations these 'belongings' seem to involve with my inner life? It seems that one of the first things I have to do as a 'social animal' is a balancing exercise between the various claims other people have on me by virtue of my membership of various groups.

One of the most important questions for my 'social conscience' in the modern world is whether I should allow myself to be identified chiefly or solely as a member of just *one* of the groups I belong to. This can go beyond getting so enthusiastic about, say, supporting a football club, that I head off to the away match first thing on Saturday morning and leave my wife to carry the weekly shopping home from the supermarket on her own.

It can go further. It can make me make me spot divisive 'issues of principle' in small things and fall out with those I was formerly loyal to, further narrowing the focus of my enthusiasm for the thing I was putting before all my other interests and loyalties.

It does not take much to make someone forget the call to ordinary friendly behaviour or the sort of gentle bettering of things Francis of Assisi was talking about, in impassioned defence of a single ideal; to turn someone into a fanatic or even a terrorist:

> The art of constructing hatred takes the form of invoking the magical power of some allegedly predominant identity that drowns other affiliations, and in a conveniently bellicose form can also overpower any human sympathy or natural kindness that we may normally have. The result can be homespun elemental violence or globally artful violence and terrorism.[4]

The Nobel prize-winning economist Amartya Sen, who utters this warning, goes on to describe recent examples of this kind of thing happening:

Actively promoted sectarian hatred can spread like wildfire, as we have seen recently in Kosovo, Bosnia, Rwanda, Timor, Israel, Palestine, Sudan, and many other places in the world. With suitable instigation, a fostered sense of identity with one group of people can be made into a powerful weapon to brutalize another.[5]

Should anything make me abandon one set of affections, loyalties and responsibilities completely in favour of another?

Close personal relationships and the right to family life

For teenagers to get drunk and have casual sex may now be regarded in a secular Western family as an ordinary rite of passage, even as acceptable behaviour, while the Muslim classmates of teenagers who behave like this may live in homes where a girl who acted in that way could be at risk of being killed by a brother to rescue the family 'honour'.

Nowhere, for most people, is 'looking after your own' more of a live issue than in family life. And in few areas of balancing moral obligations are the views of the world religions stronger or more differentiated.

You have an enemy [hostage to fortune] in your spouses and in your children... But if you overlook their offences and pardon them, then know that God is forgiving and merciful. Your wealth and your children are but a temptation.
Koran 64.12

What is a 'family'?
Modern Western expectation attaches special merits to the 'family' as something that is founded when a man and a woman marry, with the intention of forming a lifelong bond, and have children whom they bring up together. Yet this modern Western model is far from universal as an ideal. Other cultures have other notions of what constitutes a family.

Nor does this Western model of the nuclear family always work out as planned in real life. For the increasing proportion whose marriages break down or who live alone or in unconventional households containing, say, an elderly parent and a middle-aged daughter who has become a 'carer', the family model is by no means an absolute.

In ancient Roman law a family was a legal unit, defined as consisting of 'several persons, who are subject to the control of one person, either by nature or by law'.[6] These people were all legally 'free' (not slaves), although the *paterfamilias*, the male head who was known as 'father of the family', had legal power over them, extending in theory even to the power of life or death. He also owned, and could dispose of, all the *familia*'s property. So a family was a legal entity in which the power always lay with its head.

That was the theory. Real Roman families, like modern families, could be much more untidy. An adult male might marry and have children, take a later wife and have more children, and have various descendants through the male line, who would all be counted as members of the same 'family'; each of the sons who married and had children founded a new family while remaining within his father's *familia*. It was possible to be adopted into a *familia* even if you were not a blood relation, or to be formally emancipated from the legal control of its head.[7]

Human rights now recognized in European law include the 'right to family life', but that was not taken for granted in ancient Rome. Not everyone who lived in Roman society could found a family, or even belong to a family. Rome was a society with slaves, and although slaves could be freed, they could not form 'families' in the legal sense while they remained in slavery. Slaves could not have 'wives' by law and yet they formed partnerships and had children, so that if they were subsequently freed, the children were technically fatherless. They did not belong to the same *familia* as any children born to their parents after the parents were 'free' to marry. Since no one could be freed before the age of thirty,[8] this meant that a number of children not born to already freed parents could never be 'freeborn'.

Can people be property? When we read 'slaves, obey your earthly masters' (Colossians 3:22), we glimpse the expectation that there will be social differentiation and not equality of opportunity. Historically, slavery treated people as property, not persons. Any rights concerning them tended to lie with their masters. Roman legal history contains examples of lawsuits when slaves were playing a game and one master's slave injured the slave of another. The compensation went to the master, not the injured slave. The inequalities in his own society which left some in slavery and almost everyone under the legal control of the head of an extended family did not concern Cicero. Aristotle argues that there are circumstances in which it is fitting that one person should be a slave and another the master of slaves.[9]

Stoics advocated treating slaves as 'people'. Once more this is echoed in the epistles of the New Testament. There servants are exhorted to obey their masters and also to behave well in general towards them, and in return masters are expected to treat slaves well:

> And, masters, do the same to them. Stop threatening them, for you know that both of you have the same Master in heaven, and with him there is no partiality.
> **Ephesians 6:9**

> Masters, treat your slaves justly and fairly, for you know that you also have a Master in heaven.
> **Colossians 4:1**

This was a considerable breakthrough for the times, but it was to lead in due course to the enunciation of the fundamental principle of 'recognition of the inherent dignity and of the equal and inalienable rights of all members of the human family', in the Preamble to the Universal Declaration of Human Rights.[10]

Marriage and other kinds of relationship

> Marriage is basically the invention of church and state, designed around the inevitable mating and procreation ritual and evolved into an institution dedicated to defining responsibilities that existed anyway. It was for the regulation of property and affiliations. Sanctifying monogamy discourages fecklessness. It came to demand that two [people] must ask formal permission and God's blessing to live together, and insisted that without that blessing the relationship was doomed. We still half believe it.
> **Frances Fyfield, *Guardian*, 28 August 2006**

The founding of a family by forming a long-term partnership does not necessarily involve the same understanding of marriage everywhere. The 'instructions' about getting married and the theories of marriage to be found in the Old Testament (for Jews and to some degree for Muslims) and in the Old and New Testaments (for Christians) and in the Koran (for Muslims) differ.

Jesus' saying that when a man and woman marry and the woman 'cleaves to' her husband they become 'one flesh' (Matthew 19:5) is capable of being understood as a description of the transfer of the new wife from one family to another; but it came to be thought of as a mystical union, analogous with that between Christ the 'Bridegroom' and his 'Bride' the Church. The marriage was traditionally sealed by the physical consummation of sexual intercourse and an unconsummated marriage could be declared void. This view is severely tested in modern Western societies where few couples are likely both to be virgins when they marry. Every sexual act cannot make the couple 'one flesh', or every person who had multiple sexual partners would find himself or herself in a mystical union with them all. But if it is the commitment that counts, why worry about the sexual act?

Whether sexual intercourse cements or defines a relationship, and how far engaging in it outside a primary relationship constitutes the ultimate unfaithfulness, are among a mass of questions that have arisen in the climate of increased 'permissiveness' that has developed in the West from the second half of the twentieth century. Earlier generations (and other cultures) have not necessarily come to these matters with the same expectations. When John Cassian (c. 360–433) wrote of three kinds of human relationship his 'hierarchy' was not that of the modern West. At the top he put the sort of cerebral and spiritual friendship he wanted his monks to form. Below that he placed the camaraderie of colleagues, people bonded by a common working or professional interest. Lowest of all came family bonds, including that between husband and wife, for this was an era in which a wife was not expected to meet all her husband's needs for good conversation.

People are now likely to meet many more people in the course of a lifetime than used to be the case in earlier centuries. Relationships of varying depth and complexity form alongside marriages, sometimes breaking the marital bond, sometimes protecting it by meeting needs of the partners that cannot be met within the primary relationship – friendships with an erotic element, friendships without; friendships with those of the same sex or the opposite sex; brief episodes of sexual passion, sometimes so brief that the partners do not even learn one another's names; long periods of frustration; unrequited love; stalking. It is not at all easy to draw up a reliable list of rules, except perhaps by using the test of the destructive tendency of certain behaviours. Destructiveness involves an 'over-balancing' or loss of balance and when people get hurt something is manifestly wrong. Is it also wrong for me to engage in activities I keep from a partner?

Can I marry whomever I like? Without stipulating any particular approved form of marriage, or family, or mode of family life, states seeking to conform with human rights principles are expected to protect the right to marry by free consent.

The rights of the man and the woman should be the same according to the principles of human rights law, when they enter into the marriage, while it lasts, and if it is dissolved. This can be difficult to insist on in societies where women cannot hold property or where their personal rights of citizenship or nationality are considered to be swallowed up in those of their fathers or their husbands. In some societies if a father forbids it a woman will not be able to marry the husband she chooses.

In some societies marriages are arranged and in some they may even be 'forced', in the genuine belief that the preferred parental arrangements are for the good of the young couple. The age of marriage can be relevant in such situations, where a very young girl is denied future career opportunities by being rushed into a marriage. There are counter-indications medically, too, since pregnancy is not good for the health of a very young girl. Child-brides (married even before they begin to menstruate) have been common in Islam. The Koran provides for a waiting period in a divorce just in case such a bride is more mature than the husband thought and is pregnant, and he wishes to claim the child (Koran 65.4).

The right of people of different nationalities to live together in the same country as a married couple is not universally recognized.

Civil partnerships

How wide-ranging is the right to family life? Equality and anti-discrimination law seem to suggest that these rights ought to apply to same-sex couples too. The law in England now makes it possible for the state to 'recognize' civil partnerships between individuals of the same sex. The Netherlands and Belgium allow same-sex 'marriage'.[11] The lesser provision of a legally recognized partnership is more widely permitted. The Civil Partnership Act 2004 came into operation in English law on 5 December 2005. It enables a same-sex couple to register as one another's civil partner. Denmark had introduced something similar as early as 1989 and other countries such as Belgium, Canada (Quebec, Nova Scotia), Denmark, Finland, France, Germany, Iceland, the Netherlands, New Zealand, Norway, Sweden, and parts of the USA have done the same, though not in exactly the same way. The idea is to create legal duties and rights between the pair and state, and employer recognition of entitlements of partners under pensions schemes and on the death of one of the pair.[12]

Questions have recently been raised about the claim ordinary friends or siblings ought to have when they have shared a house for many years and one of them dies, leaving the other to face death duties and perhaps to have to sell their home to pay the taxes due.

The right to found a family

> I know there is no consolation. I lost a child myself once, that's enough to say that I understand your grief… What a bright creature! What a laugh, a life, a happiness! And it is all gone.[13]
> **William Makepeace Thackeray (1811—63)**

The death of a child takes parents into a far realm of grief and it seems to show that some human relationships are so close as to come 'first'. But how fundamental is this really? Jane Austen's family thought it quite usual to send a child away to live in another family. Literature has other examples that challenge this certainty about the natural closeness of family relationships:

> It was… only the utmost of parental love and indulgence (not to mention the idolatry of Nurse) which had adapted the moral and mental temperature of number 12 London Road to a fantastical little boy, who might have been a changeling in his cradle for all his resemblance to his sister and brothers… there was no actual warmth between them; no question of mourning at separations, no particular enthusiasm in reunions.[14]
> **Marguerite Steen (1894—1975)**

Family planning, the 'right' of partners in a marriage to decide how many children they have, remains controversial. For Roman Catholic Christians any interference with the procreative purpose of sexual intercourse within marriage remains problematic. There are also fears in parts of the world that family planning might be imposed on people whom the state did not wish to 'breed'; or that it would encourage promiscuity if people thought they could have sex without any danger of pregnancy resulting.

Once a child is born, society surrounds the parents with a degree of protection. A right to maternity (and paternity) leave – time allowed by society to ensure that the parents of a newborn child can give it the necessary care from the beginning – is variously recognized in the West. A woman's right to return to her job if she wishes is also protected. Teenage single mothers in the UK may be provided with flats on housing benefit.

More vexed is the question whether there is an automatic right to bring up one's own children. The medieval belief that it was the law of nature that parents should nurture and educate their children has begun to raise more complicated questions today, when marriages between individuals from different countries break down and each partner fights to keep custody of the child in his or her own country. Which country's courts have jurisdiction? What if the father is from a country where the father's rights predominate and the mother from a country where the principal consideration is the welfare of the child?

The state may interfere even when the family has not been torn apart by such a dispute. A new principle has recently emerged in English law that a child may be adopted without parental consent if his or her welfare requires it.[15] Care and supervision orders, fostering, disputes about the rights a father should have when parents divorce, resistance to social worker intervention between parents and children, and the secrecy of hearing in family courts have all been in the news.

Children of one or the other partner may be involved, and it is possible for partners of the same sex to 'have' children as a couple by various proxy arrangements. Even within the framework of heterosexual relationships there is enormous variation. Unmarried couples have children. Single mothers deserted by the father have children. Married couples have children, are divorced, remarry, and bring the children of their former marriages more or less within a new family, with perhaps more children being born to the new couple or couples.

The right to dissolve a family

A marriage is a contract. At one level it is still a property deal, as people may expensively discover when they seek divorce in the modern world – as recent examples of divorce settlements and rights of the wife or husband of the less well-off partner to a large share of the assets of the marriage show. *Miller v. Miller*[16] and *MacFarlane v. McFarlane*[17] established three principles governing redistribution of resources following divorce: the needs generated by the relationship between the parties (to be interpreted generously); compensation for disadvantage to one party generated by the relationship; and sharing of the fruits of the marriage. All three involve looking at the relationship in question (not the external factor that the husband is a multimillionaire).

Jesus seems to have taught that the contract between a couple is not simply a voluntary agreement into which they choose to enter, which is the way it is understood in modern Western legal systems. Jesus said, 'Therefore what God has joined together, let no one separate' (Matthew 19:6). God, not the consenting partners, is seen as the ultimate maker of the bond. The Old Testament prophet Malachi imputes to God a hard line on the indissolubility of marriage: 'I hate divorce' (Malachi 2:16).

Islam allows the husband to divorce the wife by saying 'I divorce you' three times (cf. Koran 2.230). The Koran strongly hints at a recognition that there are elements constitutive of a contract. There is no 'offence' in divorcing a wife before the marriage is consummated or the dowry paid. A wife thus repudiated should be treated fairly, according to the means of the husband, whether he is a rich man or a poor man (Koran 2.236). Similarly, the Koran provides that a divorced woman should wait three months before remarrying so that everyone can be sure she is not pregnant by her former husband (Koran 2.226). For if she is he may wish to take her back.

The centuries-long stream of preoccupation with the 'dangerousness' of sex, perceived as a tendency to lead people astray through strong inappropriate desires, set a high premium on chastity. This too has a biblical foundation. Jesus was asked why, if a married couple become 'one flesh', the law of the Old Testament had made provision for a man to put away his wife with a legal document of dismissal. This was, he explained, to make allowance for human fallibility. Elsewhere the Old Testament is fierce on the subject.

Yet marriage is not thought of as once-in-a-lifetime. If one partner dies the other is free to marry again:

> Perhaps there was pity in her love; certainly there was devout admiration for his mind; and so she spanned the two marriages with the two different men.[18]
> **Virginia Woolf (1882—1941)**

Jesus' own teaching was that the only circumstance in which this might be permissible was if the wife had committed adultery. And if a man divorced his wife for any other reason and then remarried he too would have committed adultery (Matthew 5:32; 19:9).

These rules were strengthened in the early church, for example, in the letters of Paul. 'The wife should not separate from her husband (but if she does separate, let her remain unmarried or else be reconciled to her husband)', says Paul, claiming that here he is not speaking for himself but for Christ (1 Corinthians 7:10). 'The husband should not divorce his wife' (1 Corinthians 7:11).

It is obviously in the interests of society if marriages are durable, and children born within marriages and brought up there. It is tidy. People know more or less where they stand. According to the early Christian writer known as Hermas, the man has an absolute duty to forgive and take back a wife who has been unfaithful even if she has behaved as badly as can be imagined, and has become a prostitute.

Remarriage after divorce is possible in the modern world. Erasmus, arguing in the early sixteenth century that the partners in unhappy marriages should not be forced to stay together, pleaded for freedom to divorce in certain circumstances and said the innocent party could legitimately remarry. 'It is legitimate for the believers to wed the wives of their adopted sons if they divorced them', for Mohammed himself did that (Koran 33.37).

The modern pragmatic view is that while marriage is an agreement entered into with the intention of permanence, it can, like any contract, be broken or dissolved by mutual agreement. When that happens, the task of society is to supervise the process by which the couple agrees what to do with joint assets and how to make arrangements for the future discharge of joint responsibilities such as the care of the children of the marriage.

So what should I regard as fundamental to forming a family and to family life?

Domestic violence

> The general principle that contact with the non-resident parent is in the interests of the child may sometimes have discouraged sufficient attention being paid to the adverse effects on children living in the household where violence has occurred.[19]
> **Dame Elizabeth Butler-Sloss**

Family morality is not straightforward even where none of these dramatic challenges occurs. Should I take the cherry in the centre of the icing or leave it for my son, the next person to cut a slice of cake? Should I pay my daughter's credit card debts or would it be better for her to learn the hard way not to live beyond her means? Should I abort the baby I am carrying now that a scan shows it will be handicapped? Should we let our elderly father who has had a stroke go into a home, which will have to be paid for by selling the house he was going to leave us in his will, or invite him to live with us, even though it will mean our teenage sons having to share a bedroom? These are dilemmas of the wealthy modern West, and they arise in the context of the life of a relatively small section of modern Western society. But they are all aspects of one of the 'oughts' that were for centuries regarded as natural laws, universally applicable to all human beings in every society. All the examples just given, except the last, could fall under the requirement of 'natural law' that parents should nurture their children. The last – does it follow that the children, once adult, have a reciprocal duty to look after their parents? – has also been a subject of frequent debate over the centuries.

There are no simple answers to moral questions, even the ones that seem to have a claim to universality. It might not be 'right' to leave the cherry for your son if he was already much too fat (suffering from 'childhood obesity').

Why do you expect your children to do the washing up?

Chapter 6

Self-sufficiency and Cooperation

Social models

Protecting your own

If anu euyl fall to any leuying man, that... euele fallys to me.[1]
[If any evil happens to any living man, that evil happens to me.]
Secretum Secretorum

What if the general good of society conflicts with the best thing for a person I love? For example, what should I do when the good of the whole community calls me to risk my safety as a fireman and I suddenly think how upset my mother will be if I am killed? How am I to balance acting for the general good and putting my family first?

Every child is my child[2]
Motto of the Concerned Parents Coalition in Uganda

Some people are *morally* offended by the suggestion that they should treat someone who is not kin as if he were a brother, or a nigger as if he were white, or an infidel as if he were a believer.[3]
Richard Rorty (1931—2007)

God ordains that blood relations are closer to one another than to other believers... although you are permitted to make bequests to your friends.
Koran 33.6

When is it right for me to protect my own?

For the individual living an ordinary family and working life the challenges of 'equal treatment' and respecting other people's 'rights' may be literally closer to home. Boundary disputes between actual neighbours, for example, about excessively tall hedges that block the light from the next-door garden, require an application of the principle of considering your neighbour's interests equally with your own, which can be surprisingly difficult. The father of a tennis prodigy was prosecuted in early 2006 for trying to cause physical harm to his child's rivals. He, too, had lost sight of the principle that his neighbours' good was as important as his own, though the consequences were much more serious.

The family and other people

Aristotle recognized that a single family – even the extended family and surrounding household of servants and slaves he was familiar with in ancient Greek society – is unlikely to be able to produce all the things it needs to sustain life, let alone live the good life. Still less can the single individual be completely self-sufficient. Economic dependency on other people – as distinct from emotional needs for company and special affection – is more obvious still in a modern West where the 'things' might reasonably include computers and mobile phones, which cannot be manufactured at home on a family small-holding or in the back garden.

It is partly for this practical, economic reason, Aristotle thought, that there need to be social arrangements such as laws and contractual agreements to enable larger groups to exchange goods and skills without wasting energy coming to blows. He saw this as a way of ensuring that people would be able to work cooperatively, but also as a recognition that a degree of specialization was going to be needed. Just as a well-made tool has a particular use or uses, so each group has a role and a purpose within the larger framework of human society. Aristotle thought rather like a modern biologist in framing his explanation of the way citizens relate to their communities. For him human beings are animals, 'social-and-political' animals, with built-in purposes that they realize best by getting together into city-states, through the natural outgrowth of their collaboration in smaller groups.

One key difference between Aristotle's picture of things and the modern one is that he did not – could not – envisage anything like the complexities of the modern world of 'partnership' deals, multiple memberships, overlapping and conflicting interests, commercial and charitable purposes. He just thought that small units needed to learn to behave collectively as larger units in order to function effectively. 'The primary community (*koinonia*) made up of several households in order to satisfy more than the merest daily needs is the village',[4] and 'villages' aggregate into towns.

Aristotle saw all this as a Greek, familiar with the life of city-states, each with an independent local city such as Athens or Corinth or Sparta at its centre, which was in political control of the surrounding region. So it was both urban and rural. For him the community that will naturally emerge from the joining together of several 'villages' is such a city-state. This is big enough to be more or less self-sufficient and it is capable of ensuring more than mere survival for its citizens. In the city-state they can find the good life.[5]

There is the important difference, though, that in most parts of the world it is no longer considered to be acceptable to deny full citizen rights to a section of the population and restrict such rights to a privileged minority, as the ancient Greeks and Romans did. The 'good life' was really only for those whose birth and wealth gave them servants and slaves and whose education encouraged them to spend their leisure in artistic, sporting and intellectual pursuits, and in contributing to citizen debate about public affairs in a 'direct' democracy (one in which the citizens were all directly involved and did not choose representatives to decide for them).

The individual Greek cities ran their societies in different ways, which could affect the treatment of those who lived in association with the community but were not full 'citizens'. The Spartans, for example, set a high premium on military supremacy and they used the Helots, or people of the surrounding country of Messenia, to farm on their behalf and produce the necessities of life, while 'citizen' Spartans concentrated on warfare. The Helots were not allowed to engage in such activities, and the Spartans considered it beneath them to do the kind of work they expected the Helots to do. No moral discomfort arose from this for the citizens themselves, for they did not seriously question the acceptability of discrimination between 'citizens' and others.

In today's world, the view of most developed societies is that it cannot be acceptable for one part of the community to exploit others in that way, or for one part to be denied access to particular activities.

In the West it is accepted that an open society ought to allow every member to move upwards and 'advance'. There should be opportunity for 'social mobility'. Yet the widening, not the narrowing, of a gap between rich and poor and the emergence of an 'underclass' of the seriously disadvantaged are visible in many Western societies.

In his *Politics*, Aristotle identifies three basic organizational structures, each with its 'good' and 'bad' version. The options he envisaged were rule by one person, rule by a small group or rule by the whole community. In each case there was room for abuse of power if the government became corrupt. He thought rule by the whole community was best, but only if it did not descend into mob rule. Ancient Greeks faced their moral choices in the context of relatively small communities, whose few hundred citizens (once the women, children and slaves had been left out) could meet comfortably in a single market square or *agora* and have a live debate about matters that concerned the future of the community and needed decisions, and then take those decisions together.

In the modern world it is not so easy to direct my social conscience to deciding what I ought to do. There is no agreed straightforward hierarchy of family first, then local community and then the state. Many other 'belongings' tug me this way and that. But something of the heritage of this Greek ideal of city life still shapes the modern conception of citizenship.

One of the balancing acts of today's world involves keeping a sense of priority among competing demands, and deciding what to care (and not to care) about.

Can I 'go it alone' or is that selfish?

Do I need other people in order to have a full life? Aristotle is clear that there is no way of finding an adequate life in economic isolation. He speaks regretfully of the disadvantaged position of someone who finds himself 'citiless'. Such a person is worse off than the modern person who is 'stateless'.[6] This is not quite the same as saying that no one can live alone and have a satisfactory life in an economy technologically developed so as to make that possible. A modern society gets over the problem that one person cannot grow and manufacture all he needs for physical survival, but leaves the profounder Aristotelian question what else it takes to make a 'good life'. He might have been dumbstruck to see so many do so in the modern West, where the trend is towards increasing numbers of single-person households. He might have had to rethink some of his arguments about the way societies come into being to satisfy economic needs with those same needs maintaining them in their original shape.

Recent press coverage in the UK suggests that the pressure on 'affordable housing' could be eased if fewer people chose to live alone. Should I take a lodger?

Good conduct in public life

The Romans contributed something of lasting importance to the debate about social 'good behaviour'. There was an assumption (largely shared by ancient Greek thinkers) that ethical questions looked different depending on whether they were considered from a personal, a domestic, or a social point of view. Cicero wrote a book on 'duty' for his son. The individual, Cicero argues, must not use for selfish ends what ought to be devoted to the common good, or society will fall apart.[7] Acting for the benefit of everyone is the ideal.[8]

Cicero wrote from the perspective of a sophisticated social and political system with high 'civic ideals' and principles about 'conduct' in public life, but also within a society with a world view and a confidence that it had a right as well as a responsibility to 'run' the world. As the Roman Republic became an empire, the Romans grew 'imperialist' in respects we can recognize from similar patterns of conduct by the 'big powers' in the modern world.

On these Roman principles have been built modern Western ideals of civic virtue and the importance of freedom from corruption and the avoidance of 'sleaze'. The principle that good conduct is desirable in social and public life is important in Islam too. The Koran points out that it is wrong to deprive others of their rights by corrupt means such as bribery (Koran 2.188). But just as Rome had its times of cruelty and exploitation, so developing societies in the modern world – and mature democracies too – may behave badly while claiming good practice and high principle.

Cicero thinks the individual should even extend this attitude beyond the duties of citizenship and act for the good of the whole 'society' of humankind,[9] for social obligations should be regarded as a law of nature.[10] Yet it is striking to the modern eye that he should talk in this way in a society that excluded so many from citizenship, including women, and saw nothing wrong with owning slaves.

When is it right to compromise?

Cicero is really thinking about the responsibilities of an experienced politician and public servant like himself. No period of life, in public or in private, whether one is dealing with one's own affairs or those of others, is without its element of *officium* (duty), says Cicero.[11] He knows very well the dangers of ambition and the corrupting effects of power and influence. These he does not regard as dangerous in themselves, unless they lead to impropriety,[12] or to acts of self-interest. Conflicts of interest are bound to arise,[13] but not admitting to them would be a betrayal of this 'social' duty.[14] If you behave well because it is expedient, or because it will serve your own interests, you will not value friendship or justice or generosity as you should, he warns.[15] One should not lose sight of the imperative to recognize the truth.[16] The good is the morally right and it cannot clash with the expedient.[17]

Cicero was clear about the importance of not losing sight of such big questions in the pressure to deal with the small ones. People should not limit themselves to wondering whether what they decide to do will make them happier or more comfortable or more powerful.[18] They should keep the bigger moral context in mind.

This is quite a demanding attitude, because it seems to discourage compromise. Compromise can mean meeting someone halfway, being willing to give up part of what you want if the other person will do the same, so that you can arrive at an agreement. It may be morally neutral. But it can also mean giving up principles, allowing a mild wrong to go unchecked in order that peace may be restored. This is what Cicero says is unacceptable public conduct.

Cicero makes a list of 'good principles' according to which to act, based on the four Roman virtues of prudence (meaning wisdom), justice, fortitude and temperance.[19] An honourable person will try to act in such a way as to ensure the conservation of society (in accordance with justice). He will aim to be truthful and honest (in accordance with prudence). He will be strong and sensible and moderate (in accordance with fortitude and temperance). His idea is that if these core principles are not compromised, there will be no danger of what we now call 'sleaze'.

Down with sleaze

Recent episodes in which politicians have acted in ways Cicero would not have approved of suggest that these principles were not a mere fashion of the moment in a political structure that collapsed many centuries ago. The UK Committee on Standards in Public Life was set up in 1994, at a time when there was mounting concern about the drift towards 'sleaze' and corruption in the behaviour of British politicians. In its first *Report* the Committee set out seven principles of good conduct for those with public responsibilities: selflessness, integrity, objectivity, accountability, openness, honesty and leadership. At the time the Committee was set up, the Conservative Party was in power, but the same sort of problem began to arise under the ensuing Labour Government after it had been in power for a short time. For example, in 2006 scandal broke about allegations that rich benefactors had made generous 'loans' to political party funds in return for 'life peerages' and seats in the House of Lords that were in the gift of the Prime Minister.

But I am not a politician

Do these rules apply if I am just running a jumble sale? Let us say that someone gives a sheepskin coat for the sale which I rather fancy for myself. I quietly set it aside to make sure no one else buys it. I have to price the items and I make sure this one is priced to suit me. That would be wrong. 'Selflessness, integrity, objectivity, accountability, openness, honesty, leadership' have all been compromised if I do. I shall find the rules about keeping clear of self-interest work in a small, personal world as they should in a larger community or a state. I should aim to conduct myself, whatever I do, in such a way that I have nothing to hide and do not act for my own advantage when I am doing something on behalf of others.

Cicero had in mind the requirements of a society in which certain adult male citizens were expected to give periods of service and to hold office in the state for a time. There was dignity in this, and it went with a certain standing within the society. In some modern societies any citizen may choose to play an active part in government. For example, in Britain someone may do this by standing for election as a local councillor or as a Member of Parliament. There is no routine expectation about this, and most people's active participation in running the affairs of the community is confined to voting for someone else to do it on their behalf.

Nevertheless, many people are involved at some time in the running of an activity, perhaps on a committee that is formed to run a Neighbourhood Watch scheme, or in a trade union, or as a youth club leader. At whatever level someone undertakes to do something on behalf of a community or part of a community, questions arise about good or right conduct in this area of public life.

The concept of 'stewardship' is involved again here, embodying the idea that someone who is entrusted with a responsibility within public or institutional life for a time (perhaps because of holding an office or position there) should be careful, holding the 'trust' with as much care as if it were a fragile piece of china. The treasurer of a club must not spend club money buying himself a fast car. The headmistress of a primary school, in a recent English case, was convicted of lavishing school funds on expensive purchases for herself.

What should be the rules of good conduct for 'public life' today, and how do they apply to me as an ordinary citizen?

Being a sound 'limb' in the 'body politic'

What should be the benefits and responsibilities of citizenship?

Christianity, as it spread through Europe from the end of the Roman empire, developed an idea that had been one of Paul's suggestions in his letters to young churches, that a group or community or society could be like a body, with parts, limbs and a head, all acting cooperatively for the good of the whole and living a shared life (Romans 12:4–5). It was an image with the advantage of giving a certain dignity to those 'parts' that were technically denied citizenship in the Greek and Roman worlds. Each part understands that it depends on the others within the body as a whole. The hand needs the foot if it is to be carried about. Christ is head of the Church (Ephesians 5:23), and the Church is his 'body' (Colossians 1:18). Christians thus became like one collective 'person' through their union with Christ, as Augustine, Bishop of Hippo, puts it.[20] So this is a social model that encourages people to develop a strong sense of their interdependence with others in serving the 'common good'.

This model does, though, expect the people with the humbler roles in the collective social endeavour not to make a fuss about their lowly status and try to get themselves into a better position. It involves everyone keeping to his or her place and not flouncing indignantly away if the place ceases to satisfy a person's ambitions.

> If the foot were to say, 'Because I am not a hand, I do not belong to the body', that would not make it any less a part of the body.
> **1 Corinthians 12:15**

The 'hand' will not aspire to be a 'foot'. Each part will continue to discharge its original function faithfully. This model is therefore not at all encouraging to 'social mobility'; it expects people to be content with their lot and regard it as virtuous not to complain or chafe or try to 'improve themselves' by getting richer or acquiring influence or moving 'upwards' in society. There may be a place for everyone but for some it will not be a very desirable place.

These ideas remained central to Christian teaching, and turned out to be durable through centuries of changing social expectations. In the eighteenth century, when Joseph Butler (1692–1752) preached on human nature[21] he took as his text for discussion Romans 12:4–5: 'For as we have many members in one body, and all members have not the same office; so we, being many, are one body in Christ, and every one members one of another.'

In the Christian monastic communities of the Middle Ages, those who became monks and nuns were understood to enter into a brotherhood or sisterhood in which they became 'one' in the sense of giving up their individual identities and wills and vowing obedience. It did not always work quite like that in real life. In *On the Steps of Humility and Pride*, Bernard of Clairvaux wrote an amusing but cutting account of the way the monks in a community can irritate one another and how easy it is for someone to lose his sense of community and begin to think himself a special case, entitled to dispensations which are not afforded to the others. Such a monk does not want to be better than the others – that is, he does not want to be a better monk. He merely wishes to be seen as different and superior. A monk can find himself descending the steps of pride when he ought to be climbing the staircase of humility.[22]

This lively tension between personal ambitions and an expectation that you will fit in and work contentedly in whatever position in life you happen to find yourself, has its counterparts today.

Is it all right for me to be ambitious even if it means
restricting other people's chances?
In what circumstances should I give up an
opportunity so that someone else can have it?

The 'corporate person'

Among the ways in which belonging to a group could involve giving up your claim to have your personal wishes met is the concept of the 'corporate person'. This enables a group with a common interest to form a collective identity as a 'body' so intimate that the law treats them as acting as one person. The early universities of Paris and Oxford were like that and so were the chapters of cathedrals and, eventually, municipal corporations.[23] Many people now work for global 'big corporations', and for smaller businesses too, some of which are also technically 'corporations'.

The medieval corporation is the model upon which the modern corporate structure of big business ultimately relies, though the modern business corporation has a structure in which only a vestige remains of the collective decision-making of the medieval corporation. Such companies are no longer like the medieval guilds in which an apprentice who became a qualified a workman could in due course become a master and a full member of the corporation. He would then take an equal part in decisions his corporation made. In a modern business corporation, a dozen or so 'non-executive directors' supervise the work of a chief executive and some executive directors. Most of those who work for the business are employees, who are expected to obey their superiors who have a line management relationship with them. 'Company loyalty' is encouraged, but this does not involve an offer of membership of the corporation. The glue holding the enterprise together is sometimes described as a 'culture'.

This can seek to impose a style the individual employee may find distasteful or absurd:

Innovation Teamwork Excellence Achievement Fun
We live and breathe our values – do you?
Our team culture is very supportive and we give structured
training from day one at a professional and personal level[24]
Badenoch and Clark, job advertisement

The employee of a big 'corporation' – or any other business – can
reasonably ask how much of him or her the employer 'owns'.

Should I work long hours out of company loyalty
even if it means I get home so late to my family that
my small children are already asleep in bed?

European law limits the number of hours a week a person can be
required to work, and that seems to suggest that it also sets a limit to
how much of a person's time is under the control of the employer.
The employer owns the employee's ideas ('intellectual property'),
and it may be difficult to prove that I had a particular idea with
commercial potential in my leisure time. Suppose I have a hobby
that is nothing to do with my job and develop a commercially
valuable idea connected with the hobby? Does that belong to the
employer too? This may become important if I go to work for some
other employer, because I shall not be allowed to take away with me
ideas of commercial value which my former employer paid for, and
hand them to the new employer to use.

Where in all this do my ideas about being good belong? Can I be
required to hand over my basic moral attitudes to be shaped by
company 'branding'? There have been some high profile cases of
whistleblowers bringing major fraud to light, as happened when Enron
collapsed. Should I obey instructions even if I can see that customers
will be cheated if I do? What if I am sacked and my family suffers?

How far should my 'company loyalty' extend? How
far do I have to 'buy in' to the culture of the
corporation or firm that employs me?

The social contract

Is it ever right to withhold payment of a tax?

Another idea of the nature of the social bond is that it is essentially
a 'contract'. The problem with this is that when the 'parties' to a

contract are not equal, one can try to impose oppressive terms on the other which the other is in no position to make reciprocal. The individual citizen may not have much say in agreeing the 'terms'.

Do I automatically agree to be bound by the laws of
a country if I choose to live in it?

'Society is indeed a contract,' says Edmund Burke (1729–97), deliberating on Rousseau's *Contrat Social* (1762) in his 'Reflections on the Revolution in France' (1790). Burke unpacks a series of special features of contracts binding on the members of a society, as he sees it.

First, contracts are mutual agreements, which are meant to be entered into freely by everyone involved. The social contract is not something I am free to dissolve. 'Subordinate contracts for objects of mere occasional interest may be dissolved at pleasure,' says Burke, but the state is different, and my 'contract' with it is not for me to seek to change as though I were an equal party to an ordinary agreement.

This 'contract' seems to involve me in a 'partnership' not only with my fellow-citizens now, he suggests, but with many generations, past and to come, in an agreement to something which embraces every aspect of life, a partnership 'in all science, a partnership in all art, a partnership in every virtue and in all perfection':

> As the ends of such a partnership cannot be obtained in many
> generations, it becomes a partnership not only between those
> who are living, but between those who are living, those who are
> dead, and those who are to be born.

This contract is not even limited to the state or society of which I happen to be a member, Burke thinks, but has features that make it universally binding because without contracts society will dissolve into confusion:

> Each contract of each particular state is but a clause in the great
> primeval contract of eternal society, linking the lower with the
> higher natures... The municipal corporations of that universal
> kingdom are not morally at liberty at their pleasure... to dissolve
> it into an unsocial, uncivil, unconnected chaos of elementary
> principles.[25]

This is what might be called a 'high doctrine' of the social contract. It is idealistic. It expects a good deal of the citizen. It poses questions for me today about the behaviour of citizens and what can be expected. The 'Wason' test of the proper behaviour of parties to the social contract, familiar in modern sociology, suggests that, in a social contract, taking the benefit without performing my part of the contract would be cheating. But the 'deal', the elements in the agreement, change with changing social expectations. In the nineteenth century owning property was a qualification for voting, partly because it was thought that only those with an investment in social stability of that sort could be trusted to choose a government. For example, the right to be treated free on the National Health Service if I am in need has now become contentious, when it is perceived that people who are not 'paying in' as UK taxpayers seek free treatment as visitors to the country.

How far does being a citizen mean being a moral guardian? I may have to do jury service. English juries of the past were encouraged to see themselves as engaged in an exercise with both the highest value for society and enormous moral implications. The medieval jury had a different job. They were character witnesses who could testify to the likelihood of the accused doing the kind of thing he was accused of. By the eighteenth century an English jury had something closer to its modern role of deciding whether the accused was innocent or guilty on their assessment of the evidence presented to them. In 1725 a charge gave a long list of sexual offences and offences arising from drunkenness and drew a graphic picture of the bad social effects of the conduct of 'Keepers of Publick Gaming-Houses and Bawdy-Houses' and 'other Lewd and Disorderly Houses'.[26] In 1797 there were special warnings about the then equivalent of terrorism, 'Men whose political Depravity may be proof against the Calls of Duty, or the suggestions of fear' and who are likely to be pursuing 'their dark Plans of Sedition and of Treason'.[27] In 1722 a jury's members were told that they were not merely expected to decide the guilt or innocence of those at whose trials they served. They were to regard themselves as having a duty to 'Suppress' 'Vice, Immorality and Profaneness', to 'Plant' 'Vertue and Religion, the Fear and Love of God'. They were to exert themselves in this 'spiritual Warfare' with the 'utmost Vigour', 'to the pulling down of the Kingdom of Satan'.[28] If I do jury service today, am I entitled to I see myself as a moral censor?

Modern citizenship

*Is it appropriate for the state to prescribe the key ideas
in the moral education of citizens?*

In the national curriculum at the time of writing, young children in English schools are taught about citizenship, in a way which reflects the current orthodoxy about the way they should be encouraged to think. There is also a requirement that immigrants applying for citizenship should 'demonstrate knowledge of both language and of life in the United Kingdom through a compulsory citizenship test'.[29]

The national curriculum syllabus makes a link between morality and good citizenship, rather as that old tradition of jury service tried to do. It seeks to ensure that the child has:

> Knowledge, understanding and skills to play an active part in
> society as informed and critical citizens who are socially and
> morally responsible. It aims to give them the confidence and
> conviction that they can act with others, have influence and make
> a difference in their communities.[30]

Accordingly, among the things even the smallest children are to be taught as prospective citizens is a sense of what is fair and unfair, and what is right and wrong. They are to be encouraged to 'realise that people and other living things have needs, and that they have responsibilities to meet them'; 'that they belong to various groups and communities, such as family and school'; and that societies and groups have rules. They are to learn to discuss differences of opinion about how to behave in the light of all this, to learn to live and work 'cooperatively' and not to bully one another (though teasing may be acceptable).

As members of a class and school community, they are to learn, at the first stage, 'social skills such as how to share, take turns, play, help others, resolve simple arguments and resist bullying. They begin to take an active part in the life of their school and its neighbourhood.' As they grow older they are expected to gain a more advanced and mature understanding of all this and 'to reflect on spiritual, moral, social, and cultural issues' as well as to learn 'what democracy is, and about the basic institutions that support it locally and nationally'.

In the curriculum as the growing child progresses through it there is a mixture of health and behavioural aspects of the broadest sort, suggesting that good 'citizenship' should include understanding of relationships and the way they work, from the closest family relationships to 'the lives of people living in other places and times, and people with different values and customs' (abutting onto the teaching of the traditional subject areas of history and geography), and an awareness of 'the nature and consequences of racism'. 'They develop their sense of social justice and moral responsibility and begin to understand that their own choices and behaviour can affect local, national or global issues and political and social institutions.'

Onward through puberty and the development of their powers of abstract reasoning the children progress, learning about 'participation and responsible action', 'the legal and human rights and responsibilities underpinning society, basic aspects of the criminal justice system, and how both relate to young people', the 'diversity of national, regional, religious and ethnic identities in the United Kingdom and the need for mutual respect and understanding', 'the importance of resolving conflict fairly', 'the world as a global community, and the political, economic, environmental and social implications of this'.

The conflation of moral and civic ideas, expectations and 'duties' in this list makes huge assumptions about the divisions of life's preoccupations and the balance to be struck between the inner and the social life of young (and presumably older) people.

Does being a good citizen impose moral obligations,
and if so, what are they?

Can I opt out?

Outward compliance and the good of the majority

If I do not join a particular club I am not bound by its rules. Is the state just a club? Can I decide not to 'join' and just ignore the needs of everyone around me in the country I live in?

'That Action is best, which procures the greatest Happiness for the greatest Numbers.'[31] This 'rule', which was later to form a core idea of nineteenth-century Utilitarians such as Jeremy Bentham and John Stuart Mill, was set out in 1725 by Francis Hutcheson. Bentham (1748–1832) thought at first that all human action is driven by pleasure and pain, which he saw as the two 'sovereign masters' governing human behaviour. Later he removed 'pain' from the list and concentrated on the 'pleasure principle'.

In his *Utilitarianism*, John Stuart Mill devised a hierarchy of pleasures in which the cultural, intellectual and spiritual pleasures are to be valued more highly because, he argues, discriminating people are right to prefer them to simple physical enjoyments. In *On Liberty* Mill claims that true utilitarianism grants each person the maximum liberty that does not interfere with the liberty of others.

Utilitarianism does not set out to treat society *en masse* but seeks to weigh the interests of many *individuals* against one another. Nevertheless, the Utilitarians of the nineteenth century thought that the right thing to do from society's point of view was what would promote the greatest happiness or benefit or welfare of the greatest number, even if some individuals suffered in the process.

The Utilitarian solution is thus quantitative, almost mathematical. It generalizes. It deliberately does not attempt to put a special value on any particular individuals and their needs. It is reluctant to allow for the possibility that some individual might be of such importance that his or her good would outweigh the good of a larger number of other individuals. If that could happen, society or some of its members might be obliged to make sacrifices for that person, not the other way round.

Should I accept that the general good is more important than what I want?

Thomas Paine (1737–1809) lists 'a system of principles as universal as truth', which he sees as deriving from the American and French revolutions. One of them is that 'Men are born and always continue free and equal in respect of their rights. Civil distinctions, therefore, can be founded only on public utility.'[32]

Yet in a team game, members of a football team play so as to give good opportunities to their best goal-scorer, and he gets the glory when he scores. In business the chief executive may be paid a very large salary, while the people who work for the business earn much more modest amounts for producing the goods or typing the letters. There are often different rules for dealing with misconduct by senior employees and junior employees, and the junior may readily be 'sacrificed' to save the job of the senior, whoever's fault the original dispute was.

In practice I have to accept the rules imposed by the laws of the country I live in as a condition of living there. If I refuse I can be punished by those laws whether I like it or not and I may eventually be deported. If I move to work for a time in another country or seek to immigrate, I shall not be allowed to take the laws of my homeland with me and insist on abiding by those instead of the laws of the host country. 'Community' living turns out to be highly territorial. I must adjust to the framework of requirements of this other place. It seems to be less a moral choice than a necessity.

'Slough is a nuclear-free zone', it used to say as you drove through this town on the outskirts of London. In practical terms opting out of society altogether by creating a little world for myself and considering myself to be almost an independent state will not be easy in the modern world. I have to live somewhere, and in most countries the land is divided up already into pockets owned and administered by individuals or groups in the society, or by the state. Only in periods of colonization has it been more or less acceptable to plant a flag, put up a fence, and claim your own space.

If I simply go onto someone else's land I could find myself in court accused of trespass. Even if I camp on common land such as a national park and drink from a stream and try to live by trapping rabbits and picking berries, I shall soon fall foul of the law and have to explain myself. Stow Horse Fair, held twice a year since the Middle Ages, became a problem for the local community as large numbers of travellers arrived ahead of the date and encamped along all the local roads, in effect extending the period of the fair considerably. Local residents felt intimidated and complained of house break-ins and fouling of the verges with human excrement. *The Stow Times* (30 July 2006) reported a meeting of the Town Council with the Parish Council of Maugersbury, the adjacent village most affected, which said, 'by and large, the public authorities are powerless to deter early arrival by the travellers'. Gypsies and travellers have found in a series of cases in the UK that if they buy land for permanent settlement they may lose the right to roam and the legal protections associated with it. To decide to give up a custom may thus be to lose a privilege.

If I am an 'illegal' immigrant I may succeed for some time in working long hours for a low wage in a sweatshop where not too many questions are asked about my nationality or how long I have lived in the country and whether I am there legally. Confronted with officialdom I shall be asked to prove that I am not in the country illegally. In countries with identity cards I may be challenged to prove that I have a right to be in the country at all.

So trying to live outside the rules as though I, and those who fall into a similar category, can be *in* a society but not *of* it is not going to be easy.

What about the inward reality of my attitudes? Am I bound to adopt all the moral norms and expectations of the society which makes the rules in the place where I live? 'Moral' and 'legal' are not necessarily the same (which is one of the drawbacks to mixing the two in a citizenship course). I might live in a country where it is legal to execute convicted murderers or to stone women for adultery, but I am not required by law to accept that either is 'morally' right or to attend executions and stonings.

Would it be right to try to change society from within?

May I object by staying in the society where I live, but where I have objections to customs or laws, and try to change it from within? Suppose I find the local laws abhorrent because they cut off the hands of convicted thieves and they stone to death women who have been raped.

Should I take a stand on points of principle and protest, perhaps try to work to get the laws changed? (But what if I am only visiting on holiday?)

The record of those who have attempted 'peaceful' or 'forced' change, other than by getting elected as Members of Parliament and working through the constitutional provisions, has been chequered. Throughout history, it has often involved holding meetings with others to discuss proposals for change or making speeches to persuade others to agree with you. That kind of meeting makes state authorities nervous, even though the European Convention on Human Rights now states the principle squarely that 'Everyone has the right to freedom of peaceful assembly and to freedom of association with others.'[33]

On 12 November 1660, John Bunyan (1628–88), the Puritan and future author of *Pilgrim's Progress*, set out for a meeting he had been invited to address:

The justice hearing thereof… forthwith issued out his warrant to take me, and bring me before him, and in the mean time to keep a very strong watch about the house where the meeting should be kept, as if we that was to meet together in that place did intend to do some fearful business to the destruction of the country. [The constable entered and Bunyan records that he was] taken and forced to depart the room.[34]

Suppose I want to start a club and hold meetings to discuss the breeding of pedigree dogs or the novels of Jane Austen, or to provide training for members in rock-climbing skills. Should I be free to do so without sending in a notice of my intention to a government agency and getting permission, or is it appropriate for the state to keep a close watch on all the activities of its citizens in case they are plotting against it? States are always only too willing to seize on an excuse to do that 'in everyone's interests'. Britain has now become one of the most 'watched' societies in the world with innumerable cameras in public places recording every move of the population 'just in case'.

Until talk of the 'war on terror' became current at the beginning of the twenty-first century, the state authorities in Western democracies had – however reluctantly – taken it for granted for a century or two that 'freedom of assembly' was a fundamental right and a necessary protection against tyranny. In early modern Britain there was an uncomfortable period when meetings ('conventicles' or gatherings) for any purpose other than worship in a Church of England church according to the forms laid down in the *Book of Common Prayer* were regarded as dangerous to the state, as John Bunyan found. Lessons had been learned.

Governments find dissent threatening and readily read into radical thinking the threat of what used to be called 'treason'. The counterpart word today would perhaps be 'terrorism'. Recent British Government attempts to create legislation to limit or supervise meetings in case they should be planning 'terrorist' attacks present a disturbing parallel with the experience of John Bunyan. The resulting mindset can read any activity as a cover for something sinister and threatening. Are those pigeon-fanciers really planning to blow us up?

'The individual is not accountable to society for his actions in so far as these concern the interests of no person but himself.'[35] John

Stuart Mill made this assertion in *On Liberty* in 1859. His argument was that there should be a presumption that governments will not interfere 'when the thing to be done is likely to be better done by individuals than by the government'. He defined 'civil or social liberty' in terms of 'the nature and limits of the power which can be legitimately exercised by society over the individual'.[36] 'The most cogent reason for restricting the interference of government' is, he thought, 'the great evil of adding unnecessarily to its power.'[37]

His concerns have since proved to be well founded. George Orwell (1903–50), author of the novel *Nineteen Eighty-Four*, foresaw an extreme of state intervention in the liberties of the citizen, which he consciously linked with the manipulation of language.[38] The fiction is now tending to become fact.

> In our time, political speech and writing are largely the defence of the indefensible.[39]
> **Steven Poole**

Terms and phrases can be 'spun' and then used as triggers and justifications for state intervention. The phrase 'terrorist suspects' seems to have emerged in British newspapers only after 1998, though it appears in Schedule 10 of the Criminal Justice and Public Order Act, 2001. The Terrorism Act of 2000 uses 'suspected terrorists', and that phrase and 'terrorist suspects' are both used in the Act passed soon after the attack in New York on 11 September 2001, the Anti-Terrorism, Crime and Security Act 2001.[40] The identification of a class of 'terrorist suspects' has made it a short step to arguing that such persons can safely be taken actually to be terrorists, to pose a threat and therefore to deserve none of the protections of ordinary civil liberties – the right to freedom from arbitrary arrest, to be told the evidence against them and to be allowed to answer it in a fair trial within a reasonable period.

John Stuart Mill's anxiety found its way into the Universal Declaration of Human Rights at Article 29:

> In the exercise of his rights and freedoms, everyone shall be subject only to such limitations as are determined by law solely for the purpose of securing due respect and recognition for the rights and freedoms of others and of meeting the just requirements of morality, public order and the general welfare in a democratic society.[41]

A balance has to be struck between the duty of governments to protect the interests of the people they govern and the personal freedom of individuals living under the government in question. It is easy for governments to alter their balance, much less easy for me as an individual to restore it.

For you and for me it may come down to the realities of what the state we live in allows us to do and say, and the scope for personal moral choice we are left with within that framework. Is there a way of living that I can adopt which is 'best for everyone', and not just for me, and that will allow me to balance these considerations of the rival claims of society as a whole and of my particular 'neighbour' in need?

Should the state interfere with personal liberty for the 'general good'?

PART III

SOME BIG QUESTIONS

*Now you may fancy that Tom was quite good,
when he had everything that he could want or
wish: but you would be very much mistaken.
Being quite comfortable is a very good thing; but
it does not make people good. Indeed, it sometimes
makes them naughty.*

Charles Kingsley (1819—75), *The Water Babies*, Chapter VI

Chapter 7

Practical Moral Decisions

Fair shares for all?

Greed and need

'I need food,' says the starving African child whose parents, living at subsistence level, can no longer feed their family when there is a drought. 'I need a new mobile phone,' says the Western adolescent insistently to his mother. This 'wealth-gap' is a conspicuous problem in the modern world, but it is not new.

> How few men in the world are prosperous? What an infinite
> number of slaves and beggars, or persecuted and oppressed
> people fill all corners of the earth with groans.[1]
> **Jeremy Taylor (1616—67)**

Rich and poor can still find themselves treated as 'classes' even where poverty is, by global standards, relative. In modern Britain or the USA the 'poor' may have mobile phones and even cars. In Africa they may not have enough to eat.

Should I buy my teenage children the trainers or fashionable mobile phones they want? If I do, will they want something else next week? If I do not, will they feel inferior to their friends, for they probably want them only because all their friends have them? Perhaps I should encourage them not to feel they must keep up with passing fashions? That expects them to show the courage to resist 'peer-pressure'. But if I give them what they want I am encouraging them to attach a profound 'value' to things which by next week will not seem valuable at all. Why does it seem important that what is 'valued' should really be 'worth it'?

We live in an era of socially sanctioned greed, when it is regarded as a good thing to be a conspicuous consumer because it is consumers, avid to shop, who keep the economy buoyant. The acquisition and frequent replacement of possessions and involvement in activities that involve spending money – for example on membership of health clubs and gymnasiums and appropriate sports clothing to wear in them – make up a 'lifestyle' for many people in the West, and may fill up much of their leisure. This can get in the way of other things in life.

To value something is to 'care' about it. This is a good example of the 'to care but not to care' rule, where things are enjoyed but can equally easily can be given up. Balancing the enjoyment against the obvious short-term value of such things can be liberating. It would be a pity to be enslaved by a lust for possessions of dubious long-term 'value'.

> *Is there a moral obligation to bring about a*
> *rebalancing of the distribution of society's goods,*
> *and how far is it my responsibility to do what*
> *I can?*

The ethics of pressurizing the gullible to buy things

With a modern world economy that depends on salesmanship goes a climate in which salesmanship can become manipulative. Whether I am a 'good' salesman in the moral sense depends how I have won the extra sales and whether I used corrupt methods or intimidated my customers. The old rule used to be a robust 'buyer beware' principle (*caveat emptor*). This has had to be modified, partly because it is not fair to expect the buyer to 'beware' if she is put under huge pressure, for example by a double-glazing salesman in her own home, who makes her afraid he is not going to leave unless she signs the agreement. The modern rule in the UK is that a purchaser should have two weeks to think again after signing such a contract. There is also a right to compensation if it turns out afterwards that someone was 'missold' something, for example, persuaded to buy a financial 'product' that was not appropriate for the buyer's circumstances, or to take out expensive and possibly useless insurance against not being able to pay the mortgage. So I may be a 'good' salesman and earn a lot of commission, but only by exploiting my customers, and that does not seem 'good' at all.

> *If my sales figures beat those of my colleagues does*
> *that make me a 'good' salesman?*

Is the consumer 'wrong' to be greedy?

The modern climate of expectation in the West makes it difficult for the individual not to be affected by the pressure to be a 'good consumer'. A whole industry of advertising energy goes into blunting the edge of any consumer anxiety that it may not be 'good' to be greedy.

In its issue of 21 June 2006, *Metro*, a free newspaper distributed in London, carried an interview with Marian Salzman, a 'trend-spotter' who 'helps marketing and advertising companies identify changes in consumer desires'. 'We're trying to anticipate what the consumer will do next,' she says. In the same article there is recognition of the interconnectedness of politics, fashionable concerns and marketing: 'We're going to see even more global resistance to brands and individuals that are American, and to American morals and values.'[2]

There is comment about the notion of moral 'retailing' in the United States, which seeks to purify greed by directing the covetous to buy things that are in themselves 'ethical' or 'ethically produced' or associated in some way with religion.

> Americans have become so decidedly religious that religion is going to become a very serious problem between the US and the rest of the world. Americans are living in a country where Christian retail is a shopping option. Christian fast food is a snack food option.[3]

A failure to be clear about definitions and categories and the ground rules of behaviour can easily make for confused ethical thinking. According to Noam Chomsky:

> It means little to say that people vote on the basis of moral values. The question is what they mean by the phrase 'moral values'. The limited indications are of some interest. In one poll, 'when the voters were asked to choose the most urgent moral crisis facing the country, 33 per cent cited "greed and materialism", 31 per cent selected "poverty and economic justice", 16 per cent named "abortion", and 12 per cent selected "gay marriage".[4]

Would it be 'right' to be moderate?

In modern marketing the moderation we have seen to be regarded as a good thing in many centuries is itself diminished to the level of a 'lifestyle choice'. The *Metro* article continues:

People want simpler lives, they want to downsize. People are
becoming very bewildered by too many choices...

In both Britain and America, young people are reporting they
don't want careers, just productive family lives.[5]

Using words that originally spoke of deep and important things in
the framework of modern marketing language and spin can send
mixed signals about values, and debase strong words such as 'belief'
and 'glory': 'Sven-Goran Ericksson has been urged to stick to his
beliefs as he bids for glory in Germany by a man who knows just
what it takes to lead England to World Cup success.'[6]

*Is it all right to indulge in 'retail therapy' if it cheers
me up?*

The morality of getting into debt

A painfully live issue for many in the West today is whether to spend
money they do not have and pay it back later, together with interest
on the debt. The exacting of interest on a loan (usury) was frowned
on by Christians in the Middle Ages. Muslim finance still avoids it.

*Does it matter I am paying in interest on my credit
card, money I could give to charity if I had not got
into debt?*

The modern West took a general decision to allow usury when it
took the form of earning interest on people's savings. Most people
who put money into a building society today do so with a clear
conscience, and even feel virtuous because they are 'savers'. We
speak of 'earning interest' although the saver does not do the
'earning' by any effort of his or her own.

In the sixteenth century the 'deserving poor' were the people who
saved for what they needed and did not get into debt. That has also
changed. It first became acceptable to take out a loan in order to buy
a house or flat, because the sums involved are so enormous that it is
only by doing that, and paying the loan back with interest over many
years, that most people can afford to buy a home at all. This is not
thought of as 'getting into debt'.

But in recent years there has been a proliferation of credit cards,
which allow me to buy items large and small, useful and frivolous,
even if I do not have the money to pay for them. The result is that a

fair proportion of the population, especially in Britain, owe money, on average thousands of pounds, on which they are paying a high rate of interest. Debt is now a problem for many, and more and more people are having to make emergency special arrangements to avoid going bankrupt.

> *Is getting into debt 'morally neutral', as long as I do*
> *not get in so deep that I cannot 'honour' my debts or*
> *ever repay them, or is it always simply 'wrong' to buy*
> *things I cannot pay for?*

Gambling

A similar shift of expectation has taken place in attitudes to the morality of gambling. That too was disapproved of in Christian Western society for a long time. There were good practical reasons; people could become addicted and gamble away all they had, and their families suffered. There was also the same objection as the one against usury: the gambler was trying to get something for nothing.

This has changed, with the introduction of National Lotteries in many European countries. In the profoundly Roman Catholic Spain, long queues can be seen waiting to buy tickets. In England, the National Lottery was introduced with the 'sweetener' that the money raised would be spent in part on charitable and other 'good' purposes, though of course there would be commercial profits too. Recent changes in the gambling laws will allow the building of casinos and even 'super-casinos'. The argument put forward by the Government in support of this change has been that casinos bring jobs and a general revival to a run-down area. This has to be balanced against the danger to local inhabitants – many of them poor and unemployed – of the convenient local temptation to use the casino themselves, and risk falling deeper into poverty.

> *Is is good or bad to buy tickets for the National*
> *Lottery?*

'Occasional half-crowns': selective and proportionate giving

> He lived among the poor, but he did not find that he got to know
> them... He did indeed visit a few tame pets whom his rector
> desired him to look after... What did it all come to when he did

go to see them?... Ernest sometimes gave [them] a little money
himself – but not as he says now half what he ought to have
given... giving occasional half-crowns was not regenerating the
universe.[7]

Samuel Butler (1835–1902) describes a scene of half-hearted
generosity I recognize only too well in my own behaviour. It is
tempting in today's world to reflect that Bill Gates can give on a
scale I cannot possibly imitate and ask why I should bother, since
anything I give can have so little effect by comparison. 'Is there
anything I can do about poverty in Africa?' I find myself asking. And
even, 'Why don't Africans help themselves?' I mutter to myself that
Third World debt is for governments or the super-rich to deal with.

In a modern Western society the majority of the population do
not belong to a distinct 'class' of the super-rich or the genuinely poor.
We are not all obvious 'givers' or 'needy would-be recipients'. On the
other hand, an entrepreneur can make a vast amount of money
through a lucky business venture. Bill Gates, the Microsoft
multimillionaire, became a major benefactor, setting up charitable
and educational projects with huge injections of capital. And some
individuals even in a generally wealthy society are destitute.

If I decide that my comparatively modest means do not let me off
giving at all, to whom should I give, or for what purposes, since I
cannot give in a wide-ranging way like a Bill Gates?

The experts have answered the question: If we had an additional
$50 billion available to improve the world, where should we
invest first? A unanimous panel of top economists recommends
that $27 billion be used to fight HIV/AIDS, $12 billion for
malnutrition and hunger, that the reduction of trade barriers,
whose costs would be modest, be initiated, and that $10 billion
be used to fight malaria.[8]

The 'experts' were a group of economists assembled at the
'Copenhagen Consensus', a conference held in May 2004. They
were arguing that these were 'worthy causes' but also that 'it is an
economically sound idea to invest in the future of humanity'. They
put proposals about climate change much lower in their hierarchy,
partly because 'for some of the world's poorest countries... problems
like HIV/AIDS, hunger, and malaria are more pressing and can be

solved with more efficacy'. But even on the matter of HIV/AIDS the experts could not come to a consensus. 'The difficult question still remains: Should we save 1,000,000 lives with condoms or 100,000 with a comparable cost outlay for clinics?'[9]

Should my giving start at home?

Do my friends and family have the first call on my generosity, whatever their particular needs are and even if people unconnected with me have more life-threatening needs? Some traditions have encouraged the giver to begin at home, with those closest to him. Ambrose of Milan, a fourth-century bishop, considered that charity should begin at home in the sense that Christians should first seek to meet the needs of other Christians, among whom the old and the ill had the first claim.[10] By the Middle Ages this was taken to mean that you should look after your own family members first, and, once they were sufficiently supplied with what they needed, you should give what remained to the poor.[11]

In the modern world this can present me with exactly the dilemma with which this chapter began. Well-fed teenage children with televisions and computers in their bedrooms, who are not at all in real 'need', clamour for the latest fashionable item. I give in to them, and do not give to Oxfam. The children themselves may pick up my sense of proportion and my priorities.

Defining neediness

When I have decided whether my family and close friends and colleagues ought to come first, should I then look to the most needy as recipients of my giving?

Can wealth be morally neutral?

One of the dangers the sacred texts sought to provide against was society's favouring of the rich – for they are likely to be the people who have the most impact and authority in a society – or of the poor just because they are poor.

The Old Testament contains the stern reminder that God made everyone, rich and poor alike (Proverbs 22:2). It also warns against the bending of the judicial process so that it favours either the rich or the poor. People ought to be treated equally when it comes to court cases:

> You shall not render an unjust judgement; you shall not be partial
> to the poor or defer to the great.
> **Leviticus 19:15**

> Nor shall you be partial to the poor in a lawsuit.
> **Exodus 23:3**

Is charitable giving different? If I give ten pounds – or dollars – to a
beggar in the street and the same to a millionaire, the benefit to the
two is going to be very different. But if I try to distinguish between
the two, I have to work out a basis for doing so that is fair and will
take into account the less obvious consequences.

Should I make moral judgements about the proposed recipients?

Can giving Aid undermine people's will to help themselves?
Augustine says that there is a danger that if you give a hungry man
food he will come to expect it and not fend for himself, so it may be
more virtuous to take bread away from him. Give in such a way as
to encourage those who are helped to help themselves, says
responsible Aid to Third World countries in our own day.

'Give to the godly and do not help the sinner', says Ecclesiasticus
(12:5). Augustine says alms should not be given to those who lead bad
or immoral lives such as prostitutes, gladiators and theatrical
performers.[12] The view was expressed in medieval canon law that if
there is a surplus to be given away you should distinguish between the
beggar you know and the beggar who is a stranger, for in the first case
you can judge whether or not he is a member of the 'deserving' poor.[13]

The Elizabethan Poor Law in sixteenth-century England took a
similar view that it was important to discourage idle and dishonest
vagrants from seeking to benefit from the charity of the parish
community. It stipulated that financial support should be restricted
to those who were known locally and whose need could be
realistically assessed. The modern British Welfare State is designed
to operate upon a similar principle, that those who are to receive
support should have to demonstrate need, and falsifying the position
so as to get money through the system by deceit is 'benefit fraud'.

But the New Testament proposes a different idea, which we have
already noted in the version in Luke's Gospel, and that is that I
should not ask questions but simply give, and more than I am asked:

'If anyone wants to sue you and take your coat, give your cloak as well' (Matthew 5:40).

Perhaps I should be open-handed in my giving? I could just see what arose, giving as I feel moved to do, without calculation, confident that an internal balancing process will provide a rough working guide.

Riches are a trap

Jesus told his disciples to look at the 'lilies of the field' when they wanted guidance on amassing wealth. He pointed out that they do not work hard or spin threads to make themselves clothes, but God makes them better dressed than King Solomon ever was, even in his finest robes (Matthew 6:28–29). Jesus had an encounter with a wealthy young man in which it quickly became clear that the young man was going to find it hard to give up his privileged position, even for the reward of a possible eternity of happiness in heaven. In the story as it is told in the Gospel, Jesus said to him, 'Sell all that you own and distribute the money to the poor, and you will have treasure in heaven; then come, follow me' (Luke 18:22).

In the wealthy modern West it is easy to sympathize with the young man's horror:

> But when he heard this, he became sad; for he was very rich.
> Jesus looked at him and said, 'How hard it is for those who have
> wealth to enter the kingdom of God! Indeed, it is easier for a
> camel to go through the eye of a needle than for someone who is
> rich to enter the kingdom of God.'
> **Luke 18:23—25**

The warning that wealth can be a kind of trap or enslavement appears elsewhere in the same Gospel: 'No slave can serve two masters... You cannot serve God and wealth' (Luke 16:13).

Jesus warned that it is important not to become too fond of money and possessions. They give a false sense of security and that leads to worries that the protection they provide could be lost. He told the story of a rich man whose lands yielded a good harvest. He gathered it all into barns. The barns were not big enough. He planned to pull them down and build bigger ones, so that he could say to himself that he was secure for years to come. But as it turned out he was going to die that very night (Luke 12:15–21).

So this call not to get too attached to possessions is a strong thread in Christianity. It is echoed in Buddhism too, in the invitation to the individual to practise detachment until he or she no longer 'needs' anything.

Not getting attached to possessions
In Britain in recent years, a householder was imprisoned for shooting a burglar. There was an outcry. Public indignation with the burglar made it difficult for people to weigh objectively what they thought a householder could reasonably do to protect life and property. People felt instinctively that the burglar was the one who should be punished. There was campaigning for the right to defend family and property in such circumstances without putting yourself in jeopardy of being punished. This example is complicated by the fact that someone attacked in that way is frightened of being hurt as well as of being robbed, but the householder had kept the gun in the first place because he feared that someone would enter his house and that the purpose would be burglary.

The problem is that, once I am rich, or even comfortably off, I have a lot to lose, and it can be difficult to maintain a detachment about my possessions so that I am not troubled at all if they are stolen. In the story of the sower who scatters seed that falls on different kinds of ground – some shallow, some rich – some falls into a thicket, and when it sprouts the plants are 'choked by the cares and riches and pleasures of life, and their fruit does not mature' (Luke 8:14).

The ease with which I become reliant on the comforts of a Western life can be one of the most noticeable daily tests of my capacity to 'care and not to care'.

Greed does not make you happy
Even if attachment to possessions does not become addictive, it has often been noted over the centuries that being wealthy does not necessarily make people happy.

> Some are, and must be, greater than the rest,
> More rich, more wise; but who infers from hence
> That such are happier, shocks all common sense.[14]
> **Alexander Pope (1688—1744)**

It remains a modern truism (tabloid newspapers love to feature examples) that becoming suddenly rich, by winning a huge prize on the National Lottery for instance, may destroy a life that was formerly quite contented, prompting the winner and his or her family to give up work and spend extravagantly for 'pleasure', only to find that the satisfactions bought are shallow and short-lived.

This is not to say that wealth is bad in itself; rather that it is easy to misuse it or to allow it to misuse me. 'There is nothing in the world so precious, but it may be abused,' regrets William Fulbecke in the sixteenth century.[15] So how should I handle it? 'To live on little with a cheerful heart' seemed a sound principle to the Roman poet Horace and also to Alexander Pope.[16] Not being shackled to wealth or the search for wealth is presented as a recipe for happiness by the nineteenth-century novelist William Makepeace Thackeray, in a letter to his mother of October 1833 from Paris, where he was studying to be an artist. 'The artists with their wild ways and their poverty are the happiest fellows in the world,' he commented.[17]

The Bible's idea, frequently repeated in both the Old Testament and the New, is that I should counter this tendency by treating my attachment to my money very lightly:

> If your enemies are hungry, give them bread to eat.
> **Proverbs 25:21**

> If anyone strikes you on the cheek, offer the other also; and from anyone who takes away your coat do not withhold even your shirt. Give to everyone who begs from you; and if anyone takes away your goods, do not ask for them again.
> **Luke 6:29—30**

'Go and sell all you have and give to the poor' was Jesus' extreme challenge to that rich young man who came to ask him what he should do to obtain 'eternal life' (Matthew 19:21). He urged him to free himself completely of the impedimenta of his possessions. He did not tell him to throw his possessions away but to use them to do good.

The Jewish ideal of righteousness includes an expectation that the righteous person will be benevolent and charitable. The Old Testament tithe or 'tenth' is a form of tax, but it has since been taken to set a benchmark for the proportion of income or wealth it was reasonable to give away. The righteous, in Islam, are seen as giving to those in need partly as an expression of gratitude for God's gifts to them; they 'give in alms from what We gave them' (Koran 2.1).[18]

The earliest Christian Church was conscious of the need to make provision to alleviate the poverty of widows and orphans, and it was quick to entrust that work to reliable people who would ensure on behalf of the community that none of their number went hungry (Acts 6:1–6). This involved a community-based charitableness rather than an expectation that individuals would give alms on a personal basis. A rough equivalent might be the modern Government promise of Aid when there is a crisis somewhere in the world. Today the charitable donation of time or money takes place in societies organized in quite a different way, where the availability of money for giving is much more fluid. When the tsunami struck the coasts of Indonesia in the last days of 2004, the money given for relief by individuals came from every level of wealth in the societies that gave.

The world religions tend to approve of the personal giving of 'alms'. The giver is usually thought to benefit spiritually, especially in the Christian tradition of almsgiving as it developed within the penitential system.[19] Giving alms involved sacrifice, since you could not keep what you gave away for your own use. The recipient benefited materially and practically. But the giver benefited too because almsgiving counted as one of the indications of the sincerity of repentance and it was deemed to 'make up' for part of the reparation the penitent owed for the sins he or she had committed. In a sense this would make charitable giving less disinterested.

Some of the money given for relief after the tsunami in Indonesia in December 2004 remained unspent more than a year later. If I give to charity, how do I know the money will be used effectively? Does it matter?

'Sheer' generosity

Was he really doing all that could be expected of him?... the Pharisees themselves in all probability did as much as the other Pharisees did.[20]
Samuel Butler

Should I give from what I can easily spare, or so that I feel the pinch, or is the only thing that matters the effect of the gift in making things better for others?

Should I expect my generosity to be noticed and approved of?

Even more important is the question whether I should I do my giving with no thought of benefit to myself. Should I expect a reward (such as feeling good about it or perhaps getting a knighthood or a peerage if I give on a really grand scale) or give disinterestedly?

The Good Man rests content with Goodness; he that is merely wise pursues Goodness in the belief that it pays to do so.[21]
Confucius (551—479 BC)

One of the lessons to be drawn from the story of the 'widow's mite' in the New Testament (Mark 12:41–44; Luke 21:1–4) concerns the value of quiet giving, with no desire to impress. There were the scribes taking care to be seen to be making big gifts in the Temple, who 'love to be greeted with respect in the market-places, and to have the best seats in the synagogues and places of honour at banquets' (Luke 20:46). There was the widow, humbly giving a tiny amount which was, nevertheless, a huge sum to her:

Who builds a church to God and not to fame,
Will never mark the marble with his name.[22]
Alexander Pope

Big benefactors, rich men anxious to have their names immortalized on a new building, big corporations or other businesses sponsoring sporting events or television programmes in return for lavish featuring of their 'brands', tend to want a visible reward for virtue. That has proved a considerable attraction to would-be benefactors. Robinson College, Cambridge, Harris-Manchester College and Kellogg College, Oxford are modern creations that recognize their benefactors by 'marking the marble with their names'. Modern benefactors can draw various further benefits from their generosity. Even the apparently free giving of time to service on boards and committees can be a route to reward by way of honour or generous 'consultant' fees.

*Can gifts with strings attached or even 'dirty' money
still do good?*

Fair treatment

What is 'fairness'?

A civilized society develops protections and requirements to try to
ensure that people in a relatively weak position are treated fairly by
those who are more powerful and influential, and that the
vulnerable are not exploited by those who are bigger and stronger,
(even if only in terms of brute force or bullying power). So fairness
requires a balancing exercise.

*What should I do if my child says she is being
bullied at school? What should I do if I am bullied
at work?*

Fairness is not the same as justice, but it is its close cousin. 'Justice'
is an idea rich with historical complexity. The Koran says I must seek
to do justice (Koran 2.188). The Old Testament is full of talk of
justice, with a heavy emphasis on the need for a righteous person to
keep God's law. 'An eye for an eye' (Leviticus 24:20) certainly
balanced things, and it might well remove the sense of injustice of the
person who lost the first eye if his enemy had to lose one too, but this
was a harsh and rigid way of arriving at a 'fair' outcome. The
Christian New Testament shifted the emphasis, for, it was claimed,
the teaching of Jesus about God's generosity and willingness to
forgive freed people from the old, rigid obligations into a world in
which there was no need to go through formal procedures to ensure
that the outcome of a dispute was fair to everyone.

One of the ways this can be done is through a formal system of
justice, using independent courts and tribunals to conduct hearings.
Justice is not quite the same thing as fairness. It is less a balancing
exercise and more a determination of a dispute between adversaries
to decide which is 'right'. Sometimes the mechanistic requirements
and the technicalities lead to outcomes which can seem 'unfair'. But
those very mechanisms are intended to guarantee that a decision is
made by someone independent enough to be fair, someone who can
be dispassionate and make a decision without fear or favouring
either side.

In the course of the evolution of judicial process two basic rules of 'natural justice' have emerged, which also have a good deal to do with ensuring fairness. The first rule is that both sides of the case must get a hearing; no one should be tried in his absence and without knowing what he is supposed to have done, and when someone is accused he must be allowed to defend himself and test the evidence. The second rule is that the person 'deciding' the case must be independent and not under the influence of either party.

A number of the Articles of the Universal Declaration of Human Rights are concerned with aspects of the right not to be subjected to arbitrary arrest and imprisonment without a fair trial, for example:

> Article 3: Everyone has a right to life, liberty, and security of person.
> Article 6: Everyone has the right to recognition everywhere as a person before the law.
> Article 8: Everyone has a right to an effective remedy by the competent national tribunals for acts violating the fundamental rights granted him by the constitution or by law.
> Article 9: No one shall be subjected to arbitrary arrest, detention or exile.
> Article 10: Everyone is entitled in full equality to a fair and public hearing by an independent and impartial tribunal, in the determination of his rights and obligations and of any criminal charge against him.
> Article 12: No one shall be subjected to arbitrary interference with his privacy, family, home or correspondence, nor to attacks upon his honour and reputation. Everyone has the right to the protection of the law against such interference and attacks.[23]

It was the blatant breach of these basic requirements, with the claim that they had to be set aside in an 'emergency', that caused such worldwide outrage about the keeping of prisoners at Guantánamo Bay at the beginning of the twenty-first century. Prisoners were held for years without their being told what they were accused of, or being allowed legal advice or any prospect of a trial with an independent judge taking place in a reasonable time (if at all).

Most people live without being accused of a crime or arrested, but that does not mean these questions of fair process will never arise in daily life. Small children develop a sense of fairness as soon as they begin to get to grips with events. The cry, 'It isn't fair!', is accompanied by the stamp of a small foot.

> *What can I do to make sure everyone is treated fairly*
> *when there is a complaint or a dispute?*

Should I be green?

A world made for humans?

> Ask for what end the heavenly bodies shine –
> Earth, for whose use? Pride answers, 'Tis for mine.'[24]

When Alexander Pope wrote these mocking words, he was challenging a longstanding presumption – that the world was created for the benefit of human beings. A key passage in the book of Genesis can be read in that way. It describes how God brought all the creatures he made to Adam so that Adam could give them names (Genesis 2:19–20). All the non-human creatures are thus portrayed as coming into existence for human benefit and remaining subordinate to human beings in their importance in the universe.

In the story as it is told in the Old Testament, the situation changed abruptly after Adam and Eve had eaten the apple. Their angry Creator drove them out of the Garden of Eden. Human behaviour damaged the earth. The ground began to sprout thistles. And human beings were henceforth going to have to work hard to get a living from the ground, toiling and sweating and growing old until at last they died (Genesis 3:17–23). But the earth and its creatures, though modified, were preserved for the benefit of human beings.

Whether relying on this story as fact or not, people have been only too happy to treat the world in that way. For centuries human beings saw themselves as the cream of creation, the reason why everything else was made. There were strong hints that this might carry some responsibilities and involved the notion of 'stewardship' once more. The Roman poet Lucretius (c. 94–49 BC) wrote a poem, 'On the nature of things', which idealizes 'a golden age of innocent reciprocities' in simple communities built on trust and the common will to protect the weak.[25]

Eventually the challenge became quite explicit. 'I was not satisfied by the many assertions made by many men concerning the outstandingness of human nature', wrote Pico della Mirandola (1463–94).[26] Alexander Pope had plenty more to say about human arrogance, and pettishness and irresponsibility, too, for example:

Destroy all creatures for thy sport or gust
Yet cry, if man's unhappy, God's unjust[27]

The emergence of modern ecological concerns has to be set against this background of centuries of arrogant human assumption that the world is ours to do with as we like. We have begun to realize that treating the world as a playground on the grand scale possible in modern times is leading to its being damaged, perhaps irreparably. So the newspapers are full of warnings about 'global warming' and man-made ecological disasters, and calls for 'sustainable development' and 'green taxes' to pay for the world of prevention and repair.

This is partly a matter of enlightened self-interest (an English expression that seems to date from early in the nineteenth century). The survival of endangered species, the preservation of the rainforests and global warming are felt to be important today at least partly because the future comfort of the human race is affected. Over-fishing of the world's oceans depletes fish stocks, so a source of food for humans is restricted. It is often not clear whether, in a campaign to save a threatened species ('Save the whale!' 'Save the tiger!'), the species is being valued for its own sake, or for its contribution to an ecosystem on which humans depend. When the discovery of the habitat of a rare tiny snail or a special kind of newt gets in the way of a proposed by-pass or planning consent for a building scheme, the welfare of the creatures in question seems paramount. But it is not unmixed with awareness that only if the widest possible range of species survives is the human race going to be able to draw on it for medical and pharmaceutical and genetic research of benefit to human beings.

People naturally do not want to live, or to leave their children to live, in a desolated world which has become too hot to handle or to live in comfortably.

Do I have a duty to future generations? What can I do to make a difference to global warming?

'Out-behaving the competition'

*'Every little helps', but what is the point of trying if
corrupt governments and big business undo my best
efforts?*

The growing power of the big global corporations and their
ruthlessness in exploiting the resources of the earth puts my
necessarily small attempts at stewardship into a depressingly modest
perspective.

The big corporations have acquired immense influence in the
world by flexing their financial muscle. They have had some success
in persuading governments to legislate in their favour, for they can
make useful 'gifts' of funding.

They exploit their 'consumers' by means of advertising,
persuading them to eat and drink things that are not good for them
and to feel that they 'must have' the latest fashionable version of
something they already own, even if that means adding to the pile of
unrecyclable computer waste full of dangerous substances, and
further poisoning the Indian workers dealing with them.

They exploit Third World producers. They have been accused of
doing harm to vulnerable communities. As an article in the
Independent newspaper claimed, 'Baby Milk Action claims Nestlé
flouts the voluntary International Code of Marketing of breast-milk
substitutes (adopted to prevent companies pushing formula milk to
mothers in countries with polluted water supplies, where
breastfeeding is safer).'

They have been accused of the exploitation of workers. 'Seven
trade unionists at Coke bottling plants have been murdered'
(referring to Coca-Cola of the USA). 'In 1999, workers in Saipan
claimed factories manufacturing for Gap [USA] had withheld wages
and forced overtime.' In Britain, trade unionists found evidence of
'"abusive working conditions" at factories around the world'.
'Charities accuse the clothing giant [Nike, USA] of using factories
that pay workers a few pence a day in dictatorial states while paying
millions of pounds in endorsements to sports stars'.

They have been accused of causing damage to the environment.
'Allegations [against Coca-Cola] include causing droughts and
poisoning water supplies.' 'Tesco's critics claim it... bullies local
authorities over planning permissions... hoards land from rivals,
erects and operates soulless hypermarkets.' '[BP] has been accused

of... destroying wildlife habitats by laying the Baku Ceyhan pipeline through Central Asia. In February, BP oil pipes were implicated in possibly the worst crude oil spill in Alaska since the Exxon Valdez.'

They are accused of the intimidation of small-business suppliers. 'Tesco's critics claim it bullies suppliers to lower prices.'[28]

Should I buy only 'fair trade' goods?

A countertrend has been set in motion by attempts to ensure that exploitation of small producers, particularly in the Third World, is replaced by the practice of paying a fair price. The first Fairtrade guarantee was made in the Netherlands in 1989. Cafédirect Fairtrade coffee in the UK was begun in 1991. The idea behind the Fairtrade Foundation and logo is to ensure that producers in Third World countries get a fair price and are not exploited. This has done some good, it seems:

> Fairtrade is raising our living standards. We used to ask managers or the government to improve our lives. Now we're doing it ourselves.
> **J. Devasagayam, tea worker, Stockholm tea estate, Sri Lanka**

> Before Fairtrade I was an exploited worker, now I have become a small-scale banana farmer and can send my children to school.[29]
> **Gabriel Salis, Banana farmer, Coopetrabasur, Costa Rica**

It has now become fashionable and even profitable for big business itself to be seen to be green or otherwise to behave ethically. *Business Ethics: The Magazine of Corporate Responsibility* lists the '100 best corporate citizens for 2006'. Among the companies recognized is Green Mountain Coffee:

> 'We take them coffee picking, and they do some hand sorting of beans in the hot sun,' says Winston Rost, Green Mountain Coffee Roaster's director of coffee appreciation, describing the annual trip he leads of a dozen employees, visiting coffee-growing cooperatives in Vera Cruz and Oaxaca, Mexico. 'With a newfound appreciation for how hard the work is, some roasters say they'll never spill another bean again,' Rost adds. This kind of attention to the human element of business offers a hint at why Green Mountain Coffee of Waterbury, Vt., is No. 1 this year on the list of the 100 Best Corporate Citizens.

Another in the top ten:

> On the environmental front, HP is reducing greenhouse gas
> emissions by cutting employee travel and using renewable
> energy.[30]

Much of the effort that can be demonstrated has a fashionable ring.
And there is the additional complication that ethical behaviour by
business is seen as something to be pursued not because it is right,
but because therein lies further commercial advantage. A business
can get 'a distinct advantage by out-behaving the competition. We
call this principled performance.'[31] Speaking on 'The power of how'
at Bentley College on 28 March 2006, the CEO of LRN (a company
that aims to develop solutions to 'address critical business needs'),
Dov L. Seidman, argued that 'how one does business or conducts
oneself is one of the few remaining great opportunities for
differentiation, competitive advantage and personal fulfillment'.[32]

Is it my fault that Third World countries are poor and undeveloped?

Amnesty International's *Human Rights for Human Dignity* gives a
comprehensive list of 'economic, social and cultural rights', to
adequate food and adequate housing (including security when these
are lost), education (free and compulsory in its elementary stage),
health, water, right to work and rights at work (including the right
to just and fair conditions, not to be dismissed unfairly and the
right to join trade unions). It is recognized that some of these are
going to be achieved only progressively in developing countries.[33]
But there are other kinds of rights that do not have to wait for a
future of economic 'equalization' between rich and poor countries.[34]

> *Does it make a difference to the number of baths I
> can conscientiously take in a week if there is no
> water shortage in my country but a shortage of
> drinking water in a country thousands of miles
> away?*

Does everyone have 'global' responsibilities or only governments
and big corporations? The reasons for the disadvantaged state of
some countries and people are very various. There may be adequate
natural resources but a political stranglehold or political corruption

preventing their being developed: 'If the poor are poor because they are lazy, or their governments are corrupt, how could global cooperation help?'[35]

In some cases a change of political climate, such as the fall of communism, has brought about a rapid emergence into full participation in the world's economy. China is the main current example, as it derives a competitive benefit from the fact that wages and salaries are still much lower than those that have to be paid to workers in the West. It so efficiently 'delivers the goods' that Western economies have begun to cry 'stop', as their own balance of trade is damaged. In other cases (the Soviet Union) the effect of the end of communism has been quite different, with an uncomfortable and patchy development of a capitalist economy. In both (and in other developing economies) human rights questions arise.

Is it selfish for the developing world to want to catch up?

Should I buy cheap clothing made in Third World factories that exploit their workers? That may be the only way for the local economy to grow. Sweatshops in Bangladesh exploit the workers but they enable the poor to begin to climb out of the poverty-trap they are in.[36] I could argue that it will keep my own family out of debt if I spend less in this way, and strengthen the economy of my own country by improving the profitability of the high street retailer which sells the jeans and sweaters in question. My 'right' response to this is not at all easy to work out. These are obviously 'balancing' questions, and they are awkward in the way they seem to make me choose between local and domestic benefit and the benefit to the wider world. On the other hand, I may be able to influence the need to strike a balance by encouraging change of practice.

It is not only big corporations in search of profits that behave in ways which damage the resources of the world. Nor is it only the greedy and economically powerful West that is responsible for exploitation. Sometimes local people do the damage themselves for what seem to them good reasons. Are poor tribes of Amazon justified in cutting down rainforests:

(a) to survive, or

(b) on a tit for tat basis (because they are exploited by a developed world which has taken more than its fair share of the earth's resources already)?

Punishing ourselves for being greedy

> We have developed a sort of compunction which our grandfathers
> did not have, an awareness of the enormous injustice and misery
> of the world, and a guilt-stricken feeling that one ought to be
> doing something about it.[37]
> **George Orwell**

The conscientious Western consumer may feel now that there is a
duty to accept a diminution of the levels of consumption which have
become usual – that it is morally necessary to stop driving a car and
flying abroad on holiday to lower the levels of carbon emissions; to
take fewer baths to conserve water; and to not add to the 'dead
computer mountain' or the thrown-away refrigerators of the world
but get things mended.[38]

*How does all this affect what I buy when I go to the
supermarket?*

Kindness to animals

The Old Testament insists that animals should be treated well.[39]
Within the Judaeo-Christian tradition the longstanding belief that
the world was made for humankind has been taken to justify various
ways of 'using' animals for human benefit: eating them; employing
them in the service of human activities (for example, plough horses
and guard dogs); keeping them as pets; using them in the testing of
drugs.

There has long been debate about the use of animals as food. The
first rule of good conduct for all Buddhists concerns not taking life,
any life. For a Buddhist, a fly is a living being and swatting it is
wrong, just as murdering one's fellow humans is wrong. Some take
this to require the adoption of a vegetarian diet, since eating meat
requires the taking of animal life.

The notion that 'flesh-eating' is somehow 'wrong' is also
associated with the various forms of dualism that have appeared
down the centuries, with the Hermetic tradition and with the
traditions of asceticism and puritanism. For dualists the basic idea
was that the two great powers at war in the universe, the powers of
good and evil, were, respectively, spiritual and material. So eating

meat meant you took matter into yourself and diminished the force of the spiritual within you. The Hermetic tradition saw human beings as standing midway between the gods and the beasts, with a 'lifestyle' choice to make. They could either aspire 'upwards' and live their lives in the most spiritual way they could; or they could bow their heads and live like animals and give in to being 'material'.

The ascetic and 'puritan' traditions have derived their concerns partly from such strands of thought. When Porphyry (234–305), a Neoplatonist philosopher of the early Christian period, wrote *On Abstinence from Killing Animals*, what he said prefigures a good deal of what later Puritans argued about simplicity of life, and staying out of the 'fleshpots':

> The fleshless diet contributes to health and to a suitable
> endurance of hard work in philosophy...[40]

> In the case of lions, wolves and wild animals in general, big and
> small alike, we cannot establish any number which would, if left
> untouched, relieve the necessities of our life, but we can for cattle
> and horses and sheep and domesticated animals in general. That
> is why we destroy the first outright, and remove the excess of the
> second...[41]

> The contemplative holds to simplicity of lifestyle... for he... is
> incapable of reaching out for luxury, and he is content with
> simple things, so he will not seek to feed on animate creatures as
> if inanimate foods were not enough for him.[42]

The 'Utopians' described in Thomas More's *Utopia* (1516) reflect some of these attitudes, when they feel that slaughtering our fellow creatures gradually destroys the sense of compassion, 'the finest sentiment of which our human nature is capable'.[43]

For different reasons, some animals may be considered fit to eat and others not. In the Judaic tradition there are 'unclean' meats, which it is considered morally wrong to eat. Early Christians took the decision not to adopt this practice. In Islam and in Judaism there are rules about the slaughter of animals for food, which do not apply in Christianity.

This all feeds into the modern debate about 'factory farming', the use of agricultural processes which make it cheaper to produce food but only at the expense of the welfare of the animals. Calves are taken from their mothers so that the milk can be sold. Battery hens are crowded into cages and denied the activities that are natural to them such as scratching up worms. Pigs are kept indoors and not allowed to root about for their food as is natural to them.[44] Some animals are given growth hormones or routine antibiotics or other drugs to encourage them to mature faster for profit.

Is it ever morally right to make experiments on animals? Small boys sometimes pull the wings off flies out of scientific curiosity or sheer mischief. When animals are used in testing and in scientific experiments, scientists can be carried away by curiosity beyond the strict limits of the planned project. 'What will happen if I just try this?' the curious researcher finds himself asking.

Christianity advances the 'stewardship' argument when considering the uses to which animals may legitimately be put. Christianity also emphasizes the importance of compassion. To accept that animals can feel physical pain and suffer stress merely raises the question how far, and in what circumstances, humans should feel entitled to inflict pain on them. To say that animals should not be made to suffer except for a purpose merely moves the discussion to what such 'purposes' should be, and how permitted experimentation can be kept within the agreed bounds.

There are protections now in Western societies, for example: requirements about the way experimental animals are kept, the size of the cages and the general conditions; ethics committees discuss the limits on what can be done, the balance of advantage to human society against pain or distress for the animals; whether simple creatures like fruit flies can be experimented on more ambitiously than intelligent creatures such as primates (but what of experimental mice?).

The idea that animal testing is justified in the development of new drugs for use in treating human diseases or for other medical purposes meets a boundary that is easy to cross into the testing of cosmetic products. Do I want my child to suffer if shampoo gets into her eyes and inflames them because it has not been tested?

There is a presumption still that humans are intrinsically more valuable than other animals. Testing on human beings is not allowed without the informed consent of the individual (though testing without consent has happened in some periods and places such as Nazi Germany).

Should I give my child drugs that have been
tested on animals if her future health depends
on it?

War and violence

Attitudes to smacking children have shifted over recent years. Parents would once have spanked their screaming toddlers without giving a thought to whether they 'should', and in earlier centuries such physical chastisement was regarded as an acceptable method of educating the soul. It might now be regarded officially as an assault, a brutal misuse of the greater power and strength of the adult against a vulnerable small human being. Two underlying questions are important for the much bigger question of the use of violence on the scale of war. One concerns the balance of power and the morality of being brutal just because you need fear no comeback. That has presented itself as a global question in the period when the USA has been the overwhelming world superpower from a military point of view, and has justified invasions of countries too weak to meet it with equal military force. The other has to do with a more pragmatic question, which is whether the use of force 'works'. The toddler may stop screaming in surprise and momentary pain, but the smack does nothing to stop the tantrums recurring. Again, recent evidence suggests that resentment and extremism may build, and that 'terrorism' may be exacerbated rather than discouraged by the extreme violence of the powerful.

Should I ever smack my children?

Not taking life
The belief that they should not take life has made Buddhists comparatively unwarlike, and it has discouraged any attempt to spread Buddhism by the sword. Nor have Buddhists used violence to resist persecution. Kindness and tolerance of those of other faiths have been encouraged. (The same attitude to the world makes Buddhists natural environmentalists.) Similarly, in modern times the Swiss and the Swedes have adopted an official neutrality as states, and they have kept out of all wars for over a century. This has enabled the Swiss to provide a geographical base for the Red Cross so that it can be understood throughout the world that it is neutral

and not under the control of any participant in the war. The Red Cross can therefore provide its battlefield medical services in comparative safety.

> *Is it ever right to kill? I might say a resounding 'no'*
> *to this until I find mice in the kitchen and slugs in*
> *the lettuces, when I become less sure about the value*
> *of other creatures' lives.*

Just and holy war

The distinction between a 'just' and a 'holy' war has become a live issue again recently. Just war is defensive, mounted in response to attack, Augustine argued. We may go to war to get back what has been unlawfully taken from us, he said. But the justification of the 'war on terror' requires a finely tuned definition of 'being attacked' in which the attack is the work of a small group, and not a nation, and the response may be to attack a nation, and not necessarily the one from which the terrorists actually came (as in the war in Iraq), or with a response out of all proportion to the initial attack (the Israel–Lebanon war of late 2006).

Within the framework of the belief that a war between nations can be just lies the expectation of unquestioning loyalty to one's country or beliefs. This flavours the well-known hymn with an emotional patriotism linked with religious fervour.

> I vow to thee, my country – all earthly things above –
> Entire and whole and perfect, the service of my love;
> The love that asks no question, the love that stands the test,
> That lays upon the altar the dearest and the best;
> The love that never falters, the love that pays the price,
> The love that makes undaunted the final sacrifice.[45]
> **Cecil A. Spring-Rice (1859—1918)**

Ideology like this is not fanaticism, but fanaticism can emerge further down the road.

Whether questions should be asked, and how insistently, has become highly topical since the 'war on terror' of the early twenty-first century began to loom so large in the world. 'The pundits had been only too happy to see the soldiers march off to war [referring to World War I], sure that that tidy affair would be wrapped up in a month.'[46] But the pundits were wrong, and soldiers who described the reality of risking the 'final sacrifice' found it a far from glorious experience. Some of them began to question the motivation and justification for what they had been sent to do, as soldiers have done in more recent wars:

> The worst moment is when you find you have survived and that all your fear was useless. You screw yourself up for a second to bear anything and nothing comes – except a curious disappointment which I suppose is also relief.[47]
> **Edward Thomas (1878—1917)**

Things can look desperate at a dramatic moment, and with the cry that the crisis is unprecedented (often heard in the course of history) governments and individuals can act in extreme ways, simplifying the issues and setting aside moral refinements, without always foreseeing the consequences. This is where it becomes apparent that I too may have a role to play in condoning or resisting war. My attitudes and responses may count, as in this description by Fidel Castro of Che Guevara:

> He was filled with a profound spirit of hatred and contempt for imperialism, not only because his political education was already considerably developed, but also because, shortly before, he had had the opportunity of witnessing the criminal imperialist intervention in Guatemala through the mercenaries who aborted the revolution in that country. A person like Che did not require elaborate arguments. It was sufficient for him to know that Cuba was in a similar situation and that there were people determined to struggle against that situation, arms in hand. It was sufficient for him to know that those people were inspired by genuinely revolutionary and patriotic ideals. That was more than enough.[48]

What sacrifices should I be prepared to make and what for? Should I object on grounds of conscience to all war? In the autumn of 1939, Dylan Thomas was wondering about such questions. He asked some of his friends to tell him what they proposed to do 'when they are told by the State to fight' people who are 'not their enemies'. His idea is that 'to undergo contemporary reality to its most extreme is to join in a war – the evil of which is the war itself and not the things it is supposed, wrongly, to be attempting to exterminate – against people you do not know, and probably to be killed or maimed'.[49] If he had not added that last thought he would have been arguing a disinterested case.

*Would it ever be right to use violence to support a
cause I believe in, and how would it affect the justice
of the cause if I did?*

What is my duty when it comes to thinking clearly about what politicians are reported as saying?

[The President] had not come out in public with one strong, clear explanation of why the United States was there, in such huge numbers, in the Gulf [in the 1990–91 Gulf War]… we were in the Gulf, the President assured us, to maintain American values, to sustain our way of life. Some of these random, additional reasons puzzled people: it was surely a little risky to go on about championing American values. How about democracy, free speech, representative government? Because everyone knew by then that Kuwait was a medieval kingdom run by sheiks, and so were an Arab ally or two.[50]

Should I be prepared to use violence if circumstances make it necessary, and how do I know when they do? And how can I be sure that extreme action that seems justified now will not look different in later years?

I just couldn't stand the look of the life in front of me. I knew the world was coming to an end. The nuclear holocaust was very real and we knew it was going to happen… I was offered a scholarship to Cambridge University, which was pretty special then, but I turned it down. What was the point when we were all going to die? Our parents couldn't understand us because we were really the first teenagers to reject society. We certainly couldn't be bothered to explain to them what we were feeling.[51]

This is what CND-supporting student Dixie Dean wrote, reflecting some decades later on his support for the Campaign for Nuclear Disarmament in 1960.

Would it ever be right to use violence to defend
someone who was being attacked? Is this the same
question as whether it would ever be right to use
violence to defend myself?

Tolerance and toleration

I have hung all systems on the wall like a row of useless hats.
They do not fit... That Marxist hat in the middle of the row, did I
ever think it would last me a lifetime? What is wrong with the
Christian biretta that I hardly wore at all?... There is a school cap,
too. I had no more than hung it there, not knowing of the other
hats I should hang by it.[52]
William Golding (1911—93)

Religious wars have occurred throughout history, within the world
religions as well as between them. They are in an acute stage in the
modern world. Many people today, especially in the West, hold
no specific religious faith. That does not mean that they have no
religious beliefs, merely that they do not see themselves as formally
belonging to any one 'faith community'. This is not necessarily the
result of not knowing about any system of beliefs in detail.
Coningsby, the golden boy with high aspirations who is the hero of
Benjamin Disraeli's 1844 novel *Coningsby*, grew up in a Victorian
society in England which offered people an 'established' Anglican
Christian religion, rather than a row of hats to choose from. Disraeli
himself was Jewish and understood the problems of living as one of
a religious minority in a society with an 'official' religion.

Nevertheless, the young man, looking for moral certainties,
'something sound and deep, fervent and well-defined', finds it just
as difficult as William Golding says he did a century later to hit on
a ready-made system that would suit him for a lifetime. And he is
not impressed by the way his elders seemed to be solving this
problem. Those in old age seemed to be 'perplexed and desponding';
those in their prime, 'callous and desperate'.[53] It is quite a common
experience that life can be busy with the attempt to do good, without
the activity being informed by religious faith or helping to sustain
that kind of faith:

During those eight years spent, so far as she had time over from
her children and house, 'doing good', nursing, visiting the poor,
she lost her faith.[54]
Virginia Woolf

By contrast, others, perhaps most notably today some communities
of Evangelical Christians and some groups in Islam, have a
passionate commitment to a belief system that includes a number of
well-defined moral expectations that they would regard as
inseparable from their religion. People reaching adulthood
intelligent, idealistic and eager to do good in the world, like
Coningsby, can be strongly attracted to the simplicities and
certainties of extreme positions within the major world religions,
and occasionally to the notion of making an ultimate personal
sacrifice for a cause.

That can fit Coningsby's brief very well ('something sound and
deep, fervent and well-defined'). But it can also be held in the form
of an assumption that the believer knows exactly what God requires
and that he or she must enforce that view at any cost:

> Many Hindu political activists today seem bent on doing away
> with the broad and tolerant parts of the Hindu tradition in favour
> of a divinely ascertained – and often fairly crude – view which,
> they demand, must be accepted by all... Why any of these
> theories – historical or religious – even if they were accepted,
> would give a licence for religious vandalism or sectarian
> destruction is not at all clear.[55]

So the relationship between morality and religion is not problematic
only for individuals. As I read the newspapers or hear broadcast
news at the beginning of the twenty-first century – with their
headlines about terrorism and 'wars' against terrorism, their
catalogues of deaths, their bewilderment at the seeming
impossibility of finding solutions to the 'principled' rancour of longstanding contests between religious communities – I am reminded
constantly that religion can strongly influence what individuals and
societies consider to be the right way to behave.

*Should I respect the beliefs of people who do not
agree with me?*

The religions of the world manifestly do not all arrive at the same conclusions about the right way to behave, or there might be less to fight about. This does not matter a great deal in a polytheistic system. The ancient Greeks and Romans had a comfortable, all-embracing view. This made room for a sophisticated set of beliefs allowing the cultivation of a profoundly moral inner life, in which 'philosophy' itself became a kind of religion. It also allowed for belief in a pantheon of national, local and domestic gods, for those who preferred that.

To these, rather than the great vague abstractions, ordinary people turned for help with their personal and family problems. Many of these little gods were reckoned to be petty and selfish and easily bribed with presents, yet were believed to be supernaturally influential in a small way. The 'broad and tolerant parts of the Hindu tradition' strike a similar balance today, in their capacity to make room for many gods while adhering to the – quite demanding – moral ideal of mutual acceptance among their worshippers.

In monotheistic religions such as Judaism, Christianity and Islam, this comfortable acceptance of many gods and their requirements is not so easy. This is partly because these religions rely for their moral teaching upon 'holy' books, the Old Testament, the Bible (composed of the Old and New Testament), the Koran. These are accepted by believers as divinely inspired guidebooks to the right way to behave, and at the same time a comfort and a reassurance. Daniel Defoe gives a description of the effect on Crusoe of being left alone with his thoughts and his fears:

> 'One Morning early, lying in my Bed, and fill'd with Thought about my danger from the Appearance of Savages, I found it discompos'd me very much.' He turned to the Bible for comfort... 'It is impossible to express the Comfort this gave me. In Answer, I thankfully laid down the Book, and was no more sad, at least, not on that occasion.'[56]

The scriptures of Christianity and Islam both draw upon the Old Testament of Judaism, and all three religions recognize the same 'one God'. But each of these major world religions points to a different set of texts as the complete and definitive word of God. Where each religious faith explains the world according to a moral system that it believes has a supernatural or divine authority or is in some way backed by a greater power, such differences begin to matter, not just in theory but in practical daily life. This becomes a fierce problem in a multicultural society, where those who practise a wide variety of religions and none live under a single government but without the cheerful syncretism of the Romans.

There can be a good deal of strain at home as children of immigrant parents grow up in the schools of a new country. The signals may become increasingly confusing when a child goes to school and meets children being reared in religious traditions in which what is considered 'right' and 'wrong' may be more straightforward, more clearly prescribed or proscribed – or much less so. In a multicultural society, these 'global' differences come home, and local and religious communities and governments feel they have to take an interest, make decisions and in some situations intervene.

For instance, a Western government might legislate against female circumcision against the strong wishes of a community of Ethiopian immigrants. Parents and children may disagree not only about what is the 'right' thing to do, but also who has the 'right' to decide. A girl who resists an arranged marriage is challenging not only the system in which it is the expected 'right' thing for a girl to accept such an arrangement made 'for her own good', but also the authority of her parents to insist that it is her duty to obey. And she is doing it in a society that has its own underlying rules about personal freedoms and the right of adults to make their own life choices: 'If a woman wishes to choose her marriage partner and paternal and religious authority align against her, a liberal society's institutions should defend her freedom.'[57]

A radio tuned to the BBC World Service, or a computer connected to the internet anywhere in the world, reveals other discordant possibilities. The issues have always been 'global' but now that is much more obvious. The resulting wider public awareness affects the behaviour of governments, as they introduce legislation designed to 'protect' one section of a multicultural population from another.

Much of a practical kind affecting people's liberties now flows from the 'polarization of moralities' linked to the suspicion of extremism, especially in the great monotheistic religions. A decade ago I might have been blown up on the UK mainland by IRA activists. Today, I stand in a long queue to pass through 'security' at

Heathrow airport, unable to take toothpaste in my hand luggage in case it is liquid explosive in disguise; everywhere I am watched by cameras, which record the scene in case it becomes necessary to identify a miscreant among the crowds; in the USA, every tap on a computer and every connection to the Internet are open to scrutiny and filing away for future reference.[58]

The choice of 'hats' William Golding puzzled over was going to affect his conduct, certainly, but mainly by way of his inner attitudes. Today, whether or not I have a religious faith of my own, I seem to have no choice but to think like a 'world citizen' and be aware of the practical importance of religious differences about morality. Insensitivity to such worldwide differences can be disastrous:

> 'We're missionaries. We're on our way to the Western Sahara to preach the gospel.'
>
> All at once, I understood why the conductor had been shadowing the couple; why he was so rancorous and unforgiving... for the first time since entering the compartment I noticed a small, open cardboard box perched between two knapsacks on the luggage rack. The box was filled with green, pocket-sized New Testaments in Arabic translation. There were three or four missing.
>
> 'Would you like one?' Jennifer asked. 'We're passing them out.'[59]

There is a considerable range of possibilities when it comes to my approach to differences of belief about profoundly important things, from open debate, to persuasion, to attempts to force my views on others. It is not a bad thing to let 'truth' make its own way, but to do that I have to be prepared to let a great deal be said, some of it things I may not like.

'Toleration' in a religious sense is a technical term that usually refers to the adoption of a 'live and let live' attitude to people who hold different beliefs. But that could also involve 'tolerance', a positive acceptance, as well as taking a decision to put the differences in a mental 'box' and ignore them.

Is mutual tolerance a 'good' thing?

Different religions and different moralities?

Would 'being religious' make me behave better?

It is possible to think about morality in its own right without *denying* religious belief. Yet it has been rare in the history of the world to reject all belief in that which is more than 'natural'. A great many people go through life with a bundle of mixed beliefs and assumptions without identifying themselves with any religious position that can be clearly labelled as Buddhist, Christian, Hindu, Jewish, Muslim, Zoroastrian, and yet without ruling out altogether the possibility that there is more to the world than its measurable physical realities. Others think everything can be explained without stepping outside those boundaries:

> I want to inspire the reader with a vision of our own existence, as, on the face of it, a spine-chilling mystery; and simultaneously to convey the full excitement of the fact that it is a mystery with an elegant solution which is within our grasp... A good case can be made that Darwinism is true, not just on this planet, but all over the universe.[60]
> **Richard Dawkins**

Atheists who see things in this way have to look for ethical principles that seem to them to be inherent in the world and its structures, and in the known patterns of human conduct. The way these are understood will depend to a degree on current vocabulary and fashions of interpretation in the relevant sciences. For example, some atheists have suggested that behaving well is just a matter of 'enlightened self-interest', learning to foresee the consequences of your actions and to act accordingly. Cooperating for everybody's good could ensure that I, the individual 'cooperating', am also able to live comfortably. 'Behave well and win yourself friends, love, support,' I might advise myself, though I might feel a twinge of concern that this would debase my best efforts to be good to the level of a trading activity.

This way of seeing things, relying on no belief in a supernatural power which is setting the standards, can allow for unselfishness, and respect for other people's needs and the common good.[61] Nevertheless, the lack of something 'higher' is sharply felt in the modern West, where the complaint is often heard that material wealth offers only hollow satisfactions, and people say that they feel dissatisfied by a life in which they may feel they are nothing more than 'consumers'.

Belief in a 'supervisory' supernatural authority has usually been associated with 'higher' moral standards. God is watching us, says Jeremy Taylor. 'We can no more be removed from the presence of God, than from our own being.'[62] He was thinking of a God conceived in the Christian tradition, who is not only good and a monitor of good in his creatures, but Goodness itself. A similar insistence on God's holiness is to be found in Judaism. Rabbinical exegetics exhorts good Jews to behave in such a way as to reflect that holiness to the world and encourage everyone who beholds it to give glory to God, for that is the meaning of 'loving God' (Deuteronomy 6:5).

On the other hand, allowing in a religious dimension is not necessarily a *guarantee* of 'higher' moral standards. The problem is that there is no universally agreed 'just and perfect Idea of that being whom every reasonable Creature ought to imitate'.[63] There have been some very unsatisfactory 'gods'. *The Spectator* in 1714 reminded its readers that the pagan gods of ancient Greece and Rome did not set much of an example. In fact, they led loose and criminous lives, so that people who set their moral compasses in imitation of that sort of God would not find religion very improving:

> The Young Man... might justify his Lewdness by the Example of Jupiter; as, indeed, there was scarce any Crime that might not be countenanced by those Notions of the Deity which prevailed among the common People in the Heathen worlds.[64]

And even where God is understood in the highest terms, in terms of all kinds of 'ultimate goods', as in the great monotheistic religions, his worshippers have proved themselves capable of acts of violence and oppression in religious wars, sometimes between adherents of different religions, but equally often in wars internal to the religion in question between sects with differing beliefs. So a good God is apparently not necessarily an effective standard setter.

What are the influences making for 'good' in my life?

Challenging wrongdoing
Having a go

> 'I didn't like to pry,' [the neighbours] told curious reporters, as
> police in black overalls carried out box after box of human
> remains [from the house where] Fred and Rose West tortured and
> murdered at least ten females.[65]

When should I be willing to take 'direct' action, as a member of
society? Is there a place for indignation, as when Jesus threw the
traders out of the Temple? (John 2:15). What would it mean to call
that 'righteous' indignation?

> But wanting to justify himself, he asked Jesus, 'And who is my
> neighbour?' Jesus replied, 'A man was going down from Jerusalem
> to Jericho, and fell into the hands of robbers, who stripped him,
> beat him, and went away, leaving him half dead. Now by chance
> a priest was going down that road; and when he saw him, he
> passed by on the other side. So likewise a Levite, when he came
> to the place and saw him, passed by on the other side. But a
> Samaritan while travelling came near him; and when he saw him,
> he was moved with pity. He went to him and bandaged his
> wounds, having poured oil and wine on them. Then he put him
> on his own animal, brought him to an inn, and took care of him.
> The next day he took out two denarii, gave them to the innkeeper,
> and said, 'Take care of him; and when I come back, I will repay
> you whatever more you spend.' Which of these three, do you
> think, was a neighbour to the man who fell into the hands of the
> robbers?' He said, 'The one who showed him mercy.' Jesus said to
> him, 'Go and do likewise.'
> **Luke 10:29—37**

The image of the Good Samaritan remains powerfully attractive.
There are 'Good Samaritan' laws in the USA and Canada, though
their function is to ensure that those who are brave enough to
intervene to help when they see someone attacked in the street are
not subject to retribution afterwards if they accidentally injure the
attacker or even cause his death. Some laws of this kind even go so

far as to impose a legal requirement not to walk past and pretend that nothing is happening, unless the passer-by would put himself or herself in danger by intervening. In some countries, such as France, Italy, Spain and Japan, there is a legal duty to contact the authorities or help directly, and in Germany the passer-by must attempt to give first aid. The kind of thing envisaged here is the giving of emergency help when someone is in danger. I might rise to that, perhaps.

When teenagers join gangs and the gangs develop bad habits of 'anti-social behaviour', attacking people and property, this can often be put down to a sense of powerlessness. Adolescents who become the subject of ASBOs in the UK sometimes say they have caused local disruption because they feel less powerless when they join a gang and can hang about on street corners in the reassuring company of others, and mock passers-by in threatening tones, and can see that people are afraid of them. The individual young people involved do not feel they can make any mark on society on their own, but together they can make quite a dent. In that mood, damage is more easily achieved than constructive change. The prowling gang can slash car tyres or mug victims to steal their mobile phones more easily than they can hope to alter the opportunities available to those who live on their home streets. The balance of power is shifted. An ASBO becomes a badge of honour. If there were 'Good Samaritan' laws in the UK, I would find myself under quite a test of courage when I met one of these gangs on a dark night.

> *You would not falsify the firm's accounts if your boss*
> *told you to. Would you report it if you discovered*
> *that someone else was doing so?*

But what of challenges to stand up for the right or the truth that present no sudden dramatic challenge and are less likely to get the adrenalin flowing? These seem to require a different kind of courage. The English Puritan Richard Baxter (1615–91) wrote a *Last Treatise* as an indictment of rack-renting (the charging of excessive rents by greedy landlords to tenants who could not afford to move), and the poverty it caused. In it Baxter tries to follow the teaching of the Gospel, and apply it to a contemporary practice he believed to be unfair and damaging to people who were helpless to defend themselves. It was a brave book, but it was not published in his lifetime. It was too 'hot' to publish if he was to avoid being accused of being a 'Leveller', one of a revolutionary group at the time of the English Civil War who wanted to create an equal society.[66]

Others have gone further, stuck their necks out, and sometimes suffered for it:

> Mahatma Gandhi and Martin Luther King Jr., did not wait for the rich and powerful to come to their rescue. They asserted their call to justice and made their stand in the face of official arrogance and neglect.[67]

I have to make difficult decisions when I think I see wrong being done. Can I do anything which will make a difference, or might I make things worse by trying to interfere, or make myself less useful in some future battle by discrediting myself by taking up an unpopular position in this one – as perhaps Richard Baxter feared he would. In some contexts the 'protester' gets only one chance, for he is executed at once.

There may be several things I can do, but I shall have to decide which would be proportionate, or justified, or right in themselves. There are situations in which the protester gets only one chance and puts his life at risk by speaking up.

Having the courage not to conform

> Believers, obey God and obey the Apostle and those in authority among you.
> **Koran 4.57**

Islam is submission, total resignation of the will in perfect obedience. Christianity has long had a similar ideal. In the old security of a hierarchically arranged world, most people probably accepted that those who were in a position of authority over them had been put there by God, and were therefore 'entitled' to give orders. That has given way in recent generations to a tendency to question all claims to authority.

The confidence of earlier generations and other societies that those in charge are to be trusted has been severely shaken and the modern West – at least in Europe – has done some radical rethinking about automatic obedience to 'authority'. In modern

Western society standing up for what I believe to be right may involve social, rather than physical, courage. What should I do when I have a clear obligation to do what I am told (for example, as an employee), but it seems to me that what I am told to do is wrong?[68]

Being a dissenting voice

Students of the way groups function have observed that group behaviour tends to go through a series of stages. The first stage involves being obliging, with members disguising their spontaneous feelings so as to appear to agree with what everyone else is saying. At a second stage members of the group may become impatient with this and begin to say what they really think, and even get angry, at the risk of losing their membership or their acceptance by the others. If an individual asks awkward questions too often, or at the wrong stage of this process in the evolution of the group dynamics, that person becomes a pariah. If the group survives that stage, it may begin to work together effectively to produce some joint or shared outcome, though that does not necessarily imply that everyone will be able to play an equal part or be equally accepted.[69] So what is my responsibility if I find I am in a group or on a committee and I think the group is weakly going along with unethical proposals?

One of the most dramatic recent examples of the importance of the individual having the courage to point the finger is the case of Enron, an American company based in Houston in Texas. This involved 'blowing the whistle' on fraud. Largely thanks to an ordinary employee with a conscience, dubious accounting practices were brought to light and the company was bankrupted, directors prosecuted for fraud, and the trustworthiness of 'big name' accountancy firms, widely relied on as auditors to pick up such malpractice, brought seriously into question. The accounting firm of Arthur Andersen, for one, faced its own dissolution as a result.

Whistleblowers do not always survive professionally undamaged. They may be sacked, though UK legislation to protect those making 'public interest' disclosures from dismissal for disloyalty to their employers has provided a partial remedy. If they have professional reputations, those are likely to be attacked in a comprehensive attempt to discredit them. So whistleblowing takes courage and can be sacrificial.

If I am a doctor, I could easily be faced with a conflict between professional standards and management instructions. Suppose my health service managers give instructions that conflict with clinical priorities? Suppose they make it clear that if I object the funding for my department will be reduced? Insisting on maintaining professional integrity can be personally and professionally costly too.

A similar set of difficulties attaches to the protection of the integrity of scientific research:

> If industry gets involved in science, it has to balance genuine hypothesis testing and transparency against commercial interests, bureaucracy of drug regulation, and the financial consequences of dishonesty.[70]

If I am an academic engaged in research that is partly funded by a commercial sponsor, say a drug company, I may find that their proposed product is faulty. The problem is that the contract signed in return for the funding may give the commercial sponsor ownership and control of the 'intellectual property', including the evidence and the right to publish the results. I find I am not allowed to raise concerns without breaking the contract. James Kahn in San Francisco, Nancy Olivieri in Toronto and others were threatened with legal action if they went public with their concerns, demonized, and their research careers damaged if they resisted. But if they did not, they would have left doctors to prescribe the resulting drugs in ignorance. So they did, but others have gone along with the terms of their contracts and not made a fuss.[71]

This kind of moral dilemma would seem remote from the concerns of people who are not scientific researchers if it were not that the use of human volunteers in the testing of drugs, and the occasional disaster when they are adversely affected, is a reminder that the trustworthiness of scientific research has everyday practical importance.

There may be small but important ways in which I can insist that the rules are kept if I can see that someone might get hurt if they are not. However modest my position in an organization, I can be the one who says 'stop'.

But in order to say it I have to have freedom of speech, somewhere to speak where the concern will be heard, and no fear of being subject to a criminal prosecution for opening my mouth. The classic arguments for freedom of speech, and the special kind of freedom of speech enjoyed by the press and the media in general, fall into three categories. One is concerned with the importance of ensuring that citizens feel free to express their opinions (within the law, so as to prevent them unfairly damaging other people by the things they say).[72]

Then there are arguments that amount to saying that freedom to speak out and challenge politicians is the only way a modern democracy can protect itself against the creeping invasion of its freedoms and the abuse of power. That argument works equally well when it comes to challenging fraudulent accounting and commercial pressure to distort the results of scientific research.

The third is the argument that unless there can be frank and free discussion and debate, truth itself will be suppressed:

> The Truth would certainly do well enough if she were left to fend for herself.[73]
> **John Locke (1632—1704)**

As Milton put it in the midst of the English Civil War of the mid-seventeenth century, given the chance, truth will always out:

> Let her and Falsehood grapple; who ever knew Truth put to the worse, in a free and open encounter?[74]

Nonetheless, Milton thought truth might need a little help from its friends.

Robin Hood in the legend robbed the rich to give to the poor. Does the achieving of good ends ever justify using means that would be wrong in themselves? Before you cry 'no!' and 'never!' think again about the way compromise works. It is very easy for those responsible for decisions, on committees and boards, as trustees or as individual executive directors, to find themselves agreeing to bend the rules a little, to let a small unsatisfactoriness slip, in order to avoid delaying things, or to get a good outcome by the most direct method available, even if it involves a minor dishonesty. Do I have the courage to stand out against that kind of compromise, and can I be effective in preventing it?

Chapter 8

Attitudes and Expectations

Telling the truth and being honest
Jesting Pilate and truth as a 'flexible friend'

Should I always tell the truth?

After three years of itinerant teaching, Jesus was arrested as a dangerous popular leader and brought before Pilate for judgement. He told Pilate, '… I came into the world, to testify to the truth', and Pilate asked him, 'What is truth?' (John 18:37–38).

Pilate's question is not easy to answer. Yet Jesus had made a stupendous claim, that the truth 'will set you free' (John 8:32). And to have no skeletons in the cupboard, to have no reason to fear that something will 'come out' that I would be ashamed to have others know about, is liberating indeed.

Can a lie be 'white'?

Augustine asks how we are to view the failures to be completely truthful with which life is fraught and which seem to be inevitable. He seems to have been in two minds about many of the key issues for he wrote two books about telling the truth which lean in opposite directions.

In one book, *On Lying*, Augustine excludes jokes as a category of lies, for everyone knows that it is obvious that a joke is not meant to be taken seriously. Puritans through the ages have been rather more severe on this point, urging the plainest of plain speaking. Although he had substantial reservations about the dangerous seductiveness of theatrical performances, Augustine thought at this time that, jokes aside, not everything that is false is a lie. The speaker may, for example, genuinely believe that he is telling the truth but be mistaken.[1] Lying requires the intention to deceive.[2] This is like the difference between accidentally picking up the wrong umbrella and the theft of an umbrella, which involves intending to deprive its owner of it permanently.

Could even the intention to deceive be forgiven if the lie was for a good cause? Augustine gives the example of someone who knows that robbers lie in wait for the unwary traveller down a certain road (a common crime in antiquity, rather like modern mugging). He is asked the way. He is afraid that the traveller will not believe him if he warns him about the robbers. Would it be more 'truthful' to tell him a lie and send him off down the wrong road in order to save him from the ambush?[3] Augustine suggests tentatively that this 'distortion' or 'amendment' of the truth for a good end may be beneficial (*utilis*) on occasion.

Could this even amount to a more profound mode of truth-telling? Jesus himself told parables, which were, on a strict definition, lies, for there was no sower who went forth to sow, and no 'wise and foolish virgins' existed in reality like those in the story. Others have recognized that it is possible to learn truths through fictions, and to understand the good through studying 'bad' examples. The plots of stories in which there is a battle of good and evil and the 'Baddies' come to a sticky end are examples. Such stories have been popular in every century and they survive in modern computer games in which the player wins by shooting down the villains or enacts battles on the screen.

Are there such things as 'white lies'?

The other book Augustine wrote on lying was called *Against Lying*. This is more absolute in its condemnation of failures in truth-telling. There are many kinds of lie, says Augustine, and now he thinks we should hate them all, for truth and lies are diametrically opposed.[4]

Anselm of Canterbury took a straightforward view of truth-telling. You are telling the truth, he said, when you say that things are as they are:

What seems to you to be the 'truth' of a saying?
When it signifies that what is is so.[5]

Truth-telling has to be attempted in all the complexity of social and personal ties, likes and dislikes, long-term wishes for a good outcome and short-term concerns for the immediate appearance of things, vanity, cowardice. Contrast Augustine's rather abstract worries about the right thing to say to the man on the road with the robbers down the next turning, with a scene from Jane Austen:

> Mr. Elliot is a man without heart or conscience; a designing, wary, cold-blooded being, who thinks only of himself; who, for his own interest or ease, would be guilty of any cruelty, or any treachery, that could be perpetrated without risk of his general character. He has no feeling for others. Those whom he has been the chief cause of leading into ruin, he can neglect and desert without the smallest compunction. He is totally beyond the reach of any sentiment of justice or compassion.[6]

These startling words explode from Anne Elliot's old friend Mrs Smith in Jane Austen's novel *Persuasion*. Anne is more than a little surprised, for at the beginning of their conversation Mrs Smith had begun by speaking well of Mr Elliot. 'My Dear,' was Mrs Smith's reply, 'there was nothing else to be done. I considered your marrying him as certain... and I could no more speak the truth of him, than if he had been your husband.'

Anne is soon saying that 'There is always something offensive in the details of cunning. The manoeuvres of selfishness and duplicity must ever be revolting.' She is not accusing her friend Mrs Smith of 'cunning' involving duplicity, but Mrs Smith has certainly been doing some manoeuvring. Should Anne be offended? Or is this an acceptable economy with the truth?

We are as likely now as in Augustine's or Jane Austen's day, to find ourselves behaving like Mrs Smith and anxiously adjusting what we say to make it more helpful to the person or people we are addressing or more acceptable in the circumstances as we perceive them. Is a partial truth in effect a lie, even if it is to spare someone's feelings? The balance between frankness and kindly tempering the truth, or withholding part of it so that it is not painful, is not always easy to strike.

Truth-telling without such 'adjustment' can lead to mistaking letting off steam for 'honesty'. When Mrs Smith in *Persuasion* feels free to say what she thinks, she delivers herself of sentiments which are not at all in the style of the usual conversational reserve of Jane Austen's characters. Communities of monks or nuns do not always live in the perfect amity which their calling expects of them. 'It is such a relief to be able to say what I really think!' said a furious young nun to an older one after hearing a sermon about honesty. A tirade of long-standing resentments followed.

It is said that 'Truth will out.' Will it? Perhaps I should try to behave in such a way that I have nothing to fear if it does. But my duty may be not only to the truth but also to the people who will hear what I have to say. Should I ever lie to spare someone's feelings? Should I tell people truths they will find uncomfortable for their own good?

> *How do I judge when being 'economical with the*
> *truth' has become a lie?*

Truth and the entertainment industry

Cool, accurate judgement becomes difficult if I am dazzled by fantasies. Imagination creates pictures in my mind, which may make it hard to be honest with myself.[7] For such reasons the Stoic Roman Emperor, Marcus Aurelius, sought to outlaw imagination (*phantasia*) as a dangerous faculty.

> *Should I give up reading novels and watching films?*
> *Should I watch 'reality shows'? Would it be all right*
> *to watch 'factual' documentaries even though they*
> *have been edited to make a point?*

The *Big Brother* series and other 'reality TV' programmes have sometimes been criticized for showing some of the worst sides of human behaviour – greed, vanity, shallowness – and for encouraging people to behave in a similar way. The possibility that pornography and violence seen in films or on television might be capable of corrupting someone led to the establishment of film censorship in the twentieth century. Films are still 'rated' as being unsuitable for children or suitable only with 'parental guidance'. The viewing of child pornography on internet websites is treated as a serious offence because of the fear that it may lead to actual paedophile attacks on children, and also because the children who appear have been exploited.

It has often been feared that attractive presentations of distorted fictions may have the effect of misleading those who are exposed to them, or even of depraving or corrupting them:

[David] Holbrook sees pornography and sadism as having been allowed to increase in our culture in recent years, with the result that a stream of hate... and debased sexuality has been thrust into our consciousness through powerful mass media. In consequence, in his view, there is now a widespread mental obsession with sexuality, a considerable degree of commercialization of sex, a growing egotistical nihilism, a preoccupation with satiation and a corruption of culture.[8]

The question whether watching 'debased' entertainment tends to have a bad effect on the audience is not new. Students in the late fourth century were discouraged by law from going to see too many of the assorted 'spectacles' or performances available in the cities of the Roman empire.[9] This was partly because the late Roman 'shows' were full of sex and violence. Augustine's friend Alypius apparently liked gladiatorial contests[10] and circuses.[11] Augustine describes how dangerously attracted he was by performances that told stories.[12] The core concern for Augustine lay in the way exciting performances stirred *curiositas*,[13] a powerful desire for extreme experience, partly because they were so enticing and addictive (that alone rang warning bells in his mind), and partly because they were designed to play to the worst characteristics of the gods in whose honour they were performed.

Yet how do such concerns mesh with the call to protect freedom of speech? There is 'a general presumption in favour of free expression, and... censorship is in its nature a blunt and treacherous instrument'.[14] History shows that it is only too easy for governments to imprison or even execute anyone who disagrees with them once freedom of speech is restricted, and that leads to tyranny and oppression.

Is there anything I should be careful not to say in case it leads someone else astray?

Spin

Do not let your perceptions be manipulated, says Marcus Aurelius. Think straight.

How easily led am I?

Any travel representative who has led a group on a holiday will tell you that its members quickly become dependent.

Headmistresses and business executives hand over responsibility for their lives and begin to ask the group leader's permission even to buy a newspaper. It is a well-observed fact of 'group dynamics' that even normally independently minded people behave differently when they are in different groups, to the point of being so eager to go along with what the group is telling them that they are prepared to deny the evidence of their own eyes, and so eager not to be excluded that they do things they would consider wrong if they were on their own. A mob will lynch someone although few of its members would be aggressive on their own. A shy, awkward teenage boy is capable of doing things as a member of a gang which he would not think of doing by himself.

This means that an eloquent leader may be able to sway our way of seeing things and make us lose sight of the basic principles we would normally rely on. Julius Caesar (100–44 BC) was murdered by Brutus and a group of fellow politicians who were afraid that he had ambitions to make himself emperor and destroy the democratic republic of ancient Rome. In Shakespeare's *Julius Caesar*, Mark Antony makes a speech designed to calm down the mob, which is dangerously excited by the news of the assassination, shouting for blood and revenge. Antony plays cleverly on their feelings and beliefs until individual citizens, uncertain what to think, begin to be swayed and the mass hysteria is fragmented:

> First Citizen: Methinks there is much reason in his sayings.
> Second Citizen: If thou consider rightly of the matter,
> Caesar has had great wrong.
> Third Citizen: Has he, masters?
> I fear there will a worse come in his place.
> Fourth Citizen: Mark'd ye his words? He would not take the crown;
> Therefore 'tis certain he was not ambitious.

Antony ends with a show of pious emotion to underline the fact that nothing he has said is to be taken to suggest that he does not take this murder seriously, or was not himself loyal to Caesar:

> Bear with me;
> My heart is in the coffin there with Caesar,
> And I must pause till it come back to me.

The citizens are duly moved:

> Second Citizen: Poor soul! His eyes are red as fire with weeping.
> Third Citizen: There's not a nobler man in Rome than Antony.[15]

Lance Price, a former BBC correspondent and journalist, became a special advisor and Alistair Campbell's deputy in the press office at No. 10 shortly after the 1997 election:

> I thought a lot about the truth. Would I have the same relationship with it that I had enjoyed while I was employed by the BBC? I had seen the Labour spin doctors at work close up so it seemed unlikely. Not that they were habitual liars. They weren't... But most spin doctors would stand uneasily in the dock with a Bible in their hands. They might just about manage 'the truth and nothing but the truth'. The bit about 'the whole truth' would be more of a problem.[16]

Modern Western society is full of spin, in politics and in all sorts of presentation and advertising. Professional public relations experts use verbal trickery and we no longer feel offended. Marketing could not succeed without spin, for it cannot work unless it persuades the potential consumer not only to buy something, but also to prefer one version of the product to another.

Is it all right to exaggerate to make my point? When does spin become lying?

Spin has altered the style of public discourse in the modern West so that everyone feels obliged to 'boast' in order to get an advantage over their rivals.

Is this 'free market' approach right? Should it extend to every part of life?

Augustine was not really speaking out against what the modern world would see as artistic creativity when he objected to the theatrical performances of his day, but against something much closer to a combination of modern spin and the kind of advertising which seeks to persuade people that they should feel entitled to buy an expensive cosmetic because they somehow deserve it. The tricks of modern advertising are often designed to appeal to the belief that someone is defined, given status, made to be of importance in the world, by buying the latest thing. Such manipulation of people's perceptions encourages them to believe statements by politicians who sometimes later turn out to have been economical with the truth, or to spend money. In a press interview of 2003 with President George W. Bush we read:

> [Diane] Sawyer: Again, I'm just trying to ask, these are supporters, people who believed in the [Iraq] war who have asked [whether it was right to state] as a hard fact, that there were weapons of mass destruction[,] as opposed to the possibility that he could move to acquire those weapons still.
> Bush: So what's the difference?[17]

One of the features of 'creative accounting' about telling the truth is the development of a moral relativism. Sceptics suspend belief because when they balance the arguments on either side they see no reason to declare for any particular view. In the ancient world this could be one of the ways of achieving tranquillity. In the modern world it can become a licence to adopt any opinion with any degree of adamant conviction just because you feel it or like the look of it,[18] but without testing it.

How do I know whether to believe anything
politicians say?

Am I honest?

> I think stealing from a supermarket is totally moral. One hundred per cent... They rob from you so rob from them.
> **Student overheard in caf**

How would you have answered him? Anselm would have seen it in black and white. 'When an action does as it ought, can that be appropriately said to be "doing the truth"?'[19] he asks, and unhesitatingly answers that it can. Stealing from a supermarket would not seem to him to be that kind of action, so it would not be 'true' and therefore not honest.

This notion of an integrity that compels one to act in accordance with how things are in their rightness is to be found in Confucius, too:

One who really cared for Goodness would never let any other
consideration come first. One who abhorred wickedness would
be so constantly doing Good that wickedness would never have a
chance to get at him.[20]

These are modern problems but they are not essentially new.
Dictionary definitions (as in the OED) of cheating include 'to
defraud; to deprive of by deceit; to trick'. A 'deceiver' is an
'imposter', a 'swindler'.

Is it all right to do personal photocopying or make personal
phone calls at work and not bother to record it? If I am a student, is
it all right to download a ready-made essay from the internet and
adjust it a bit for my coursework? What else do I do that is dishonest
when I come to think about it in comparison with this high standard
of straightforward behaviour?

The modern dictionary definition describes an honest person as
one who is honourable, who has moral excellence in general; what
he does is fitting, having 'decency, decorum'. An honest person has
'uprightness of disposition and conduct; integrity, truthfulness,
straightforwardness: the quality opposed to lying, cheating, or
stealing' (OED). These characteristics ought to create norms for
their possessor, so that not countenancing corruption, or getting
advantage by bribery or corruption, comes automatically.

A Buddhist rule is not to take what one is not offered. This is an
even stronger idea than not stealing what is someone else's property,
and one which arises from a different conception of property. In
Judaism a high premium is put upon honesty and truthfulness.
Stealing, lying and perjury are forbidden; even delaying in paying
bills to small tradesmen would be frowned on, as analogous with
holding back overnight the day's wages a hired labourer had earned
in Old Testament times.

*Is it 'true' that murder is wrong? What kind of truth
status can a moral assertion have?*

Kindness and the place of severity

Ye have heard that it hath been said, Thou shalt love thy
neighbour, and hate thine enemy. But I say unto you, Love your

enemies, bless them that curse you, do good to them that hate
you, and pray for them which despitefully use you.
Matthew 5:43—44

Does this call to be magnanimous and behave generously in the
face of other people's mistreatment of me mean that I should
always be gentle, mild and kindly? Mothers have to learn to resist
the impulse to be so kind and helpful to growing children that they
do not learn to do things for themselves and become independent.
Respecting the dignity of someone else and not smothering them
with misplaced kindness could be important when dealing with
adults too.

Sunday school pictures of Jesus used to show him with children
about his knees in an atmosphere of somewhat saccharine
'sweetness'. But there is another tradition, of uncompromising
loving severity.

He had... a sense of being looked at by things which had a right
to look. His feeling was less than fear; it had in it something of
embarrassment, something of shyness, something of submission,
and it was profoundly uneasy.[21]

In his science fiction trilogy, C.S. Lewis hints that beings like these
(he has something like angels in mind) might make you feel
uncomfortable by the terrible clarity with which they would see into
the real motives for your actions. His idea seems to be that these
beings mirror, like the Christian angels, the way God himself
behaves.

That does not mean that the tender pictures of a gentle Jesus in
conventional Sunday school pictures are 'wrong'. It means that I
ought to consider the possibility that they may not tell the whole
story. 'God is not loving kindness,' remarks a nun of many years'
experience. Nuns often find prayer quite a struggle, because doing a
lot of it takes them to uncomfortable places where they feel rather
like the hero of C.S. Lewis's novel when the angels or 'Eldils' are
looking into his mind.

But I am no angel and neither are you. If we are to practise this
'loving severity' it will have to be from the perspective of recognition
of our own frailties.

Is it right to rebuke someone else when I am far from perfect myself?

Tough love

The modern expression 'tough love' strictly means something slightly different from this discomfiting process of being forced to be realistic about myself.[22] The 'tough love' method of helping families dealing with adolescent children who got completely out of control was initiated by two American family therapists, who had a 'problem child' of their own. After their daughter was arrested for armed robbery, they took the extreme measure of refusing to let her return home until she had given up drugs and got a job. This involved cutting off direct relations with her themselves, though they asked others to keep in touch with her. They found that this strategy helped to break patterns of negative behaviour and destructive response within a family. Such severity can be seen as a form of 'to care and not to care', which allows kindness to pull no punches when that may actually be the most 'loving' thing.

Small children grow up into a world in which much of what they want to do turns out to be 'right' or 'wrong' in the opinion of their parents and teachers, for reasons which may be opaque to their minds in extreme youth (and which they may still not agree with when they grow up). There is likely to be external correction to enforce the adult point of view. This involves withholding the expression of natural affectionate impulses, at least for a moment, for another's good. A mother snatches a box of matches from a toddler's hand (with or without a slap, depending on the expectations of society at the time about the physical punishment of children).

Train up a child in the way he should go: and when he is old, he will not depart from it.
Proverbs 22:6

In this way, the child learns the 'rules'.

But as a punishing parent I do not see as clearly as Lewis's angelic beings, and I lack the ability to think consistently with the same loving detachment. Sometimes I am angry and unreasonable. The child begins to engage in inner struggles before doing what he or she knows will be disapproved of. Knowing his mother or teacher is not allowed to hit him may embolden one child to daring; anxiety about causing his mother distress and a wish to please may restrain another. Another may be indignant at being treated in a way he thinks is unfair, and respond by testing how far he can go, justifying disruptive and challenging behaviour by telling himself it is the parent's fault. And perhaps it is.

At the other extreme, and perhaps intermittently with periods of angry blame and punishment, a child may be indulged with everything it asks for by parents eager to express their love, until it becomes a monster of unreasonableness, discontented and selfish.

> *Can 'tough love' work for grown-ups too? How*
> *should I respond if someone tries it on me?*

Compassion

> Rejoice with those who rejoice, weep with those who weep.
> **Romans 12:15**

> [By sympathy] we enter into the concerns of others... we are moved as they are moved, and are never suffered to be indifferent spectators of almost any thing which men can do or suffer. For sympathy must be considered as a sort of substitution, by which we are put into the place of another man, and affected in many respects as he is affected.[23]
> **Edmund Burke (1729—97)**

Compassion of this sort is not inconsistent with loving severity, since its objective is to do good, to do the best for someone else as an act of love:

> There is a natural principle of benevolence in man which is in some degree to society, what self-love is to the individual. And if there be in mankind any disposition to friendship; if there be any such thing as compassion, for compassion is momentary love; if there be any such thing as the paternal or filial affections; if there be any affection in human nature, the object and end of which is the good of another; this is itself benevolence, or the love of another.[24]
> **Joseph Butler (1692—1752)**

But this is bound to raise the question of the disinterestedness of compassionate feelings, in which there may well be an admixture of secret pleasure in someone else's distress, known as Schadenfreude: 'Of these two, delight in the prosperity of others, and compassion for their distresses, the last is felt much more generally than the former', remarks Joseph Butler shrewdly.[25]

Should kindness involve compassion?

The danger of doing more harm than good

Yes, I can do something to make a difference, but what if it backfires?

In the spring of 2006, a refugee Afghan father, who had become a Christian in the West, returned to Afghanistan, it was reported, with the intention of recovering his children and taking them away with him to join him in his new life. He found himself in prison and under sentence of death on the grounds that he had turned away from the Islamic faith. The religious authorities in Afghanistan claimed they had no choice but to punish the man's apostasy as their faith required. The Pope, as worldwide head of the Roman Catholic Church, pleaded for clemency. The President of the USA intervened with counterclaims about the absolute right of all people to religious freedom.

The Afghan authorities bowed to this international pressure and 'released' the father, on the grounds that he was mentally unfit to plead. Rather as happened in Soviet Russia under communism, in the period when political dissidence was deemed to be a sign of insanity, he was taken off to have his 'illness' investigated.

Should the father have returned for his children, given the dangers he faced? It has been held for centuries to be a natural law that parents will bring up their children and take care of them. Isidore of Seville (c. 560–636) says as much in the sixth century. On the other hand, the attempt to do so was going to get this father executed or incarcerated, so that he would not be able to look after them at all.

Towards the end of March 2006, Norman Kember, the British peace campaigner who had been kidnapped in Iraq with three companions four months earlier, was released as a result of a raid by the SAS in association with other military forces. He had been working with a group called Christian Peacemaker Teams (CPT). Once the straightforward delight at the successful rescue began to ebb, the world's press observed that he had not seemed very grateful. It also began to comment that the CPT were 'putting at risk the lives of British soldiers and ordinary Iraqis by sending its members to Iraq'. Norman Kember's first public statement included the guarded words, 'I do not believe that a lasting peace is achieved by armed force, but I pay tribute to their courage and thank those who played a part in my rescue.' He added that he would now need to 'reflect' on whether he had been 'foolhardy or rational' in going to Iraq. As press comment moved on, it began to be suggested that this bearing of personal witness had had integrity in a period when the official responses of the 'free world' had been deadened by the catastrophe which had followed the war in Iraq. It was asserted that an awkward sense of being compromised was making it difficult for the leaders who might otherwise have done so, to speak out about human rights disasters such as 'ethnic cleansing' and oppression elsewhere in the world. Did Norman Kember do more harm than good in Iraq by working for the obvious 'absolute' goods of peace and reconciliation?

What is involved in setting an example to others?

Apology and forgiveness
Sorry!

The word 'sorry' is almost my way of saying 'Hello'. It is probably the word I habitually use most often – sometimes as a way of hailing a waiter… I want to give my support to acts – verbal utterances – which represent revulsion against wrongdoing, to accept that forgive and forget is the better part and to acknowledge the enchanting power of language to bring about changes in the air.[26]
Marina Warner

Saying sorry can amount to a mere nod to convention, little more than a form of words, which does not necessarily mean I am sorry at all. I have felt no shame, no remorse, no regret, no compunction, no wish to make reparation. The other sort of 'sorry-saying' is much more heavyweight, so heavyweight in fact that it became a positive encumbrance in the eyes of the Reformation. The Christian penitential system took the view from an early date that if I want to be forgiven, I ought to be willing to do something to show I am truly sorry. The sixteenth-century reformers in the West reacted strongly against that, claiming that the institutional Church was imposing requirements that were really only human requirements, that God's forgiveness was free and generous and did not have to be earned. They cited the New Testament: 'The prayer of faith will save the sick, and the Lord will raise them up; and anyone who has committed sins will be forgiven' (James 5:15).

Should I always say 'sorry' if I have been in
the wrong?

Purge the wrong, punish the offender, put the wrong right – or just forget it, let it go?

Judaism lacks the Christian concept of forgiveness; it finds it more natural to think in terms of justice and righteousness, the balancing of punishment against offence.

By contrast, acts of kindness or restoration or free forgiveness repair the damage. 'Love your enemies,' said Jesus (Luke 6:35). Marcus Aurelius said you should be ready to be reconciled as soon as the person with whom you have fallen out shows signs of rapprochement.[27] Jesus said the same. Do not let the sun go down on your wrath; make up your quarrels at once, was his advice:

> So when you are offering your gift at the altar, if you remember
> that your brother or sister has something against you, leave your
> gift there before the altar and go; first be reconciled to your
> brother or sister, and then come and offer your gift.
> **Matthew 5:23—24**

Which of these approaches is right?

Slobodan Milosevic died before he could be found guilty of the wrongs it was widely held that he had inflicted on the people he ruled, and he was therefore not punished by the law. Perhaps that did not really matter. Punishment would have been an acknowledgement of the seriousness of what he had done, and in that way it would have sent a message. This might have restored a sense of fair play.[28] But even seen as a form of officially approved revenge, punishment would not have put the original wrong right. It could even have created fresh resentments or set in train a sequence of vendetta in which each side felt obliged to take revenge in turn.

Should I try to 'let it go' when I feel someone has wronged me? What steps can I take to bring matters to an end?

Forgiveness

> If another disciple sins, you must rebuke the offender, and if there is repentance, you must forgive. And if the same person sins against you seven times a day, and turns back to you seven times and says, 'I repent', you must forgive.
> **Luke 17:3—4**

When saying sorry meets overtures of forgiveness and reconciliation there can be healing and restoration. Therapeutic benefits of forgiving your enemies are well recognized in the modern world. The Forgiveness Project is the work of a contemporary organization which describes itself as non-political and non-religious, promoting conflict resolution and restorative justice and the 'healing of memories', partly by collecting and publishing examples, some of which are touched on below.[29]

Responding with forgiveness makes you feel better even in the most appalling situations. It helps in dealing with the complex negative reactions that can include an irrational guilt. This was expressed by the parents of the child Victoria Climbié who was tortured and killed: 'We were tormented by guilt, anguish and hatred, and could not understand how our daughter's life could have been destroyed by someone who had promised to take care of her.'[30]

It seems that this is not necessarily easy, or even possible, for everyone. On 22 March 2006, *The Times* carried an article on the contrasting responses of two British women whose children had been murdered. The one who found she could not forgive was a Christian priest, Julie Nicholson, whose twenty-four-year-old daughter was killed on a tube train in one of the terrorist attacks in London on 7 July 2005. She resigned because she did not see how she could continue to preach a ministry of forgiveness when she could not put her own teaching into practice. 'It's very difficult to stand behind an altar and lead people in words of peace and reconciliation and forgiveness when I feel very far from that myself,' she said.

The other was the mother of the teenager Anthony Walker, who had been attacked by his schoolfellows with an axe, in a killing apparently motivated by racial hatred. Mrs Walker responded by publicly forgiving her son's killers, consciously excluding the option of hating them: 'I just haven't got any room for [hate].'

Another famous example of heroic 'public' forgiveness cited in this *Times* article was that of Gordon Wilson, whose daughter died as a result of a bomb attack on Enniskillen Remembrance Day in 1987. He was quoted at the time as saying, 'I have lost my daughter and we will miss her, but I bear no ill will, no grudge. Dirty sort of talk is not going to bring her back to life.'

In South Africa in the period of Apartheid the priest Michael Lapsley discovered that he was on the Government's hit-list:

I had long ago come to the conclusion that there was no road to freedom except via the route of self-sacrifice, but nothing could have prepared me for what was to follow. Three months after Nelson Mandela's release from prison, I received a letter bomb hidden inside the pages of two religious magazines that had been posted from South Africa. In the bomb blast I lost both hands, one eye and had my eardrums shattered... Quite early on after the bomb I realised that if I was filled with hatred and desire for revenge I'd be a victim forever.[31]

Mrs Walker tried to tackle the problem which had led to her son's attack, so that nothing like it would happen to anyone else. She launched the Anthony Walker Foundation, 'a charitable organization to promote racial harmony in schools, the workplace, sport and society generally'. This urge to bring something good out of the bad thing which has happened is common among the positive responses people attempt in order to make a personal disaster more bearable. One way of doing that is to demonstrate that the lost life has not been wasted.

Part of being human is rolling up your sleeves and taking an active part in repairing harm.[32]

That's why we're opening a school in the Ivory Coast. It will be a centre of excellence providing education for children from all around the world. The sole reason for Victoria coming to England was to get an education. This school is our way of immortalising the spirit and the name of our child.[33]

Forgiveness is certainly a solution to stopping cycles of violence. It is about drawing a line under the dogma of vengeance. It doesn't lessen your own pain, but it makes you less at war with the world.[34]

How far should I go to put things right when I have done something wrong?

PART IV

TWO GREAT UNDERLYING ISSUES

You have asked me why, if a providence rules

the world, it still happens

that many evils befall good men...

Seneca (c. 4 BC–AD 65), *De providentia*

Chapter 9

The Problem
of Evil

Why do I find it so difficult to do the right thing?

> Steve betrays many of the tell-tale signs of a problem gambler. He
> says he thinks about poker 'pretty much all the time', gets 'a real
> buzz' from a good hand of cards, and admits the game distracts
> him from his college work and social life. [Steve is 17, and an
> underage player of internet poker.][1]

Steve might accept that his gambling is 'bad' for him but say that
it would be very hard for him to give it up, even though it is
costing him much more than the money he loses. The
compulsions that drive addicts are a vivid modern reminder of a
pattern of behaviour that became central to the moral theology of
the Christian religion in its first centuries – the expectation that no
one will be able to become good and stay good, for everyone will
become a 'backslider'. I may not be a problem gambler, or in and
out of prison, but I recognize that something keeps stopping me
from doing what I know is the right thing. 'Something' means that
when I try to be good, I take two steps forward and slip back one
instead of making steady progress. That is the classic 'problem
of evil'.

The idea that something has gone wrong with human nature
which makes everyone liable to behave badly was not fully
articulated until the late fourth century in the West, although the
threads that were going to come together in the idea can be seen
much earlier. Human beings have long recognized the sense of
being 'pulled both ways', of being 'torn', of wanting to do the right
thing and repeatedly doing the wrong thing. We are all life's

'problem gamblers' in that way. This is common experience, but explanations for it have varied among the world's religions and those who do not believe in a God at all.

A mixed bag of supernatural influences?

Religions that admit the possibility that there are numerous supernatural powers in the universe are able to envisage a distribution of functions among them. These polytheistic systems often have mischievous or destructive gods balancing good and benevolent ones. Some gods can be thought of as responsible for the dark side of life and some for the rest. It is then relatively easy to explain the tug I feel to do the wrong thing when I know perfectly well what would be the right thing to do, by blaming it on the influence of a bad god or spirit.

An out-and-out war of good and evil?

Another explanation positions the power of evil at a much higher level, as a cosmic force. Before the time of Christ, the Gnostics or dualists were already exploring the theory that the universe is ruled by two great primeval powers, Good and Evil, eternally at war, striving for supremacy. The 'good' is spiritual and light and the 'bad', material and sensual and dark. A mythology grew up in which colourful supernatural characters waged war in the cosmos.

This war of good and evil had its later counterparts in mythological battles of personified virtues and vices, conducted on the battlefield of the human soul, because people have always confirmed that that is how it feels inside. A long sequence of attempts to use the same basic idea to solve the problem of evil followed, by the Manichees in China[2] and Persia (Iran) and the ancient Middle East and north Africa; later by the Albigensians and Cathars and Bogomils in southern Europe in the late twelfth and thirteenth centuries.

Even witchcraft belongs to this tradition insofar as it involves choosing to worship the Devil, who is recognized as the 'god of evil'. This allows for the possibility that people may consciously choose, of their own free will, to join the 'dark' side. There are stories of those, such as Dr Faustus, who have sold their souls to the Devil in return for wealth and power while they live.

The continuing story of Harry Potter as he works his way through his school years at Hogwarts School of witchcraft and wizardry has at its heart an unresolved battle between the evil Voldemort and Harry, the champion of the Good.[3]

If there is only one all-powerful God, how can evil exist?

The great monotheistic religions cannot use this device for explaining where evil comes from and how it works. The one God of Judaism, Christianity and Islam is all-powerful and wholly good. So if bad things happen, it looks as though this cannot be correct. If there is evil, either God cannot be all-powerful, or he cannot be completely good.

The origin of evil and the beginning of sinful behaviour require a different explanation for these monotheistic religions. There can still be an evil power; however, it will not be seen as a rival power or god, but as a fallen creature in troublesome – but ultimately impotent – rebellion against the one supreme Good and Almighty God.

In the Old Testament, God is sometimes said to send spirits to do his work, but independent supernatural powers with evil intentions all of their own are a quite different concept. The nearest to them to be found in the Old Testament is Satan in the book of Job. Satan, the Devil, appears in the person of a fallen angel. In the Old Testament, Isaiah 14:12 describes the fall of a star or heavenly being, who came to be identified with this 'Lucifer' figure and also with Satan. The first chapters of Job describe the court of heaven, in which God is portrayed as a great king and the angels as his courtiers. There is Satan among them, making trouble, trying to persuade God to test his faithful servant Job to destruction.

The idea of more small-scale 'evil spirits' or 'devils' seems to have arrived on the Judaeo–Christian scene in the time of Christ (Mark 5:1–20). There are episodes in the Gospels in which evil spirits are seen as real and actively working to lead people astray or make them ill.

Christian tradition inherited the story of the first wrongdoing, which is told in Genesis, when it adopted the Jewish scriptures as the 'Old' Testament of the Christian Bible. Led astray by a serpent, also later identified with the Devil, Adam and Eve, the first people, ate the forbidden fruit of one particular tree (Genesis 3). The way the story is told, what they did 'wrong' was to disobey God's clear instructions, and as a result they began to understand things which had not been apparent to them before, such as the fact that they were naked, and that being naked was now somehow a bad thing.

'Sin' could thus be defined as acting against the will of God, but also as wishing to be something God had not intended you to be. In the story, God responds by punishing Adam and Eve, and Genesis describes the adverse consequences for the whole of creation: how thistles sprang up with uncomfortable prickles; people had to work for a living; and it became painful for women to bear children (Genesis 3:16–18).

Fear of the active malevolence of evil spirits

Interpretation of the Genesis story, in which the serpent is the tempter, led to the framing of an explanation of the origin of Satan. The Christian tradition was that he had become, as a consequence of his own sin, the enemy of God; one of the results was that he was hungry to capture the human race for himself. That was why he took the form of a serpent in the Garden of Eden.

The idea that temptation was the work of supernatural tempters – instigated by their leader, the Devil – developed a good deal further in the first Christian centuries. This was partly influenced by the active interest of Origen (c. 185–c. 254), the Greek philosopher and theologian in demonology. Origen argues that demons take an active interest in the ruin of mankind and that there are specialist devils, who concentrate on gluttony or pride or other specific vices.[4] Augustine took seriously in his book *City of God* the idea that the air is full of spirits, good and bad, who affect our lives. There are many stories in early monasticism of combat with demons. It was generally felt in monastic circles that the proper place to do battle with your demons was by yourself in the desert. Evagrius of Pontus (345–99) in the late fourth century developed a theology of the monastic life of which battling with distractions in the form of demons forms an unavoidable component.[5]

Such trends have created a climate of fear about the active malevolence of evil spirits, forces beyond my control, positively eager to trip me up – motifs which make their modern appearance in children's computer games and in films.

The subjugation of the flesh

Could it be morally wrong to enjoy the scent of a rose too much?

The belief was widespread among ancient philosophers that the ascetic was a more virtuous person than someone who thoroughly enjoyed food and drink and the pleasures of the senses, even in moderation. They thought like this on the basis of assumptions widely held for many centuries – that matter is somehow evil. This would mean that all the pleasures of the senses must be 'bad', for they involve responding to the material world. No delight should be taken in that; it is far too dangerous, argued writer after writer. What was the danger? That such pleasures would be seductive, and that they would distract people's attention from what they should really be doing, which was cultivating their spiritual and intellectual interests.

Early Christianity also tended to favour this cult of asceticism. A moral and spiritual 'anorexia' could result, in which a person could become trapped, obsessed with self-denial. One of the recognized features of the extreme asceticism of the early Christian monastic life was that the tempted soul could go on struggling for a lifetime, temptation never entirely overcome; another was that even temporary failures could cast the struggling soul into depression.

Demons driven by anger were believed to tempt humans by fostering inordinate 'fleshly' desires, causing them to become obsessed with longings they felt, also obsessively, that it would be wicked to give in to. 'Wicked' thoughts of forbidden pleasures continually obtruded upon prayer. Problems in getting free of the passions were commonplace, and the Christian who thought he had ceased to enjoy the sight of naked women would find them parading through his fantasies and distracting him. Jerome reported something of the sort when he had gone to live in the desert in search of a simple life. Evagrius thought it all starts with gluttony because if you are well fed you will have the energy to feel the other temptations. Only the hungry and weak are likely to be uninterested in fleshly lusts because they will not have the energy.[6] He said that it is wise not to go to places where you may see women, but if even the thought of a woman arouses you, you should walk briskly round your cell praying hard and wearing scratchy clothing to distract yourself from feeling desire.[7]

To the modern reader the preoccupation with sex as a danger, likely to turn sensible people into monsters, rapists, stalkers, paedophiles, may seem strikingly up-to-date; but in reality, it has been a concern in every century, and not only in Christianity. Islam, too, has inherited something of this tradition in regarding women as tempting and dangerous, and tried to ensure that they could not be a temptation to anyone likely to be inclined to have sex with them unlawfully:

Enjoin believing women to turn their eyes away from temptation
and to preserve their chastity... to draw their veils over their
bosoms and not to display their finery except to their husbands,
their father, their husbands' fathers, their sons, their stepsons, their
brothers, their brothers' sons, their sisters' sons, their women-
servants, and their slave-girls; male attendants lacking in natural
vigour, and children who have no carnal knowledge of women.
And let them not stamp their feet when walking so as to reveal
their hidden trinkets.
Koran 24.30

A similar sense that sensual enjoyments are somehow morally 'bad'
is to be found in most centuries. William of Auvergne in the early
thirteenth century criticized the Islamic heaven because it offered a
paradise of sensual pleasures, though Muslims themselves tended to
try to defer such enjoyments beyond this life.[8]

When, in seventeenth-century England, Oliver Cromwell's
'puritan' armies defaced statues and broke the medieval stained glass
windows in English churches, they believed themselves to be
fighting on the Lord's side in a battle against idolatry, in which the
representation of holy things by material objects, such as pictures or
statues, was dangerously likely to tempt believers to worship the
objects their senses could perceive instead of God himself. The
'puritan' tradition also disapproved of music in worship and the use
of vestments and rituals. It encouraged people to dress plainly, not to
go to the theatre even for recreation, and to observe Sunday
rigorously, refraining from work and pleasure.

Should I enjoy the pleasures I experience through my
senses as much as I can or is there virtue in
moderation?

The consequences of the first sin

What would make wrongdoing a sin?

It took until the time of Augustine of Hippo for two principles to be
clarified in the Western Christian tradition. His first and immensely
influential idea was that evil was 'nothing'. It did not exist. It could
not exist, for there is only one God and God is good. So evil can only
be an absence of good. Evil was not to be thought of as an

independent power in the universe which could be fought by the valiant supporters of the good power. Only good was a power in the universe, and those who lost touch with it or turned their backs on it lost its controlling benefits. As Augustine described it, they became twisted in their thinking, distorted in their actions, and incapable of seeing straight, let alone doing the right thing. Evil separates us from God, and the further we find ourselves from God the more miserable we shall be.[9]

This explanation has such a ring of psychological truth that it has been embraced for centuries as a convincing explanation of the sense of being pulled both ways when a decision has to be taken, and the frequent experience of doing wrong when the right thing to do is quite obvious, and then feeling guilty and miserable.

In Buddhism the inevitable outcome of doing wrong is also seen as disturbance of peace of mind. There is a recognition here too that the inward disposition and the outward action may be linked in significant ways.

The second Augustinian insistence was the belief that the very make-up of human beings had been changed by the supreme act of arrogance which that first sin in the Garden of Eden represented. He described what has come to be known as the doctrine of 'original sin'. His idea was that the change in Adam and Eve had been passed on to their children and it had made them, too, recidivist sinners, for now human beings had lost the capacity to make free personal choices and were more or less helpless to do the right thing unless God assisted them.

It does not necessarily matter for the person trying to be good whether this explanation is the right one or not. Augustine was describing a common human experience – of being too weak-willed to do the 'right' thing, even when the desire is there. The modern experience of trying to break a pattern of compulsive or addictive behaviour is a vivid illustration of what he meant. Someone trying to give up smoking has a cigarette in a moment of weakness and one cigarette leads to another, and the process of giving up has to be started all over again. Alcoholics Anonymous teach that there will never be 'just one drink' for an alcoholic.

Moreover, said Augustine, the first sin had left each human being with an inherited burden of guilt with which every child was born and which condemned it in the sight of God even before it had had the opportunity to commit any sins of its own. Augustine describes how even tiny babies show jealousy.[10] His autobiographical *Confessions* is full of turbulent feeling and his own sense of being pulled this way and that by events, and by his own response to them, which he understood in the light of this explanation.

These are powerful ideas and they have continued to have a strong emotional attraction. They chime well with human experiences. The Christian Churches have developed immense structures of doctrine and practice on these notions of sin and its effects, and on the belief that God requires something to be done to put the consequences right.

One result, for many, has been the creation of a burden of guilt and anxiety. It was part of the theology of 'original sin' that it had inescapable results, consequences which might stretch into eternity and send you to hell:

> The good and bad consequences which follow our actions are [God's] appointment, and our foresight of those consequences is a warning given us by Him how we are to act...
>   [God] has appointed satisfaction and delight to be the consequence of our acting in one manner, and pain and uneasiness of our acting in another, and of our not acting at all.[11]
> **Joseph Butler**

'Is any man among you without sin?' asked Augustine,[12] referring to the passage included in some versions of John's Gospel, where Jesus, confronted by the Pharisees with a woman 'taken in adultery', calls whoever is without sin in the watching crowd to cast the first stone (John 8:7). No one takes up his challenge. One by one they all creep away. There follows, in Augustine's little book on the possibility of any human being behaving so well as to be 'perfectly' righteous, a discussion of a series of passages of the Bible which throw a various and contradictory light on the question. For example, Deuteronomy 9 has God himself declaring that his commandments are not impossible to observe. Nevertheless, Augustine concludes that no one but Christ can be perfect in this life,[13] even if God chooses to overlook this fact in the case of some individuals.

Would doing good works make up for being sinful?

Martin Luther (1483–1546) argued that the institutional Church in the West was exacting too many observances from the faithful and misleading them into thinking that if they did not comply with all these 'human impositions' they would not get to heaven. He took this position in reaction against the way the medieval penitential system had evolved, along highly formulaic lines, apportioning a specific quantitative penance to be done for each confessed act of wrongdoing. By their time, in the early sixteenth century, Lutherans claimed, ordinary people were thrown into a state of extreme anxiety about doing the right things.

The problem with a 'works-based' approach to doing good was that it tended to become mechanical and burdensome. Luther proposed a revolutionary new view. Faith was enough on its own. God required nothing at all by way of good behaviour but would accept as righteous or just anyone who had faith. It was all God asked. This doctrine of 'justification by faith' became, and remains, the keystone of Lutheranism. All this prompted an energetic debate in the sixteenth century about the function of good works. If they do my prospects no good, why should I bother?

Those Christians who have seen things in this way have not necessarily set aside all moral considerations as a consequence. Some have argued that even if it is true that God has already chosen those he plans to 'reward', the 'elect' will still behave well, even though there is no need for them to do so to please God. Wanting to do good flows naturally from an inward state or attitude in which God is thought to be doing most of the 'work' of encouraging his 'elect' in that direction. Good works should thus be seen as expressions or effects, rather than meritorious acts designed to earn heavenly brownie points: 'The lively and true faith... causeth not a man to be idle, but to be occupied in bringing forth good works, as occasion serveth.'[14]

From the point of view of practical morality there is no need to take a position on all this; rather the opposite, for it has been the source of a great deal of personal pain and struggle. Religious wars have been fought over the rights and wrongs of it. Two things seem to matter: I shall keep making mistakes and failing to be as 'good' as I meant; I should not waste time worrying about that but simply try again. I try to be good because it is right and not worry whether a scorecard is being kept.

Should I try to make up for ('balance') my wrong acts with right ones or put it all behind me and make a fresh start?

The eternal context

'In every action reflect upon the end; and in your undertaking it, consider why you do it, and what you propound to yourself for a reward.'[15] This freedom from anxiety is not what moralists have tended to urge. Jeremy Taylor's book, from which this exhortation comes, is keen to encourage a salutary nervousness. 'I shall entertain you in a Charnel house, and carry your meditations awhile into the chambers of death,' he says.[16]

His overriding idea is one which has been strongly influential in Christianity over the centuries – that we really live in a world which is much more long-lasting than the one we can see, and that it is in this eternal world that the important things happen, the things which determine our future.

> Reckon but from the spritefulnesse of youth, and the fair cheeks
> and full eyes of childehood, from the vigorousnesse, and strong
> flexure of the joynts of five and twenty, to the hollownesse and
> dead palenesse, to the loathsomenesse and horrour of a three
> days burial.[17]

Looked at from this point of view, there is no time to waste in not being as good as you can, he thinks, and certainly no benefit in clinging to the satisfactions of the present life, for those are few: 'As our life is very short, so it is very miserable, and therefore it is well it is short.'[18]

There is, however, a quite different way of seeing the eternal future, not in terms of reward and punishment, but simply as the wider and far more 'real' dimension in which I do what I do now, though I cannot at present see how far it stretches.

Can I confine moral questions to here and now?

Doing good and being good: the possibility of growth

With something like this in mind, the possibility that emerged in Christian thought was that one purpose of behaving well might be to shape and edit people so that they grew more capable of appreciating a better life than this. There would not be much point in arriving in heaven and being uncomfortable there because you did not fit in. Heaven was understood as a state more than a place, in which being happy in God's presence would involve a form of 'friendship' with God. That expectation underlies this kind of comment:

> The great design of Christianity was the reforming Mens Natures, and governing their Actions, the restraining their Appetites, and Passions, the softning their Tempers, and sweetning their Humours, the composing their Affections, and the raising their minds above the Interests and Follies of this present World, to the hope and pursuit of endless Blessedness.[19]
> **Thomas Burnet (c. 1635—1715)**

All this threw into a new perspective the question whether moral rightness necessarily has to do with good conduct, and with it the idea that the world is a 'vale of soul-making',[20] in which people can learn how to be good as a result of the way they live and the way they think.

One underlying idea here is that any experience can be turned to good and made to be of value to others if not to oneself. Thomas de Quincey (1785–1859), as an early nineteenth-century addict of the fashionable drug of the day, defends his opium addiction, which he admits was extreme ('I have indulged in it to an excess not yet *recorded* of any other man'). He claims that the 'benefit resulting to others' from his recounting what he has learned in the heightened states of perception he has experienced, outweighs any fault in his own conduct.[21] He points out that opium-takers are very numerous, and he is rendering a service to the whole class in telling his story. He names some prominent figures known to him to take opium, such as William Wilberforce and Isaac Milner.[22]

Learning from practical experience of bad behaviour and good works, mine and those of others, has been seen as important in more than one religion. Sikhs approve of work and service, in the community and the family. Most religions encourage something similar, often as a way of earning divine approval, and the reward of a better life to come, though Judaism offers no eternal future as Christianity does, only a pattern of right conduct now.

Why should I try to 'grow better' if I do not believe there is a heaven to look forward to?

Chapter 10

Freedom of Choice

How free am I to choose what I do?

If there is God, could he be running the universe like a model train set, laying out the tracks on which the trains of individual human lives must run, changing the points and directing them to their destinations whether they want to go there or not? Perhaps he is running it like an interactive computer game which he has designed so that the player can make choices, some of which can change the way the game ends, moving it to higher or lower levels of difficulty on the way? Perhaps the universe is a great 'if/then' sequence presenting a finite range of options to creatures like me. Perhaps it is just a 'learning environment', and I am a mere rat in the maze.

In order to make moral decisions, surely I have to have a will, and freedom to use it to make choices? If I am living helplessly in a great scheme where everything I do is already decided for me, and if the rules of the game are not of my devising, and if my best hope is to make choices which will lead along better, not 'worse', pathways, surely my bad behaviour is not my fault? I am a victim, not a villain, whatever I do.

Machines of providence?

'My son...' said the kindly old man... 'We are the machines of Providence...'[1]
'We are in the power of the Eternal Being, just as the stars and the elements are; that he controls everything we do and are, that we are little cogs in the huge machine!'[2]
Voltaire (1694—1778)

The English word 'providence' comes from *pro-videre* in Latin, which means 'to see ahead'. Christians, like Jews and Muslims, believe in a God who sees everything in advance, for he is believed to be omniscient. If he knows everything that will happen and is also all-powerful (omnipotent) nothing can happen that he does not expect. That would put me in a difficult position because if that is true my free choices do not seem to be free at all. It will be no good my changing my mind since God knows about that in advance too.

The modern discussion about 'intelligent design' – the idea that a power with a mind, not a blind force or process, made the universe – is in part a continuation of this ancient debate. The problem is that what can be 'proved' scientifically is limited to those things that can be tested by experiment. Some things cannot be tested in that way and remain at the level of hypothesis and speculation, even where a 'model' is used to predict the future on the basis of the past. Much of the current discussion of 'climate change' is inevitably of this kind. The history of science is full of predictions that turned out to be wrong. But the urge to guess the future remains strong.

But because of the inherent limitations of its methods and of the evidence available to it, science cannot establish beyond question whether the universe is a natural accident with no one in charge; or part of a giant and carefully orchestrated divine plan; or something in between, a complex and delicate machinery designed by a God who then stood away and watched it run by itself, perhaps intervening at intervals to make adjustments, a God who designed the 'software'. I know only that my actions follow one another in a sequence, and that sometimes the consequences are not obvious at once and I learn about them years later, or not at all. I am bound to wonder whether this sequence is random; determined by me; determined by others; determined by God; predetermined in part or altogether; or some combination of these.

*'I couldn't help it!' begins to seem a reasonable
excuse. Is it?*

There are strands in several world religions today that see the universe as predetermined, under the control of a providence that already has everything worked out.

He admits into his mercy whom he will: but for the wrongdoers
he has prepared a woeful punishment.
Koran 76.31

I like to think I have a choice. But do I?

'Personal' predestination?

This morning I am tempted to do something I realize
is wrong. Does God know? Is he going to stop me? If
he could stop me and he does not stop me, is it my
fault if I do it?

If whatever you decide to do is a foregone conclusion to God, did
you really decide to do it? This seems to make divine foreknowledge
amount to the same thing as divine predestination. It also brings
home to me as an individual the question where I would fit into a
predetermined universe. If there is a God who designed the
machinery, does he 'care' about all the cogs revolving within it?
Does it make any difference to my moral choices whether I believe
in such close control of my affairs?

If someone or something cares, is it a reliable something or
might it exercise control over my activities for fun or even out of
malice? All these possibilities have been seriously entertained, and
they are not dead yet. In the ancient world, people were as keen to
foretell their futures as the readers of modern horoscopes, and some
saw 'fate' and 'fortune' as independent supernatural powers
affecting their lives, and capable of being capricious; others thought
even fate and fortune were the mere instruments of one great
providential power who had a grand plan which he was steadily
unfolding. Modern readers of newspaper horoscopes and followers
of 'lifestyle' gurus are submitting themselves to the possibility that
there may be 'powers' to be placated and ways of influencing their
futures.

The question that exercised Greek and Roman philosophers most
was whether there was a power great enough to supervise everything
down to the last detail and to bring everything to a guaranteed
conclusion, which would include the particular events of every
single life, even down to those of sparrows. Those whose idea of God
was most elevated of all tended to think a truly Supreme Being
would be so 'high' that even to use the word 'was' would be to say
something unworthy of him. He could certainly not be expected to
have direct contact with the earth and its small, muddy affairs. The
Christian tradition came to the opposite conclusion in the emphasis
it placed on a God so caring that he had gone to unimaginable
trouble to rescue his afflicted, sinful people.

*Do I believe there is a God who cares about me? Or
am I on my own?*

Paul seems to say quite clearly that God makes choices among individuals, that he even 'predestines' each individual before that person is conceived and born, and for no reason other than his own preference. There is nothing these chosen ('elect') have done to deserve it:

> For those whom he foreknew he also predestined to be
> conformed to the image of his Son, in order that he might be the
> firstborn within a large family. And those whom he predestined he
> also called; and those whom he called he also justified; and those
> whom he justified he also glorified.
> **Romans 8:29—30**

Augustine said that the way God makes that choice, and the identity of the people he chooses, are veiled in mystery. He made it seem quite impersonal. The chosen do not know they are chosen and cannot smile gratefully back at God. They simply have to toil through life like everyone else and wait and see.

John Calvin (1509–64), another extreme predestinationist, writing a thousand years later, thought the chosen did 'know', that the mark of the 'elect' was their certainty that God had saved them. When someone stops you in the street and says 'Are you saved?' he is asking you a question Calvin would have thought quite reasonable.

It is one thing to say that God chooses who he wants for heaven, another to suggest that he predestines particular people for hell. Augustine and the Carolingians resisted that idea vigorously, because it seemed to imply that God could be the author of something evil. Calvin thought differently. In his view God divides the human race into those he accepts and those he rejects, and he himself does the rejecting as well as the accepting before the individual is even conceived, let alone born.

There were drawbacks to the Calvinist view, for both categories, for it implied that whatever the 'elect' did, God would never reject them, so in principle they could behave as badly as they liked. And those who did not enjoy this inner certainty would suffer a despair from which nothing could rescue them, for whatever they did God would not accept them.

*If God has already decided whether I am one of his
chosen people will it make any difference what I do?*

It is up to God to make me behave in the way he wants, if I am
helpless to do so myself. And if that is how things stand, God could
surely leave out the requirement to do the right thing, if he intends
to approve of those he chooses to approve of anyway. And,
conversely, there emerged the interesting possibility that there might
be people who can do no wrong, however 'wrongly' they actually
behaved. Some even claimed that 'there is no crime for those who
have Christ'.[3]

*How can I make moral choices if I am not free to
make choices at all?*

Conclusion

Keeping it simple inwardly

Modern life can be over-stimulating, even overwhelming. Too many aspects and options present themselves. How am I to strike a balance amidst all these complexities? How am I to 'care and not care' in the right proportions?

It can look as though it was easier in earlier centuries. 'The congregation usually consists principally of servant girls... often with market baskets in their hands. But they are very devout and quiet... it makes one feel better to be with them', wrote Francesca Alexander to John Ruskin from Venice on 27 June 1889, about her daily half hour of morning prayer in the church of S. Stefano.[1] But she was struck by the calming effect of this experience only because she, in the nineteenth century, seems to have experienced life much as you and I do now. The quotations in this book show that a 'big complicated psychological buzz... travels around with' each of us in every century.[2]

We have to find a way to calm this buzz and keep things simple. Freedom from more than passing anxiety, and an ability to deal with upsets as rapidly as possible, are important to the flexibility needed for keeping a moral balance of the kind sketched in this book. Here is Jeremy Taylor in the seventeenth century warning about the same danger of allowing fuss and worry to get in the way of seeing what matters:

> Let your imployment be such as may become a reasonable
> person; and not be a business fit for children or distracted people;
> but fit for your age and understanding. For a man may be very
> idley [sic] busy, and take great pains to... little purpose.[3]

A few generations later, Jane Austen was wryly conscious that sometimes the scale of the events in her life was quite absurdly small and fussy, and it was possible to lose a sense of their real importance. 'I shall get foolishly minute unless I cut the matter short', she wrote.

But she also understood the reassurance to be found under the surface of apparently superficial exchanges. 'Mrs. Harrison and I found each other out and had a... very comfortable little complimentary friendly Chat', she wrote in a letter to her sister Cassandra, in November 1813.[4]

> One should do simple separated things. Don't imagine you are that big complicated psychological buzz that travels around with you. Step outside it. Above all, don't feel guilt or worry about doing right.[5]
> **Iris Murdoch (1919—99)**

The 'big complicated psychological buzz' is an inner environment it is possible to step out of. If I can do that, even briefly, I can perhaps look 'over the heads' of the complications and uncertainties, do my best, not worry overmuch about getting it wrong.

Wouldn't it be easier just to follow the rules?

Mavis, one of the characters in Iris Murdoch's novel *An Accidental Man*, from which the above quotation comes, sometimes talks as though moral questions can be cut and dried: 'Mavis talked sometimes, her eyes far away, a little embarrassed, preaching to her, about simple duties simply understood, about obvious needs and obvious claims.'[6]

She knows, really, that it is not always as simple as that, yet she suspects that somewhere in each dilemma are aspects which are fundamentally 'simple' and 'obvious'. They need to be sought for.

One of Augustine's most frequently misunderstood remarks is 'love and do as you like' (*dilige et quod vis fac*). He did not mean that there are no 'rules'. He would probably not have answered 'Yes' to the question, 'Can I do what I like as long as it does not harm anyone else?' He did think that there are things it is simply 'wrong' to do.

He was confident, though, that the rules become self-interpreting when the context in which they are to be applied is approached in a spirit of simple goodwill which is essentially loving. The principle that 'love covers a multitude of sins' (1 Peter 4:8) suggests that there may be room to get it wrong (and put it right as far as possible), without wasting time and energy on self-reproach and fear of the consequences, and without feeling obliged to approach moral decision-making in any expectation that it will always be obvious or straightforward what to do.

Spreading goodness?

The eighteenth-century moralist Joseph Butler described an idyll of:

> ... universal goodwill, trust, and friendship, amongst mankind, if this could be brought to obtain; and each man enjoyed the happiness of others, as every one does that of a friend; and looked upon the success and prosperity of his neighbour, as every one does upon that of his children and family.[7]

This suggests that I may be able to aim not only at *doing* the right thing as well as I can but also at *being* in the right way. Many writers have spoken of a 'quiet goodness'. Perhaps I can try to create around me an environment in which others can live like that too, and we can all rub along together without envy or rivalry. But what shall I do when it turns out that that does not work, and the inability of my friends and workmates to enjoy the happiness of others unreservedly, leads to quarrels and resentments and the usual bad behaviour? Just as freedom from inner torments and tuggings this way and that is likely to be hard-won for me as an individual, so it is a long, slow process, subject to set-backs when it concerns relations with and among others.

Here 'quiet goodness' may turn out not to be as passive as it looks. We saw in looking at 'tough love' that being kind does not necessarily rule out rigour and tough-mindedness and making oneself hold back from an immediate impulsive display of affectionate forgiveness towards someone else. The same probably applies to being always 'gentle'.

The right moral choice may be to do nothing, but even that may be a form of 'doing'. I may need to be pretty active in helping to maintain a peaceful 'balance' among the people with whom I live and work. What sort of impression will that create? Will that be compatible with 'quiet goodness'?

I may also need to practise patience as a positive self-restraint when I am eager to get results. Built into a policy of practising 'quiet goodness' is an expectation that 'gratifications' will be deferred where necessary.

So there may be a great deal of mental detaching to be done, from things and people I may care about a good deal, before life can be seen in a satisfactory moral perspective, as the essayist William Hazlitt realized when he wrote about how 'to set a just value on life':

> If we merely wish to continue on the scene to indulge our
> headstrong humours and tormenting passions, we had better
> begone at once: and if we only cherish a fondness for existence
> according to the benefits we reap from it, the pangs we feel at
> parting with it will not be very severe.[8]

New problems of today

Completely new moral dilemmas present themselves from time to time in the modern world, which make it important to have thought out fundamental principles ready to use in deciding what to do about them 'for the best', since there may be no 'always-right' answer.

Until comparatively recently there was no such thing as a 'frozen embryo', a child conceived in a glass dish and frozen for future use when it consists of only a few cells. What are the rights of such a child and its parents? Are these frozen embryos human beings, and if so what are the 'rights' of the ones which do not get implanted in a womb with the chance of being born? Now that science can detect a genetic abnormality before a baby is born, should the law allow the abortion of the foetus, and who should decide whether the unborn child's life would be worth living? These are new dilemmas, but they concern much older beliefs about the value of human lives.

Then there is trying to decide what matters and what does not matter in the face of changing social trends. Some acts are sometimes seen as morally 'indifferent', innocent enjoyments and neutral activities; some are not. Some fall into that category only within certain norms. Others fall outside it altogether. Drug-taking for recreation is 'allowed' by society if the drug is alcohol, even if people binge-drink; if it is cocaine or heroin a series of different considerations apply, both socially and legally.

I shall also need to have my moral wits about me when I am suddenly faced with certain choices.

Is 'if in doubt, don't' a good rule?

How do I apply 'principles' and which principles?

In the end, though, I shall need to have the confidence of my convictions, be ready to learn from mistakes but not worry at them and allow them to get in the way of fresh, creative and active living. When my inner life – balanced, compassionate, but not tortured – is expressed in what I do, I shall occasionally have a delighted sense of making progress. I shall not grow smug about it, for the next moment I shall be conscious of failing again.

References

PREFACE
1. Elizabeth Jane Howard, *After Julius* (London, 1965; repr. 1967), p.62.

CHAPTER 1: WAYS OF LIVING
1. T.S. Eliot, 'Ash Wednesday', *Collected Poems 1909–62* (London, 1963).
2. Anselm of Canterbury, *Proslogion VIII, Anselmi Opera Omnia*, ed. F.S. Schmitt (Rome and Edinburgh, 1938–68), 1.106.
3. Marcus Aurelius Antoninus, *The Communings with Himself*, ed. C.R. Haines (London, 1969).
4. Seneca, *Epistulae Morales*, 4.1, ed. R.M. Gummere (London, 1917), Vol.I, pp.12–13.
5. The system was adopted and also taught by Chrysippus, who probably did more than Zeno to establish its place in the array of philosophical options Greeks could choose from, which included Platonism and Aristotelianism. Of Chrysippus only fragments survive. See Josiah B. Gould, *The Philosophy of Chrysippus* (Leiden, 1970).
6. Aristotle, *Problemata*, Book XXVII, 1–3, ed. H.S. Hett (London, 1937).
7. Boethius, *The Consolation of Philosophy*, I.pr.ii., in *Theological Tractates*, eds J. Stewart and E.K. Rand (Loed, 1973).
8. Ibid., I Pr.iv.
9. Ibid., I Pr.v.
10. Ibid., I Pr.vi.
11. George Chapman, *Chapman's Homer, The Iliad*, ed. Allardyce Nicoll (Princeton, 1984). Chapman's dedicatory lines to the King, p.3.
12. Alain de Botton, *The Consolations of Philosophy* (London, 2006).
13. Alexander Pope, *Essay on Man*, II.iii.101–104, ed. Mark Pattinson (Oxford, 1884).
14. James Boswell, *Boswell's London Journal* (1762–63), 25 February entry, ed. Frederick A. Pottle (London, 1950), p.202.
15. John Ruskin, 'Letter to Francesca Alexander', 1 July 1889, *The Brantwood Diary*, ed. Helen Gill Viljoen (Yale, 1971), p.362.
16. Salley Vickers, *The Other Side of You* (London, 2006), p.217.
17. Thomas B. Strong, *Christian Ethics*, Bampton Lectures, University of Oxford, 1895 (London, 1896), p.31.
18. Thomas Traherne, *Christian Ethicks* (1675), I, eds Carol L. Marks and George Robert Guffey (Ithaca, NY, 1968), p.17.
19. Carol Shields, *Unless* (London, 2002).
20. Epicurus, *Epistola ad Menoecem*, 135, tr. R. Waterfield (London, 1993).
21. Seneca, *Epistulae Morales*, 78, 11–12.
22. Marcus Aurelius, *The Communings with Himself*, I.6.
23. Ibid., I.7.
24. Henry Sidgwick, *The Methods of Ethics*, ed. G.J. Dalcourt (Lanham, Maryland, 1927), pp.380–82.
25. Ibid.
26. Cicero, *De officiis*, III.vii.33–34, tr. Walter Miller (London, 1913).
27. Elizabeth Jane Howard, *After Julius* (London, 1965; repr. 1967), p.42.
28. Richard Hooker, *Of the Laws of Ecclesiastical Polity*, I.V.1 ff., ed. Arthur Stephen MacGrade, *Cambridge Texts in the History of Political Thought* (Cambridge, 1989), pp.66–67.
29. *British Moralists: being selections from writers principally of the eighteenth century*, ed. L.A. Selby-Bigge (New York, 1965), Vol.I, p.3.
30. Steve Redgrave and Nick Townshend, *You Can Win at Life!* (London, 2005), pp.10–11.
31. Ibid.
32. Matthew Arnold, *Letters*, ed. Cecil Y. Lang (Charlottesville and London, 1996–2001), 6 vols., Vol.I, p.5.
33. James Mackintosh, *Discourse on the law of nature and nations, Vindiciae Gallicae and other writings on the French*

Revolution, ed. Donal Winch (Indianapolis, 2006), p.203.

34. R.W. Chapman (ed.), *The Works of Jane Austen* (London, 1954), Vol.VI, *Minor Works*, pp.453–57, here p.455, p.456.

35. Jeremy Taylor, *Holy Living*, ed. P.G. Stanwood (Oxford, 1989), Vol.I, p.19.

36. Ibid., p.22.

37. Ibid., p.21.

38. William Schweiker (ed.), *The Blackwell Companion to Religious Ethics* (Oxford, 2005), p.279.

39. John Betjeman, 'Devonshire Street', *Collected Poems* (London, 2003).

40. Jenny Joseph, 'Warning' (London, 1997).

41. Cicero, *De officiis*, I.xx.69–70.

42. Cicero, *De officiis*, I.xxi.71.

43. Cassiodorus, *In Psalmos*, CCSL 98, p.3.

44. Bernard of Clairvaux, *De Consideratione, Bernardi Opera Omnia*, ed. Leclercq, Talbot and Rochais, Vol.III, I.1–II.2, Book I, Chapters 1–2.

45. Daniel Defoe, *The Political History of the Devil*, ed. Irving Rothman and R. Michael Bowerman (New York, 2003), p.220.

46. John Evelyn, *Diary*, 30 October 1680, ed. D.t. de Beer (Oxford, 1955).

47. William Hazlitt, 'On the Fear of Death', Essay VIII, *Table Talk* (London, 1952), p.329.

48. Ibid., p.330.

CHAPTER 2: WAYS OF BEHAVING

1. Simon Blackburn, *Think* (Oxford, 1999), p.287.

2. Ibid.

3. Prudentius, *Psychomachia*, ed. H.J. Thomson (London, 1948).

4. Toshihiko Izutsu, *Ethico-Religious Concepts in the Qur'an* (Montreal, 1966), Chapter V. Surah 70.22–35 lists the things to do so that God will approve of you: worship, almsgiving, belief in the Last Judgement, fear of God, sexual continence, faithfulness, truthfulness, thankfulness, repentance.

5. Macrobius, *In Somnium Scipionis*, I.8.8, ed. I.Willis (Stuttgart, 1970), p.38.

6. The theological virtues have an order of priority – faith, hope, charity – suggests Aquinas. Aquinas, *Summa Theologicae*, Iii q.62 a.4, Dominican English tr. (London, 1911).

7. Thomas Browne, *Works*, ed. Geoffrey Keynes (Chicago, 1964), 4 vols., I.247.

8. William Fulbecke, *A Booke of Christian Ethicks* (London, 1587), no pagination.

9. Robert Boyle, *The Christian Virtuoso*, I (1690–91), *Works*, ed. Michael Hunter and Edward B. Davis (London, 2000), Vol.XI, p.365.

10. James Russell Lowell, 'Once to Every Man and Nation', published in the *Boston Courier*, 11 December 1945.

11. André Comte-Sponville, *A short treatise on the great virtues (Petit traité des grands vertues)* tr. Catherine Temerson (Metropolitan books, 2001; Vintage, 2003), p.4. French text published in Paris, 1966.

12. William Schweiker (ed.), *The Blackwell Companion to Religious Ethics* (Oxford, 2005), p.279.

13. Thomas B. Strong, *Christian Ethics*, Bampton Lectures, University of Oxford, 1895 (London, 1896), p.101.

14. *Virtus est animi habitus naturae modo atque ratione consentaneus*, Cicero, *De inventione*, II.liii.159.

15. Peter Abelard, *Ethics (Scito te ipsum)*, ed. David Luscombe (Oxford, 1971).

16. Aquinas, *Summa Theologicae*, Iii q.63.a.1, Dominican English tr. (London, 1911).

17. Ibid., Iii q.63 a.2.

18. Even if God infuses virtues into us, these are, he claims, of a different kind from the virtues we acquire through our own actions. Aquinas, *Summa Theologicae*, Iii q.63 a.3 and a.4.

19. Robert Boyle, *Works*, II.287.

20. André Comte-Sponville, *A short treatise on the great virtues*, p.2.

21. Aquinas, *Summa Theologicae*, Iii q.66 a.1.

22. Ibid., Iii q.64 a.1.

23. Patrick Delaney, *Fifteen sermons upon social duties* (London, 1744), p.3.

24. *Qui unam virtutem habet, omnes habet et, qui unam non habet, nullam habet.* Augustine, Letter 167.ii.4, *Epistulae*, ed. A. Goldbacher, CSEL 44 (1904), p.591.

25. Aquinas, *Summa Theologicae*, Iii q.65 a.1 and aa.2–5.

26. 'An homily against idleness', *The Homilies* (1562), (London, 1833), pp.359–62.

27. André Comte-Sponville, *A short treatise on the great virtues*, p.7.

28. Lynne Truss, *Talk to the Hand* (London, 2005), p.14.

29. Thomas Traherne, *Christian Ethicks* (1675), eds Carol L. Marks and George Robert Guffey (Ithaca, NY, 1968), p.3.

30. Francis Hutcheson, *An Inquiry into the Original of Our Ideas of Beauty and Virtue in Two Treatises* (1725), II, 1, ed. Wolfgang Liedhold (Indianapolis, 2004), pp.85, 95.

31. Daniel Defoe, *The Political History of the Devil*, eds Irving Rothman and R. Michael Bowerman (New York, 2003), pp.274–5.

CHAPTER 3: PERSONAL RESPONSIBILITY

1. Joseph Butler, Sermon III (Rolls Chapel), *Sermons* (London, 1849), p.28.

2. Jean Barbeyrac, *Spirit of the Ecclesiasticks of all sects and ages as to the doctrines of morality* (London, 1722).

3. William Kidd, *Thoughts on Individuality* (London, 1863), p.5, quoting Addison.

4. Ibid., p.iv.

5. John Ruskin, 10 October 1877, *The Brantwood Diary*, ed. Helen Gill Viljoen (Yale, 1971), p.55.

6. William Golding, *Lord of the Flies* (London, 1962), pp.28–29.

7. Milton, *Paradise Lost*, III.194–5.

8. Jeremy Taylor, *Holy Living*, ed. P.G. Stanwood (Oxford, 1989), Vol.I, p.37.

9. C.S. Lewis, *Studies in Words* (Cambridge, 1959), pp.199–202.

10. Ibid., p.187. See Horace, *Epistles*, 1.i.61.

11. Thomas de Quincey, *Confessions of an English Opium-Eater*, Original preface, 1821, *The Works of Thomas de Quincey*, ed. Grevel Lindop (London, 2000), Vol.II, p.95.

12. Benedictus de Spinoza, *Tractatus Theologico-Politicus*, XIII.4, *Spinoza on Freedom of Thought: Selections from Tractatus Theologico-Politicus and Tractatus Politicus*, ed. and tr. T.E. Jessop (Montral, 1962), p.23.

13. Ibid., XIV.13, p.27.

14. Anthony Trollope, *Barchester Towers* (Basingstoke, 1987), Chapter 26.

15. Interview with Rowan Williams, *Guardian*, 21 March 2006.

16. www.theforgivenessproject.com/stories/peter-tatchell, accessed 2007.

17. Benedictus de Spinoza, *Tractatus Theologico-Politicus*, XIV.3, p.25.

18. Ibid., XV.26, p.35.

19. Benedict of Nursia, *Règle*, Prologue, ed. and tr. A. de Vogüé and J. Neufville (Paris, 1972), Vol.I, p.413.

20. Ibid., p. 412.

21. Bernard of Clairvaux, *On precept and dispensation*, IV.9 and V.11, *Opera Omnia*, eds J. Leclercq, C.L. Talbot and H.M. Rochais (Rome, 1957–77), Vol. III, pp.253 ff.

22. Monica Baldwin, *I Leap Over the Wall: A Return to the World After 28 Years in a Convent* (London, 1949; repr. 1987), p.15.

23. www.theforgivenessproject.com; name has been changed to protect identity.

24. *Guardian*, 21 March 2006.

25. Ibid.

26. T.S. Eliot, 'Ash Wednesday' 6, *Collected Poems 1909–62* (London, 1963).

27. The full version of the prayer is as follows:

> God, grant me the serenity to accept
> the things I cannot change;
> courage to change the things I can;
> and the wisdom to know the difference.
> Living one day at a time;
> enjoying one moment at a time;

accepting hardship as the pathway to
peace.
Taking, as He did, this sinful world as
it is, not as I would have it.
Trusting that He will make all things
right, if I surrender to His will.
That I may be reasonably happy in this
life,
and supremely happy with Him forever
in the next.

CHAPTER 4: OTHER PEOPLE

1. Voltaire, *Candide and Other Stories*, ed.
and tr. Roger Pearson (Oxford, 1990),
p.116.

2. Jonathan Swift, *Gulliver's Travels*, ed.
Colin McElvie (1976), p.96.

3. Ibid., p.97.

4. Ibid., pp.96–97.

5. Alexis de Tocqueville, *Democracy in
America* (London, 1994), II, p.335.

6. Cf. Boethius, *The Consolation of
Philosophy*, I.pr.vi , II.pr.1., in *Theological
Tractates*, eds J. Stewart and E.K. Rand
(Loed, 1973).

7. *The Observer*, 12 March 2006.

8. Voltaire, *Candide and Other Stories*,
p.249.

9. Julia Neuberger, *The Moral State We're
In* (London, 2005), p.ix.

10. Mary Alcock, *Poems*, ed. Joanna
Hughes (London, 1799).

11. Universal Declaration of Human
Rights (1948), Preamble, Philippe Sands,
Lawless World (London, 2005),
pp.290–93.

12. Ibid.

13. Ibid.

14. Neil A. Lewis, 'Interrogators Cite
Doctors' Aid at Guantánamo', *New York
Times*, 24 June 2005.

15. Steven Poole, *Unspeak* (London,
2006), p.150.

16. Human Rights Law does not create
human rights. It treats them as already
existing. Michael Arnheim, *The Handbook
of Human Rights Law* (London, 2004), p.2

17. Jonathan Swift, *Gulliver's Travels*,
pp.181–83.

18. Article 14, Universal Declaration of
Human Rights.

19. 'Thoughts on various subjects, LXX,
Miscellanies in prose and verse', *The Prose
Works of Alexander Pope*, ed. Rosemary
Cowler, II (Oxford, 1986), p.161.

20. John Evelyn, *Diary*, 27 April 1693, ed.
D.S. de Beer (Oxford, 1955).

21. *Essays of George Eliot*, ed. Thomas
Pinney (London, 1963), p.55.

22. Daniel Defoe, *An Essay upon Projects*,
eds Joyce D. Kennedy, Michael Seidel,
Maximillian E. Novak (New York, 1999),
pp.108–109.

23. Henrik Ibsen, *A Doll's House*,
translation as quoted in Toril Moi, *Henrik
Ibsen and the Birth of Modernism: Art,
Theatre, Philosophy* (Oxford, 2006), p.243.

24. On racial equality in the Koran see
Bruce Lawrence, *The Qur'an: A Biography*
(London, 2006).

25. Amartya Sen, *The Argumentative
Indian* (London, 2005; 2006 edition),
p.154.

26. Charles Lamb's ' Imperfect
sympathies', first published in *London
Magazine*, August, 1821, and entitled 'Jews,
Quakers, Scotchmen, and other imperfect
sympathies', later see *Elia* (1823).

27. Ibid.

28. Ibid.

29. David Miles, *The Tribes of Britain*
(London, 2005/2006), pp.442–43.

30. Alistair Cook, *Letter from America*, 29
June 1993 (London, 2004; 2005 edition),
pp.358–59.

31. Ibid., p.360.

32. www.canadianheritage.gc.ca/progs/
multi/inclusive_e.cfm, accessed 2007.

CHAPTER 5: A TANGLE OF TIES

1. Richmal Crompton, *More William*
(1922; repr. Macmilliam, 1995),
pp.120–21.

2. Jerome, Letter XIV, *Epistulae*, ed. I.
Hilberg, CCEL (Vienna, 1996), vol.
54–55.

3. John Stuart Mill, *On Liberty*, ed.
Gertrude Himmelfarb (London, 1974).

References

4. Amartya Sen, *Identity and Violence: The Illusion of Destiny* (London, 2006), p.xv.

5. Ibid.

6. Ulpian, in Justinian, *Digest*, 50.16.195.2, ed. T. Mommsen (Berlin, 1870).

7. Jane F. Gardner, *Family and Familia in Roman Law and Life* (Oxford, 1998), pp.3 ff.

8. Ibid., p.179, citing the *Lex Aelia Sentia* of AD 4.

9. Aristotle, *Politics*, I. 1255a , ed. F. Susemihl (Leipzig, 1909).

10. Universal Declaration of Human Rights (1948), Preamble, Philippe Sands, *Lawless World* (London, 2005), pp.290–93.

11. www.womenandequalityunit.gov.uk, accessed 2007.

12. Ibid.

13. Thackeray 'Letter', 25 December 1862, *The letters and private papers of William Makepeace Thackeray*, ed. Gordon N. Ray, (London, 1946), Vol.IV, p.279.

14. Marguerite Steen, *William Nicholson* (London, 1943), p.45.

15. President's Guidance (Adoption: the new law and procedure) [2006] 1 FLR 1234.

16. [2006] UKHL 24.

17. [2006] 1 FLR 1186, HL.

18. Virginia Woolf, 'A Sketch of the Past', in *Moments of Being: Unpublished Autobiographical Writings*, ed. Jeanne Schulkind (Oxford, 1976), p.91.

19. Dame Elizabeth Butler-Sloss, quoted in at 973 in Re H (Contact: domestic violence) [2005] EWCA Civ 1404 [2006] 1 FLR 943.

CHAPTER 6: SELF-SUFFICIENCY AND COOPERATION

1. *Three prose versions of the Secretorum Secretorum*, ed. Robert Steele, EETS (London, 1898), p.1.

2. Cited in Judith Ferster, 'The Family of Origin versus the Human Family: Universal Love in Literature', *Mindful Spirit in Late Medieval Literature*, ed. Bonnie Wheeler (New York and Basingstoke, 2006), p.258.

3. Richard Rorty, 'Human Rights, Rationality and Sentimentality', in *On Human Rights*, ed. Stephen Shute and Susan Hurley (New York, 1993), p.125.

4. Aristotle, *Politics*, Book I.i.7 1252b, ed. F. Susemihl (Leipzig, 1909).

5. Ibid., Book I.i.8 1252b.

6. Ibid., Book I.i.11 1253a.

7. Cicero, *De officiis*, III.vi, 28, tr. Walter Miller (London, 1913).

8. *Utilitas uniuscuiusque et universorum*, Cicero, *De officiis*, III.vi.26.

9. *Communem humani generis societatem*, Cicero *De officiis*, III.vi.28.

10. Cicero, *De officiis*, I.xvi.50.

11. Ibid., II.ii.4.

12. Ibid., I.viii.25.

13. Cicero himself says he chooses to follow the Stoics rather than other earlier ethical philosophers. Cicero, *De officiis*, I.iii.8.

14. Cicero, *De officiis*, I.ix.30.

15. Ibid., I.ii.5.

16. Ibid., I.iv.13.

17. *Non utilia cum honestis pugnare aliquando posse dixerit*, Cicero, *De officiis*, III.vii.33–34.

18. Cicero, *De officiis*, I.iii.9.

19. Ibid., I.v.15.

20. Augustine, *Enarrationes in Psalmos*, 30(2) I.4, CCSL 38, p.193.

21. Joseph Butler, Sermon I 'Upon Human Nature' (Rolls Chapel), *Sermons* (London, 1849).

22. Bernard of Clairvaux, *De Gradibus Humilitatis*, XIV.42, *Bernardi Opera Omnia*, eds Leclercq, Talbot and Rochais, Vol.III, p.48.

23. The OED defines 'corporation' as 'A number of persons united, or regarded as united, in one body; a body of persons' and 'A body corporate legally authorized to act as a single individual; an artificial person created by royal charter, prescription, or act of the legislature, and having authority to preserve certain rights in perpetual succession.'

24. *Sunday Times*, 3 September 2006.

25. Edmund Burke, 'Reflections on the Revolution in France' (1790), pp.143–47.

26. *Charges to the Grand Jury, 1689–1803*, ed. George Lamoine, Camden Society, 4th Series, 43 (London, 1992), (1725), p.208.

27. Ibid., (1798), p.609.

28. Ibid., (1722), p.161.

29. As stated in the Nationality Immigration Act 2002, with effect from 1 November 2005.

30. Qualifications and Curriculum Authority, www.qca.org.uk/7907.html, accessed 2007.

31. Francis Hutcheson, *An Inquiry into the Original of Our Ideas of Beauty and Virtue in Two Treatises* (1725), II.3.viii, ed. Wolfgang Liedhold (Indianapolis, 2004), p.125.

32. Thomas Paine, 'Freedom of Posterity', *The Rights of Man, Part I* (1791), pp.8–10.

33. European Convention of Human Rights, Article 11.

34. John Bunyan, *Grace Abounding and Other Spiritual Autobiographies*, eds John Stachniewski and Anita Pacheco (Oxford, 1998), p.98.

35. John Stuart Mill, *On Liberty*, Chapter V, ed. Gertrude Himmelfarb (London, 1974), p.163.

36. Ibid., pp.180–81.

37. Ibid., p.59.

38. George Orwell, 'Politics and the English Language (1946) in *George Orwell: Essays*, ed. John Carey (London, 2002), pp.954–67, and *George Orwell: Essays* (London, 1984), p.356.

39. Steven Poole, *Unspeak* (London, 2006), pp.143 ff.

40. Ibid.

41. Universal Declaration of Human Rights (1948), Philippe Sands, *Lawless World* (London, 2005), pp. 290–93.

CHAPTER 7: PRACTICAL MORAL DECISIONS

1. Jeremy Taylor, *Holy Dying*, Epistle Dedicatory, ed. P.G. Stanwood (Oxford, 1989), Vol.II, p.41.

2. *Metro* article of 21 June 2006.

3. Ibid.

4. Noam Chomsky, *Failed States: The Abuse of Power and the Assault on Democracy* (London, 2006), pp.227–28.

5. *Metro*, 21 June 2006.

6. Ibid.

7. Samuel Butler, *The Way of All Flesh*, ed. Daniel F. Howard (London, 1965), p.215.

8. *How to Spend $50 Billion to Make the World a Better Place*, ed. Bjørn Lomborg (Cambridge, 2006), pp.xvi–xviii.

9. Ibid.

10. Brian Tierney, 'The Decretists and the "Deserving Poor"', *Comparative Studies in Society and History*, 4 (1959), pp.362–63.

11. Peter the Chanter, *Verbum Abbreviatum, Textus conflatus*, II, ed. M. Boutry, CCCM 196, p.656. I am grateful to K.R. Chambers for this reference.

12. Augustine, *Enarrationes in Psalmos*, 102.13, CCSL (Brepols, Turnhout, 1956), Vol.40, p.1463.

13. Rufinus in *Gratian's Decretum* as discussed in Brian Tierney, 'The Decretists and the "Deserving Poor"', *Comparative Studies in Society and History*, 4 (1959), pp.363–64 and p.372, Appendix A.

14. Alexander Pope, *Essay on Man*, IV.II.49–51, ed. Mark Pattinson (Oxford, 1884).

15. William Fulbecke, *A Booke of Christian Ethicks* (London, 1587), no pagination.

16. Alexander Pope, *The sixth satire of the second book of Horace* in *Collected Poems* (London, 1924), p.341.

17. *The letters and private papers of William Makepeace Thackeray*, ed. Gordon N. Ray (London, 1945), Vol.I, p.267.

18. The Koran promises a reward in the life to come (Koran 4.57).

19. B. Poschmann, *Penance and the Anointing of the Sick*, tr. F. Courtney (London, 1964).

20. Samuel Butler, *The Way of All Flesh*, p.216.

21. *The Analects of Confucius*, IV, 2, tr. Arthur Waley (London, 1938), p.102. cf. tr. D.C. Lau (Penguin Classics, 1979), p.72.

22. Alexander Pope, *Moral Essays in Collected Poems* (London, 1924), p.243.

23. Universal Declaration of Human Rights (1948), Philippe Sands, *Lawless World* (London, 2005), pp. 290–93.

24. Alexander Pope, *Essay on Man*, I. V.130–32.

25. Lucretius, *De rerum natura*, V,1019–27, cf. Phillip Mitsis, *Epicurus' Ethical Theory: The Pleasures of Invulnerability* (Ithaca and London, 1988), p.105.

26. Pico della Mirandola, *On the Dignity of Man*, tr. Charles Glenn Wallis (Indianapolis and Cambridge, 1965), p.3.

27. Alexander Pope, *Essay on Man*, I. IV.115.

28. All cited from the *Independent*, 8 June 2006.

29. From a Fairtrade notice in a café 2006, referring to www.fairtrade.org.uk

30. *Business Ethics: The Magazine of Corporate Responsibility*, 20 (Spring, 2006).

31. www.lrn.com, November 2006.

32. http://forum.wgbh.org/wgbh/forum.php?lecture_id=3088, accessed 2007.

33. Amnesty International, *Human Rights for Human Dignity* (London, 2005).

34. Geoffrey Robertson, *Crimes against Humanity: The Struggle for Global Justice* (London, 1999), Chapter 4, pp.131 ff.

35. Jeffrey Sachs, *The End of Poverty* (Penguin, 2005), p.226.

36. Ibid., pp.11–12.

37. George Orwell, 'Writers and Leviathan', *George Orwell: Essays* (London, 1984), p.454.

38. *Ethics in an Age of Technology: The Gifford Lectures*, 1981–1991, ed. Ian G. Barbour (SCM, 1992).

39. For example, Exodus 23:4–5.

40. Porphyry, *On Abstinence from Killing Animals*, tr. Gillian Clark (Duckworth, 2000), p.31.

41. Ibid., p.35.

42. Ibid., I.56, p.54.

43. Thomas More, *Utopia* (1516), Book II, ed. and tr. George M. Logan, Robert M. Adam, Clarence H. Miller (Cambridge, 1995), p.139.

44. Neville Gregory, *Physiology and Behaviour of Animal Suffering* (Oxford, 2004).

45. Cecil A. Spring-Rice, www.cyberhymnal.org/htm/i/v/ivow2the.htm

46. Jeffrey Sachs, *The End of Poverty*, p.214.

47. Letter 181, 23 March 1917, *Letters from Edward Thomas to Gordon Bottomly*, ed. R. George Thomas (London, 1968), p.279.

48. Fidel Castro, *Che: A Memoir*, ed. David Deutschmann (Melbourne and New York 1994; 2nd edition, 2006), p.84.

49. Dylan Thomas, *The Collected Letters*, ed. Paul Ferris (London, 1985), pp.424–28.

50. Alistair Cook, *Letter from America*, 30 November 1990 (London, 2004; 2005 edition), pp.343–44.

51. Dominic Sandbrook, *Never Had it So Good: A History of Britain from Suez to the Beatles* (London, 2006), p.265.

52. William Golding, *Free Fall* (London, 1959), pp.6–7.

53. Benjamin Disraeli, *Coningsby* (1844; repr. Pennsylvania, no date), pp.138–39.

54. Virginia Woolf, 'A Sketch of the Past', in *Moments of Being: Unpublished Autobiographical Writings*, ed. Jeanne Schulkind (Oxford, 1976), p.90.

55. Amartya Sen, *The Argumentative Indian* (London, 2005; 2006 edition), pp.47–48.

56. Daniel Defoe, *The Life and Strange Surprizing Adventures of Robinson Crusoe* (Oxford, 1927), p.182.

57. 'Equality entails privileging the individual rights of women over claims of obedience grounded in religious faith and paternal authority. If a young woman wishing to study at university is opposed by a father who wishes her to stay at home, and she seeks legal assistance to prevail, a liberal society will side with her against her father's wishes. If a woman wishes to choose her marriage partner and paternal and religious authority align against her, a liberal society's institutions

should defend her freedom. To the extent that women wish to remain obedient to the religious and family values of their culture of origin, they should remain free to do so.' Michael Ignatieff, in *Free Expression is No Offence*, ed. Lisa Appignanesi (Penguin, 2005), pp.132–33.

58. Patriot Act 2001, renewed 2006, also known as 'The Uniting and Strengthening America by Providing Appropriate Tools Required to Intercept and Obstruct Terrorism Act of 2001', www.epic.org/privacy/terrorism/hr3162.html

59. Reza Aslan, *No God but God: The Origins, Evolution and Future of Islam* (Arrow Books, 2006), p.xiv.

60. Richard Dawkins, *The Blind Watchmaker* (1986), Preface.

61. Cf. Cicero, *De Officiis*, III.vi.

62. Jeremy Taylor, *Holy Living*, ed. P.G. Stanwood (Oxford, 1989), Vol.I, p.35.

63. *The Spectator*, 634, 17 December 1714, ed. Donald F. Bond (Oxford, 1965), V, p.638–39.

64. Ibid.

65. Jeremy Paxman, *The English: A Portrait of a People* (London, 1998, 1999), p.118.

66. See F.J. Powicke, 'The Revd Richard Baxter's Last Treatise' (Manchester, 1926), *Bulletin of John Rylands Library*, 10.1.

67. Jeffrey Sachs, *The End of Poverty*, p.365.

68. Onora O'Neill, *A Question of Trust*, Reith lectures (London, 2002).

69. W.R. Bion, *Experiences in Groups: And Other Papers*, (Tavistock, 1961; repr. Routledge, 1989).

70. Aubrey Blumsohn, 'Authorship, Ghost-Science, Access to Data and Control of the Scientific Literature: Who Stands Behind the Word?', *Professional Ethics Report*, 19(3) (2006), 1–3 (American Association for the Advancement of Science).

71. Ibid.

72. Onora O'Neill, *Rethinking Freedom of the Press* (Dublin, 2004).

73. John Locke, *Letter concerning Toleration*, ed. Gough (1948), p.151.

74. www.bodley.ox.ac.uk/external/cross/areopagitica.pdf

CHAPTER 8: ATTITUDES AND EXPECTATIONS

1. Augustine, *De mendacio*, I.1, ff., ed. J. Zycha, CSEL XXXXI (1900), pp.413 ff.

2. Ibid., III.4, p.416.

3. Ibid., III.4, p.417.

4. Augustine, *Contra mendacium*, III.4, ed. J. Zycha, CSEL XXXXI (1900), p.474.

5. Anselm, *De veritate*, II, Anselm of Canterbury, *Anselmi Opera Omnia*, ed. F.S. Schmitt (Rome and Edinburgh, 1938–68).

6. Jane Austen, *Persuasion* (Leicester, 1993), Chapter IX.

7. Cicero, *De officiis*, VII, 17, and elsewhere.

8. Report of the Committee on Obscenity and Film Censorship, 6, Chaired by Bernard Williams (Cmnd 7772, 1979), 6.74, p.92.

9. The Theodosian Code, 14.9.1 (370), tr. C. Parr (New York, 1969).

10. Augustine, *Confessions*, VI. viii.13, tr. Henry Chadwick (Oxford, 1991).

11. Ibid., VI.vii.11–12.

12. Ibid., XXX.ii.2.

13. Ibid., VIII.x.23.

14. Report of the Committee on Obscenity and Film Censorship, 5.24, chaired by Bernard Williams (Cmnd 7772, 1979), p.56.

15. *Julius Caesar*, Act 3 scene 5.

16. Lance Price, *The Spin Doctor's Diary*, (London, 2006; 2nd edition, 2006), p.xxiii.

17. Justin A. Frank, *Bush on the Couch* (first published, 2004; London, 2006), p.128, press interview of December 2003.

18. Simon Blackburn, *Truth* (New York, 2005; 2006 reprint), pp.xiv–v.

19. Anselm, *De veritate*, II, V, pp.178 and 181–82.

20. *The Analects of Confucius*, IV, 6, tr. Arthur Waley (London, 1938), p.103.

21. C.S. Lewis, *Out of the Silent Planet* (first published, 1938; London, 2000), p.111.

22. www.4troubledteens.com/
toughlove.html, accessed 2007.

23. Edmund Burke, 'Enquiry into the
Sublime and Beautiful', Section XIII, *The
Writings and Speeches*, ed. Paul Langford
(Oxford, 1997), I, pp.220–21.

24. Joseph Butler, *Sermons* (London,
1849), pp.3–4.

25. Ibid., Sermon V (Rolls Chapel), p.47.

26. Marina Warner, 'Who's Sorry Now:
Personal Stories, Public Apologies', *Sex
Rights: Oxford Amnesty Lectures*, ed.
Nicholas Bamforth, (Oxford, 2005).

27. Marcus Aurelius Antoninus, *The
Communings with Himself*, I.7, ed. C.R.
Haines (London, 1969).

28. Matt Ridley, *The Origins of Virtue*
(1996; Penguin, 1997).

29. www.theforgivenessproject.com,
accessed 2007.

30. Ibid.

31. Ibid.

32. Katy Hutchison,
www.theforgivenessproject.com, accessed
2007.

33. www.theforgivenessproject.com/
stories/francis-berthe-climbie, accessed
2007.

34. Marina Cantacuzino, founder of The
Forgiveness Project, quoted in *The Times*,
22 March 2006.

CHAPTER 9: THE PROBLEM OF EVIL

1. *The Observer*, 12 March 2006.

2. S. Lieu, *The Diffusion and Persecution of
Manichaeism in Rome and China: A
Comparative Study* (Rome, 1981), Oxford
D.Phil thesis (1981), Ms D.Phil c.3571.

3. For example, J.K. Rowling, *Harry Potter
and the Chamber of Secrets* (London, 1998).

4. Origen, *On First Principles*, 1.6–8, and see
David Brakke, *Demons and the Making of
the Monk* (Cambridge, Mass., 2006), p.12.

5. Evagrius of Pontus, *Traité pratique ou
Le moine*, eds A. Guillaumont and C.
Guillaumont (Paris, 1971), and see David
Brakke, *Demons and the Making of the
Monk* (Cambridge, Mass., 2006), p.48.

6. David Brakke, *Demons and the Making
of the Monk* (Cambridge, Mass., 2006),
p.60.

7. Ibid.

8. William of Auvergne, *De legibus*, 1,
Opera Omnia (Paris, 1674; repr.
Frankfurt-am-Main, 1963), p.22.
Chapter XVIII contains a hostile life of
Mohammed with the usual accusations.
Chapter XIX criticizes his idea of
paradise with its fleshly pleasures.
Chapter XX compares the Judaic law
(*lex fortunae*) with the Muslim
(*lex naturae*) and the Christian (*lex
gratiae*).

9. See my *Augustine on Evil* (Cambridge,
1983).

10. Augustine, *Confessions*, tr. Henry
Chadwick (Oxford, 1991).

11. Joseph Butler, *Analogy*, I.ii.1 (London,
1907).

12. *De perfectione iustitiae hominis*, eds
C.F. Urba and J. Zycha, CSEL, 42 (1902),
p.4.

13. Ibid., XX.I44, pp.46–47.

14. 'A Sermon of Good Works Annexed to
Faith', *The Homilies* (1562) (London,
1833), p.31.

15. Jeremy Taylor, *Holy Living*, ed.
P.G. Stanwood (Oxford, 1989), Vol.I,
p.29.

16. Jeremy Taylor, *Holy Dying*, Epistle
Dedicatory, ed. P.G. Stanwood (Oxford,
1989), Vol.II, no page number.

17. Ibid., p.25.

18. Ibid., p.41.

19. Gilbert Burnet, *Sermon*, Sermon,
31–32.

20. Letter to George and Georgiana
Keats, 21 April (1819), *Letters of John
Keats*, ed. H.E. Rollins (1958),
Vol.II.

21. Thomas de Quincey, *Confessions of an
English Opium-Eater*, Original preface,
1821, *The Works of Thomas de Quincey*, ed.
Grevel Lindop (London, 2000), Vol.II,
p.95.

22. Ibid., p.96.

CHAPTER 10: FREEDOM OF CHOICE

1. Voltaire, *Candide and Other Stories*, ed. and tr. Roger Pearson (Oxford, 1990), p.235.

2. Ibid., p.237.

3. Michael Gaddis, *There is No Crime for Those Who Have Christ* (Berkeley, 2005), pp.283 ff.

CONCLUSION

1. John Ruskin, *The Brantwood Diary*, ed. Helen Gill Viljoen (Yale, 1971), p.364.

2. Iris Murdoch, *An Accidental Man* (Faber, 1971), p.94.

3. Jeremy Taylor, *Holy Living*, ed. P.G. Stanwood (Oxford, 1989), Vol.I, p.22.

4. Jane Austen, *Letters*, 6–7 November 1813, ed. Deirdre le Faye (3rd ed., Oxford, 1995), p.251.

5. Iris Murdoch, *An Accidental Man*, p.94.

6. Iris Murdoch, *An Accidental Man*, p.84.

7. Joseph Butler, Sermon V (Rolls Chapel) *Sermons* (London, 1849), p.51.

8. William Hazlitt, 'On the Fear of Death', Essay VIII, *Table Talk* (London, 1952), p.330.

Index

Acknowledgments

Bible acknowledgments

pp. 12, 173–74, 175: Extracts from the Authorized Version of the Bible (The King James Bible), the rights in which are vested in the Crown, are reproduced by permission of the Crown's Patentee, Cambridge University Press.

pp. 17, 34: Scripture quotations are from the Revised Standard Version published by HarperCollins Publishers, copyright
© 1989 by the Division of Christian Education of the National Council of the Churches of Christ in the USA, and are used by permission. All rights reserved.

pp. 35, 50, 62, 64, 71, 75, 89, 93, 94, 99, 100, 110, 131, 132, 133, 134, 136, 159, 165, 176, 179, 180, 198: Scripture quotations are from the New Revised Standard Version published by HarperCollins Publishers, copyright © 1989 by the Division of Christian Education of the National Council of the Churches of Christ in the USA, and are used by permission. All rights reserved.

Text acknowledgments

pp. 8, 61: Extract from 'Ash Wednesday VI' by T. S Eliot. Permission granted by Faber and Faber.

p. 28: Extract from 'Devonshire Street' by John Betjeman ©, The Estate of John Betjeman, published by John Murray (Publishers) Ltd. Used with permission.

pp. 47–48: Extract from *Lord of the Flies* by William Golding. Permission granted by Faber and Faber.

pp 52, 61, 92, 102, 161, 189, 196: Extracts from *The Koran* translated by N. J. Dawood (Penguin Classics 1956, Fifth revised edition 1990). Copyright © N. J. Dawood, 1956, 1959, 1966, 1968, 1974, 1990, 1993, 1997, 1999, 2003.

pp. 58–59: Extract adapted from material from www.theforgivenessproject.com